CHARLES HILLINGER'S AMERICA

CHARLES HILLINGER'S
AMERICA
PEOPLE & PLACES IN ALL 50 STATES

with a foreword from
Charles Kuralt

CAPRA PRESS
SANTA BARBARA

For my five little girls:
Hayley, Kristina, Brittani, Carlie and Nicole Arliene

Cover design, book design, typography and image scanning
by Frank Goad, Santa Barbara.

LIBRARY OF CONGRESS CATALOGING-IN-PUBLICATION DATA
Hillinger, Charles [America]
Charles Hillinger's America : people and places in all 50 states
/ Charles Hillinger : with a foreword by Charles Kuralt.
p.   cm.
ISBN 0-88496-405-1 (paper)
l. United States—Description and travel—Anecdotes.
1. United States—History, Local—Anecdotes. I. Title. II. Title: America.
E169.04.H55 1996   96-11113
973—dc20   CIP

Capra Press
Post Office Box 2068
Santa Barbara, CA 93120

CONTENTS
&
PHOTO CAPTIONS
(All photos by the author unless otherwise noted.)

Foreword by Charles Kuralt / 9

About the Author / 11

Delaware / 13 Delaware is a state sprinkled with tiny hamlets called cross roads and corners. An Amish buggy whizzes by in a tiny town called Dinahs Corner.

Maryland / 18 Maryland's red-brick Capitol with its 181-foot high white wooden dome is the only statehouse that has served as America's Capitol. *(Photo credit: Maryland Office of Tourism)*

Washington, D.C. / 21 Charles Lindbergh's Spirit of Saint Louis looms above Paul E. Garber in Smithsonian National Air and Space Museum. Garber is responsible for museum's marvelous collection of flying machines.

Virginia / 28 Guard on duty at Tomb of Unknowns at Arlington National Cemetery.

New Jersey / 35 Archivist Mary Bowling of Edison National Historic Site in West Orange, New Jersey, in front of replica of the Black Maria, the first movie studio built by Thomas A. Edison.

New York / 40 Linda Canzanelli, supt. Women's Rights National Historic Park in Seneca Falls, N.Y. outside park's visitor's center holding copy of Elizabeth Griffith's biography, *In Her Own Right: The Life of Elizabeth Cady Stanton.*

Connecticut / 45 Mystic Seaport is the home of the Charles W. Morgan, the only surviving wooden whaling ship.

Rhode Island / 48 Brown and Hopkins Country Store in Chepachet, R.I., founded in 1809, reportedly oldest continuously operated general store in America. That's Carol Wilcox, with her husband, Paul, 21st owners of store waiting for a customer.

Massachusetts / 52 "Just imagine 10,000 men of Gloucester lost at sea (while fishing)," mused author-historian Joseph E. Garland, on the back porch of his home overlooking Gloucester Harbor and the Atlantic Ocean.

Vermont / 55 A tidy Vermont Village against a mountain backdrop,

Washington, Vermont. *(Photo credit: Vermont Travel Division)*

New Hampshire / 60 Virginia Irwin with Sarah Josepha Hale doll.

Maine / 63 Lighthouse on Maine's Machias Seal Island. *(Photo credit: Maine Office of Tourism)*

Pennsylvania / 69 Edwin Wolf 2nd, librarian emeritus of oldest public library in America, holds one of Benjamin Franklin's books.

West Virginia / 73 Storyteller Bonnie Collins picks up her mail at her log cabin home near the hamlet of Mountain, the only place in America where someone actually made a mountain out of a molehill.

North Carolina / 79 Replica of Wright Brothers plane that flew at Kitty Hawk Dec. 17, 1903 on North Carolina Outer Bank where flight took place.

South Carolina / 85 Confederate cannons at Fort Sumter.

Georgia / 89 Giant wheel and grist mill on Berry College campus to grind corn and grain.

Florida / 94 Photographer photographing shore birds at J.N. (Ding) Darling National Wildlife Refuge on Sanibel Island.

Alabama / 100 Tuskegee University is not only a university but a national park as well. Carnegie Hall is school's Media Production Center. *(Photo Credit: Tuskegee University)*

Tennessee / 104 Charlie Jones, son of Casey Jones, outside Casey Jones' home in Jackson, Tenn.

Kentucky / 109 George B. Wright, the officer in charge of the U.S. Bullion Depository, Fort Knox, outside building where America's gold is stored.

Ohio / 114 George R. Smith holds copy of *The Budget* at newspaper's pub lishing offices in Sugarcreek, Ohio. Paper has 500 reporters who file their reports in long hand.

Indiana / 118 A selection of Johnny Appleseed records, books and sheet music.

Michigan / 122 Orville and Wilbur Wright's bicycle shop at Henry Ford's Greenfield Village in Dearborn, Mich. Shop was gift to Ford from Orville.

Wisconsin / 126 Wisconsin is America's milk and cheese state. In the office of *Hoard's Dairyman*, bible of the dairy industry, a large cow looms over editor William D. Knox's desk.

Minnesota / 133 Minnesota poster promoting donations to loon programs made possible on state tax forms. Minnesota is the looniest state in the lower 48.

Iowa / 136 Meredith Willson leading the parade down Main Street in Mason City, Iowa, Music Man's hometown. *(Photo credit: Mason City Convention & Visitors Bureau.)*

Illinois / 140 In Illinois "Land of Lincoln" there are more statues of Abraham Lincoln than in any other state. This one in New Salem shows Lincoln reading while riding a horse.

Missouri / 145 Harry and Bess Truman's 19th century home in Independence where the President and his wife lived from 1919 to their deaths— except for when they lived in the White House.

Arkansas / 150 Elsie Ward demonstrating how to make lye soap at the Ozark Folk Center.

Mississippi / 155 Bigger than life portrait of Astronaut Ronald E. McNair at theater named in his honor at Davis Planetarium in Jackson, Miss.

Louisiana / 159 Trapper Victoria Toupes with row of muskrat hides to dry at her home on Bayou La Fourche.

Texas / 165 "When you say longhorn, you're talkin' Texas," said J.D. (Jack) Phillips shown here with Big Red.

Oklahoma / 170 "The Race" into Cherokee Outlet, 1893 to claim land in an Oklahoma Run. (*Photo credit: Oklahoma Historical Society*)

Kansas / 175 Amelia Earhart (1898-1937) was the first woman to fly across the Atlantic Ocean in May 1932. She is shown here boarding the Lockheed Vega which is now on display in the Pioneers of Flight gallery of the National Air and Space Museum. (*Photo credit: National Air and Space Museum*)

Nebraska / 180 Vesper Einspahr at her sod house with bucket of corn cobs for her potgut stove.

South Dakota / 185 Rare Italian stringed instruments on exhibit at the Shrine to Music in Vermillion, South Dakota. (*Photo credit: S.R.H. Spicer Shrine to Music, University of South Dakota*)

North Dakota / 190 North Dakota Farmer chopping through ice on frozen lake so his cattle will have water to drink.

Montana / 196 Charlie Russell at work on his painting "When the Land Belonged to God" in his studio at his Great Falls home. (*Photo credit: Montana Historical Society, Helena*)

Wyoming / 204 Wyoming's Albany County Sheriff Ted Burnstad visits bunkhouse cowboy Phil Rathbun in Jelm. "Old Phil," 88 at the time and still going strong, spent his life working cattle.

Colorado / 208 Durango-to-Silverton train chugging through the mountains of Colorado along the Animas River on a 45.2 mile run through wilderness.

New Mexico / 215 Spectacular ceremonial dances take place throughout the year at all the Indian Pueblos of the Rio Grande Valley. Many dances and costumes such as these at the Indian Pueblo Cultural Center in Albquerque are very realistic in the representation of nature and animals. *(Photo credit: Albuquerque Convention and Visitors Bureau)*

Arizona / 223 Harvesting fruit of saguaro cactus at 145-acre Desert Botani cal Garden in Phoenix.

Utah / 227 Haunting, elongated, ghostly bigger-than-life figures were etched high on the pink sandstone cliff forming the mysterious mural known as The Great Gallery, a magical art exhibit left over from the distant past. *(Photo credit: National Park Service)*

Idaho / 231 Basque Center in Boise, Idaho. Idaho's 20,000 Basques form the largest Basque community in America as well as the largest Basque commu nity outside Spain and France.

Washington / 238 Hayley Kenny, 14, and author's wife, Arliene, in Hoh Rain Forest.

Oregon / 244 Pittock Mansion in Portland, Oregon's Forest Park...Portland has 12% of its total area dedicated to parks...*(Photo credit: Portland Parks and Recreation)*

Nevada / 248 Longest, loneliest bookmobile route in America serving one third of Nevada, an area larger than 13 states.

California / 253 Mary Hill holding Mary Hill rose.

Hawaii / 257 Margaret Kupihea, Big Kahuna of Kauai.

Alaska / 263 Eagles in snowy tree overlooking Chilkat River.

Puerto Rico / 267 Firemen from across America beat a steady path to Ponce, Puerto Rico's second largest city. They come to Ponce because of its *bomberos* (firemen) and the city's colorful 1883 fire station. *(Photo credit: Bob Krist for the Puerto Rico Tourism Company)*

Virgin Islands / 270 Windmill and other relics of a Danish plantation on St. Croix Island. *(Photo credit U.S. Virgin Islands Dept. of Tourism)*

FOREWORD

by

Charles Kuralt

Charles Hillinger has been a hero of mine since I first started reading his stories in the *Los Angeles Times* back in the sixties. (I discovered him pretty late; I hate having missed all the stories he wrote in the forties and fifties.) He was always on the go, like the wandering scribes of yore, and like the other well-known traveling writers of our time, the likes of John Steinbeck, James Agee, Calvin Trillin, William Least Heat Moon, Jules Loh, John McPhee. But it seemed to me right from the beginning that Chuck Hillinger was a direct spiritual descendent of the greatest of them all, Ernie Pyle. As Ernie Pyle did, this Hillinger leaves himself out of the stories. He doesn't draw cosmic conclusions from his travels, or bother to puzzle out deep meaning. He shows up and listens and understands, discovers things he didn't know before, then sits down and writes plain stories about plain people which tell the readers things they didn't know before, either, or hadn't thought about. About the time a sniper's bullet ended Ernie Pyle's travels toward the end of World War II, Chuck Hillinger was just preparing to set out for himself. It's as if Ernie handed on his suitcase and typewriter to Chuck.

Now, Hillinger has had a full career of his own. After 45 years of nearly non-stop wandering, you'd think he might have had enough of trains and planes and rental cars. I happen to know that after he retired from his traveling job on the *Times* in 1992, he and his Arliene have toured Eastern Europe, Scandinavia, Thailand, Mexico, Canada, both U.S. coasts and the Caribbean. Those are just the trips I know about. He said to me one time, "I never tire of travel."

I was a traveling man myself, *On the Road* for CBS News, seeking out the same sorts of people and places which drew Hillinger's attention, and I figured that sooner or later, our paths would cross. It happened in Pueblo, Colorado, where we both showed up to cover a reunion of retired rodeo cowboys. A few of the old-timers, having marinated themselves in bourbon, decided to climb aboard wild Brahma bulls just one more time. I remember the stricken expression on Hillinger's face as, one after another, those drunk old men went flying up into the blue Colorado sky and came thudding down into the brown Colorado sawdust. Only after the last of them had dusted himself off and staggered bowlegged to safety did Hillinger permit himself a relieved smile. The man is a humanitarian.

He's also a historian. If you think Johnny Appleseed was purely a figure of myth, you'll learn in these pages that he was no such thing. He was a real man, John Chapman, a gentle New Englander who traveled barefoot into the frontier with a coffee sack for a shirt, sowing apple seeds and giving away religious books. Hillinger admired this wandering eccentric enough to spend a few days in Ohio and Indiana chasing down the truth about Johnny.

And Casey Jones, the famed engineer of the Cannonball Special who "died at the throttle . . . with the whistle in his hand"—he was a real man, too, you know, not just a country ballad. In Tennessee, Chuck Hillinger found Casey's pocket watch and engineer's cap, not to mention Casey's son, Charlie, who told him all about the wreck, just as it happened in the spring of 1900.

In fact, not one of these stories by my old hero is without its local history and its pungent local flavor. A 70-year-old Hawaiian woman, mother of 27 children, tells how she heals illnesses with her touch and catches fish with her bare hands. A North Dakota farmer remarks on a 15-below-zero day, "One good thing about a day like this, the mosquitoes aren't biting." A mountaineer woman in West Virginia, who lives without plumbing or electricity, plays Hillinger a tune on the banjo she made from the transmission of a 1935 Buick.

The names on the land obviously make Chuck Hillinger's heart beat faster. He can't stay out of Pitchfork or Spotted Horse, Wyoming; or Rabbit Hash or Hell for Certain, Kentucky. They say America is becoming homogenized, but the people who say that never bother to get off the Interstate Highways. Chuck Hillinger celebrates the glorious uniqueness of American places—the loons of the Minnesota lakes, the seashells of the Florida beaches, the lonely islands of Maine. And a wonderful odor of cooking food wafts through these essays— bread baking in the outdoor ovens of New Mexico, catfish stewing in green onions in a kettle on a Louisiana bayou, peach butter simmering over an oak fire in Arkansas, johnny cakes frying on a Rhode Island griddle.

Charles Hillinger's America is not the crisis-ridden, argumentative, highly politicized country that we read about on the front pages. It's much more neighborly and much more interesting than that. If you ask me, it's much truer to our real lives, too. If some historian of the future wants to know what we Americans were like in the second half of the twentieth century, he'll find us in this book.

ABOUT THE AUTHOR

For 45 years Charles Hillinger roamed California, America and the world doing nearly 6,000 human interest stories on whatever he wanted to write about for the *Los Angeles Times*. His features and column "Charles Hillinger's America" were syndicated by the Los Angeles Times and Washington Post news services to more than 600 newspapers.

Hillinger is known as the Charles Kuralt of print by his peers throughout the United States. In fact, he and Kuralt are friends. At times their paths have crossed gathering material about unusual people, places and events.

Within these pages is a unique slice of America—stories from all 50 states; Washington, D.C.; Puerto Rico, and the Virgin Islands. They capture the flavor of this great country of ours in a way you have never experienced before. These stories are updated versions of his columns, in some cases a combination of two or more features from a state.

You will spend time with the Outer Bankers of North Carolina; attend the Sheepherders Ball, one of the biggest social events of the year in Idaho; visit America's most fascinating cemetery, and peek into the editorial offices of a national newspaper boasting more than 500 correspondents, all of whom file their copy in longhand.

There's a story about Paul Garber, who single-handedly collected all the flying machines for the Smithsonian Air and Space Museum; a profile of the Pueblo Indians of New Mexico, and a look at the largest gathering of bald eagles on Earth in Alaska.

Hillinger takes the reader along the East Coast, then across the nation on an entertaining and enlightening adventure. He explains what "Mary Had a Little Lamb" had to do with Thanksgiving. He visits Mountain, W.Va., once called Mole Hill—perhaps the only place in the world where someone actually made a mountain out of a mole hill.

He explores Johnny Appleseed country; the looniest state in the Lower 48; the musical state with more bands than all the others; the nation's richest county per capita, where you can't even buy a loaf of bread or a pint of milk, and Tuskegee, the university that's a national park. He visits Hawaii's Big Kahuna and the Cha Chas of the Virgin Islands.

Hillinger thinks he has just about the best job anyone could ever dream of: never going to the office and commuting from his bedroom a couple of steps to his studio where he does his writing.

As a feature writer and columnist for *The Times*, he spent a week or two on the road, came home and wrote a dozen stories or more. Then he would be back on the road again.

Hillinger's writing has taken him around the world twice, to the North and South poles, Mt. Everest, all 50 states, all the Canadian provinces, all the Mexican states, Central and South America, Russia, China, all of Europe, much of Africa, the Middle East, the Far East, Australia, New Zealand and throughout the Pacific Islands.

His datelines are from such exotic places as Niue, Nauru, Andorra, Magadan, Xian, Sharjah, Addis Ababa, Bombay, Anadyr, Tuleneut, S'gogogsig and the Galapagos Islands. He has interviewed kings, queens, prime ministers, presidents and skid-row bums.

Like the life of all reporters and writers for major newspapers, Hillinger's has been one adventure after another. He survived five airplane crashes.

He was one of six pool reporters for NASA aboard the aircraft carrier *Hornet* in the Pacific for the recovery of the *Apollo 11* astronauts Neil Armstrong, Buzz Aldrin and Michael Collins on their return to Earth after man's first flight to the moon. When three towering undersea mountains were discovered the day Armstrong and Aldrin first set foot on the moon, it was Hillinger who named them for the astronauts.

Hillinger was the first American journalist to travel throughout Siberia. He has won numerous writing awards, is past president of the Greater Los Angeles Press Club and author of *The California Islands* and *Bel-Air Country Club, A Living Legend* as well as scores of stories for national magazines. He was one of the creators of the NBC prime-time television show "Real People," which featured more than 100 segments based on his newspaper articles.

Born in Evanston, Ill., he grew up in Park Ridge, both Chicago suburbs. In the 7th through 10th grades he was a columnist and the youngest circulation manager of an accredited newspaper in America, the weekly *Park Ridge Advocate*. He was a copyboy and feature writer for the *Chicago Tribune* as a high school junior and senior. A graduate of Maine Township High School in Des Plains, Ill., and of UCLA, Hillinger served nearly three years in the Navy during World War II aboard the aircraft carrier *Attu* and the attack transport *Garrard*. His ship took part in the April 1, 1945, invasion of Okinawa and was with the Third Fleet when it sailed into Tokyo Bay as the war ended.

He and his wife Arliene, listed in Who's Who of American Women for her club and philanthropic work, were married in 1948. They have a son, Brad; a daughter, Tori Lindman, and four granddaughters.

ABOUT THE AUTHOR

ONE

DELAWARE
America's First State

"THE FIRST STATE," proclaims Delaware's license plates. Why Delaware? Because on Dec. 7, 1787, Delaware became the first state to ratify the U.S. Constitution.

Only 96 miles long and 9 to 35 miles wide, Delaware, America's second smallest state, is rural, mostly farmland. The state flag is emblazoned with a cow and a farmer holding a hoe.

This is a state sprinkled with tiny hamlets called crossroads and corners, quaint communities with names from the earliest days of colonization along the mid-Atlantic coast. You find names like Anthony's Corner, Cabbage Corner, Big Oak Corner, Stumps Corner, Kings Crossroads, Queens Crossroads, Lords Crossroads and Milford Crossroads. You also find Blackbird, Alms House, Hour Glass, Little Heaven, Rising Sun, Blue Ball, Cocked Hat, Mermaid, Old Furnace and Shortly.

Delaware is the only state that has "hundreds," a throwback to a unit of English local government in size between a village and a shire, or county. Hundreds date back to King Edmund I (939-946) and continued to be used in Great Britain into the 1800s. They're still in use in Delaware today.

Delaware is divided into 33 hundreds. Blue posts with the names of hundreds in yellow letters mark the boundaries throughout the state.

Historians believe that the designation hundred originally signified an area with enough people to provide 100 men for battle in wartime.

In the early days of Delaware there were hundred constables, hundred courts, hundred school districts, hundred tax assessors and hundred tax collectors.

Now there are only hundred polling places. *Hundred* is primarily a geographic term, referring to locations such as Appoquinimink (Indian for "Wounded Duck") Hundred and North and South Murderkill hundreds (from the Dutch *Moeder*—"Mother"—and *Kill*—"Creek").

"Hear ye! Hear ye!" shouted town crier Ronny Dodd, 52, in his high, whiny Southern Delaware twang, as he stood on a balcony of the 1837 colonial-style, red brick Sussex County Courthouse. "Here are the official election returns!"

Dodd, the Georgetown undertaker and longtime town crier, was decked out in an 18th-Century black top hat, white dickey and tails. He was carrying on a tradition dating back to 1791.

It was Return Day in Georgetown, population 1,800, Delaware's biggest and most venerated celebration. It takes place two days after the November election every other year.

More than 20,000 Delawareans were on hand from all over the tiny state (1990 population, 666,168), from Wilmington, the state's largest city, and Dover, its capital, from hamlets like Dinahs Corners and Dutch Neck Crossroads.

They had come as they always do, to enjoy the public peacemaking ceremony by political opponents, to see the winners and losers of the state's political races ride side-by-side in a parade of horse-drawn carriages a mile down Market Street and around the town circle in front of the courthouse.

They had come to hear band concerts, to munch on Delaware delicacies such as barbecued ox, slippery dumplings, muskrat, oyster and soft crab sandwiches, funnel cakes (sugarcoated fried dough), crab cakes and clam chowder.

They had come to see Democrats and Republican political leaders bury a symbolic hatchet in a pile of sand and to see opponents shake hands with one another on a platform in front of the Georgetown courthouse.

Of course, those assembled in the town circle knew from listening to the radio, reading newspapers and watching television who had won Delaware's lone U.S. House of Representatives seat, state legislative posts and other state, county and local offices long before the town undertaker made his announcement.

But Dodd's declarations are part of the time-honored tradition of Return Day, a public holiday in Delaware. There's nothing like it anywhere else in the nation.

Delaware's governor, Mike Castle, and the state's two senators, Joseph Biden, Jr., and William Roth, Jr., rode in a horse-drawn carriage in the two-hour parade—but not beside opponents. They were not up for reelection this particular year.

"This is a day with a lot of virtues," the governor said. "It's a time of healing for us. The candidates worked hard against one another for several months. Now they are pulling together for the greatest good of the state.

"Return Day could only happen in a state the size of Delaware, where we all know each other so well."

As always happens in American politics, there was bitterness in many Delaware campaigns, heated rhetoric, pointed accusations.

Atty. Gen. Charles M. Oberly, 39, and his challenger Dallas Winslow, 42, a Wilmington attorney, engaged in a tough tug-of-war. Oberly won the election by only eight-tenths of 1%. At first Winslow said he was going to demand a recount.

Delawareans wondered if Winslow would show up. They knew Oberly would. Winners always do. But sometimes losers just can't swallow their pride.

"Of course I have every intention of riding in an open carriage seated next to my opponent on Return Day," Winslow said after he lost the election. "Delaware is lucky indeed to have such a tradition. This is a nice way to calm things down."

During the campaign, Oberly demanded Winslow publicly apologize to his father for accusing him of illegally contributing to Oberly's campaign.

Winslow accused Oberly of violating election laws in permitting 15 major drug dealers to plea bargain and avoid jail sentences.

Although the two grew up in the same neighborhood and have known each other all of their lives, both said they're not sure their relations will ever be the same again. But they smiled and waved to the crowds as the carriage moved along the parade route.

They did not, however, look at each other or engage in casual chitchat.

"I give Mr. Winslow a good deal of credit for being here," said the attorney general. "It's easy to be a winner. It shows a lot more character to be a loser on a day like this."

Another spirited race was that between state Treasurer Janet Rzewnicki, 33, and the defeated Bonnie Benson, 29, a Milton attorney.

"I wasn't the one doing the mud slinging," Rzewnicki told reporters before the parade.

"I'm proud of my campaign," said Benson. "I have no regrets."

"Those losers who don't come and ride in the parade next to the winner might as well forget about running for political office again," said Joe Conaway, a Sussex County administrator who served as master of ceremonies at the event. "The people of Delaware expect both winner and loser to be here."

When Joe Flickinger, 40, victor in the race for New Castle County registrar of wills, passed by in his horse-drawn carriage, parade spectators shouted: "Where's the loser?" Flickinger shouted back: "Maybe he's sick. Who knows? I don't know where he is...."

John Romanowski, 55, defeated in his efforts to win a seat in the state House of Representatives, admitted before the parade he had not congratulated his opponent. "I'm not going to be humble," he said, laughing. "I'm a poor loser. But we won't come to blows."

In the early days of the celebration, scuffles and arrests were common. In 1844, one politician was killed by an opponent in a furious fight in Georgetown on Return Day.

"Oh, it was hard fought in the old days. We're getting more genteel, more civilized," insisted Georgetown Mayor W. Layton Johnson, 60. In office 25 years, he credits his long tenure to "having 45% of the people in town relatives and 25% owing me money.

"You know, it's amazing that for six months these people slug it out, then 48 hours later they hop into a carriage together and bury the hatchet. Return Day makes us a better community, a better state. It's too bad this doesn't happen all over America."

Part of the tradition is to roast two oxen at the Georgetown Circle, then pass out free sandwiches to everyone.

Henry Vogt (pronounced Vote), 69, operator of the town newsstand for 30 years, was in charge of roasting the two oxen. The oxen barbecued over charcoal briquettes on two huge spits. For 30 hours, there had to be someone at the cinder-block pit to turn the animals every half-hour.

Return Day got its start when voters came to Georgetown, the county seat of one of Delaware's three counties, to cast their ballots. The votes would be tallied the next day. On the third day, the people would return to learn the results from the town crier

They came to Georgetown in buckboards, on horseback, on foot and in horse- and oxen-drawn wagons. After the politicians "buried the hatchet," there would be a big party. There has been one ever since.

In the parade, in addition to the politicians, were a dozen bands from all over the state. There were floats, antique cars, fire trucks, the First Delaware Regiment armed with flintlock rifles and wearing Colonial uniforms. Men marched in long, blue crushed-velvet coats, knickers and tricornered hats. Women marched in Colonial gowns, ascots, bonnets and feathered hats.

Winning state Sen. Thurman Adams, 58, a seed and grain dealer from Bridgeville, summed up Return Day this way:

"We Delawareans bury the hatchet as if nothing negative has ever been said. Everyone tries to be sociable. Sometimes, in the heat of the campaign, things were said that should not have been. But now, it's time to forgive and forget and become friends again."

TWO

MARYLAND

The British Colonial Legacy Is Everywhere

HUGE PORTRAITS of King Charles I of England and his wife, Henrietta Maria, flank the fireplace of the Governor's Reception Room on the second floor of Maryland's Capitol.

The paintings of the 17th-Century royal couple are quite appropriate in America's oldest capitol in continuous legislative use. It was Lord Baltimore who named Maryland in honor of King Charles' wife, after the king granted Baltimore a charter for a colony in the New World.

Annapolis is named for Queen Anne, who ruled Great Britain from 1702 to 1714 and issued the capital its charter in 1708.

Streets in Annapolis, population 32,000, are named Duke of Gloucester, King George, Prince George and Hanover, for the royal house of the same name.

Annapolis is filled with reminders of America's early history. The city boasts more pre-Revolutionary War homes than any other. Block after block of cobblestone and brick streets and alleys are lined with preserved and restored Colonial red-brick homes and shops.

Maryland's pillared, red-brick Capitol, with its 181-foot-high white wooden dome, is perched on Annapolis' highest hill. It looms above the capital's historic district, above the sprawling U.S. Naval Academy on the shores of the Severn River. The Capitol was built between 1772 and 1779.

This is the only statehouse that has served as the nation's Capitol. From Nov. 26, 1783, to Aug. 13, 1784, this same building, which continues to house Maryland's legislative chambers and executive offices, was the seat of the new country's government.

It was in the Old Senate Chambers, on Dec. 23, 1783, that George Washington appeared before the Continental Congress and resigned his commission as commander in chief of the Continental Army. Five years and four months later, he was inaugurated as President.

On Jan. 14, 1784, the Treaty of Paris was ratified by the Continental Congress at the Capitol in Annapolis, officially ending the Revolutionary War. Thomas Jefferson and James Monroe were members of the Continental Congress when the Maryland Statehouse served as the nation's first peacetime Capitol.

Every day, guards climb the 149 steps of the steep spiral staircase to the top of the dome to raise and lower the U.S. and Maryland flags. Maryland's is the only state flag with the colors and coat of arms of a state's founding families.

The Capitol dome, the nation's largest wooden dome, is constructed of Maryland cypress and held together with wooden pegs. The dome is crowned with a huge carved acorn, a symbol of wisdom.

Almost every day, fourth graders studying Maryland's history are bused in from schools throughout the state to tour the Capitol. "The fourth graders get quite excited about being able to stand on the exact spot where George Washington stood and delivered his farewell address from the Army," veteran guide Judy Housley said.

The Annapolis Capitol is one of Maryland's most popular attractions. Tour guides wear Colonial costumes.

Above the grand staircase is an 1859 painting by Edwin White of Gen. Washington resigning his military commission.

Every state honors two of its most famous citizens with statues in Statuary Hall in the U.S. Capitol. Smaller versions of Maryland's two statues of John Hanson and Charles Carroll stand in the New Senate Chamber of the Maryland Capitol.

Hanson is often called the "first President of the United States" because he represented Maryland in the Continental Congress and was elected by that body in 1771 as the "first President of the United States in Congress Assembled."

Carroll, one of Maryland's four signers of the Declaration of Independence, was the only Roman Catholic to sign the document. Of the 56 signers, he survived longest and was one of Maryland's first U.S. senators. At 90, on July 4, 1828, Carroll presided at a ceremony that began construction of the Baltimore and Ohio Railroad.

In 1781, the Legislature commissioned famed Maryland painter Charles Wilson Peale to paint a full-length portrait of Gen. Washington, "in grateful remembrance of that most illustrious character." Peale's painting hangs in the Old Senate Chamber. A mannequin of Washington stands there, too.

A plaque in the rotunda salutes Maryland native Matthew Alexander Henson, the African-American hero who co-discovered the North Pole with Adm. Robert E. Peary in 1909.

Behind glass is a miniature Maryland flag carried to the moon and back by the *Apollo 11* astronauts, along with several small flakes of moon rocks.

Numerous historic paintings adorn the walls of the statehouse. One painting that attracts considerable attention is *The Burning of the Peggy Stewart*. Depicted is Anthony Stewart, owner of the ship, shown putting a torch to the vessel at the Annapolis waterfront Oct. 19, 1774.

Like Boston, Annapolis had its tea party. When Revolutionary patriots learned Stewart had brought a cargo of tea from England and paid taxes on it, they demanded he burn his ship and its contents. They threatened to burn his warehouses and other holdings in town if he refused. History records that Stewart did put a torch to his ship, a ship he'd named after his daughter Peggy Stewart.

"From time to time over the last 100 years there has been talk of moving the capital to Baltimore," said Chris Allan, administrator of the State Archives, "but it was never pursued very seriously.

"There is something especially nice about using the old statehouse so long, about that kind of utility, where other states have moved to new locations several times and constructed massive complexes devoted to state government."

But Maryland has stuck with its old Capitol and its original plan for its capital city, laid out by a royal governor, Francis Nicholson, who ruled from 1694 to 1699. Nicholson moved the Colonial capital from St. Mary's to Annapolis in 1694 and laid out the city's baroque street plan that continues to distinguish Annapolis as one of the finest examples of a Colonial city in America.

THREE

WASHINGTON, D.C.

Statuary Hall and
Paul Garber's Amazing Flying Machines

ACH YEAR as many as 10 million visitors view the bronze and marble statues of America's heroes in the U.S. Capitol. Some are well known. Many are not.

Since 1864, each state has been entitled to donate statues of two of its most distinguished deceased citizens for permanent exhibit in the Capitol.

Once a state legislature decides who is to be honored, a statue is created and accepted by Congress for a place in National Statuary Hall—America's hall of fame.

"People are always anxious to see the statues from their state," said Barbara Wolanin, curator of Statuary Hall since 1978. "But often they're surprised and disappointed because they have no idea who the people depicted in the statues are.

"Members of Congress call my office from time to time asking, 'Who are our two statues?' When I tell them, they often reply, 'Who's that?' or 'Who are they?'"

Only three Presidents are here—George Washington (Va.), Andrew Jackson (Tenn.) and James A. Garfield (Ohio).

One would expect to see Abraham Lincoln representing Illinois. But the state known as "Land of Lincoln" has statues of Frances E. Willard and James Shields instead. Willard founded the Women's Christian Temperance Union; Shields was an Army general, governor of Oregon Territory and U.S. senator from Illinois.

Three states have statues of vice presidents—John C. Calhoun (S.C.), George Clinton (N.Y.) and Hannibal Hamlin and William King, both from Maine.

Thirty-six statues depict former U.S. senators. There are 23 members of the House of Representatives, 30 governors and 32 military heroes. (Some honorees held more than one of these titles.)

There are statues of four signers of the Declaration of Independence. There are six physicians. There's a king—Kamehameha (Hawaii)—and a famed cowboy artist—Charley Russell (Mont.). Oklahoma honors two American Indians: Sequoya, inventor of the Cherokee alphabet, and Will Rogers, humorist, newspaper columnist and movie star.

In keeping with Rogers' famous advice to "Always keep an eye on Congress to see what they're up to," his statue is the only one facing the House chamber.

The feet of many of the statues gleam from constant rubbing by visitors for good luck. Will Rogers has the shiniest feet of all.

There are statues of the president and vice president of the Confederacy, Jefferson Davis (Miss.) and Alexander Hamilton Stephens (Ga.), as well as of the "Father of Refrigeration" John Gorrie (Fla.) and steamboat inventor Robert Fulton (Pa.).

Six statues honor women: Dr. Florence Sabin (Colo.), author of the Sabin Health Laws that modernized the state's public health system; Illinois' Frances Willard; Marie Sanford (Minn.), educator and champion of women's rights; Jeannette Rankin (Mont.), the nation's first congresswoman; Mother Joseph (Wash.), a Catholic nun who contributed to the fields of health care, education and social work, and Esther Hobart Morris (Wyo.), the first woman to hold judicial office in the nation.

Some of America's best-known historic figures are here as well: Henry Clay (Ky.), Huey Long (La.), Daniel Webster (N.H.), William Jennings Bryan

(Neb.), Robert E. Lee (Va.), Samuel Adams (Mass.), Roger Williams (R.I.), John C. Calhoun (S.C.), Sam Houston and Stephen Austin (Tex.) and Ethan Allen (Vt.).

Lesser known are: Jabez Curry (Ala.), Uriah Rose (Ark.), Edmund K. Smith (Fla.), George Shoup (Ida.), Samuel Kirkwood (Iowa), George Glick (Kans.), Zachariah Chandler (Mich.), Zebulon Vance (N.C.) and Jason Lee (Ore.). Most visitors to Statuary Hall haven't the slightest idea who they were.

"People pass away who are much more famous than many in Statuary Hall," said curator Wolanin, "but the states are stuck with those selected at an earlier time. If we were to let states substitute statues they would rather have now, it would open a Pandora's Box."

California's statues, both dedicated on the same day, March 1, 1930, are of a minister and a priest.

Most visitors recognize Father Junipero Serra, the Franciscan priest who established nine California missions before he died in 1784. Father Serra's bronze likeness holds a little mission in his left hand. His right hand holds a cross high above his head.

Thomas Starr King is not so familiar. "What did he do?" Californians typically ask when they see the statue.

King, a Unitarian minister, came to California in 1860 from Boston to serve as pastor of the First Unitarian Church of San Francisco. It was during the Civil War, and many Californians favored the Confederacy. Of more than 100 newspapers in the state, only 24 supported Abraham Lincoln.

"King traveled throughout California championing the Union cause," curator Wolanin explained. "He is remembered as the man whose matchless oratory kept California in the Union."

King lived in California only four years before dying at age 40 in 1864.

Fourteen of the statues are of religious leaders, including Father Damien (Hawaii), who devoted his life to lepers on Molokai; Father Kino (Ariz.), a Jesuit missionary, and Brigham Young (Utah), the Mormon Church leader.

Five states—Nevada, North Dakota, Wyoming, Colorado and New Mexico—have contributed only one statue each so far.

On May 2, 1990, Utah became the latest state to present its second statue, a 7-foot, 7-inch bronze likeness of lanky Philo T. Farnsworth (1906-1971), known as the "Father of Television." The statue shows Farnsworth holding one of his first cathode-ray tubes. He transmitted his first electronic TV picture in 1927.

Students at Ridgecrest Elementary School in Butler, Utah, under the guidance of Principal Bruce Barnson, led the effort to put the Farnsworth statue in the Capitol.

In a statewide poll conducted by the students, residents favored Farnsworth over 20 other Utahans, including Eliza Snow, poet and wife of Brigham Young; Mormon leader Ezra Taft Benson; hotelier J. Willard Marriott, and heavyweight boxing champion Jack Dempsey.

Among those present for Utah Gov. Norman Bangerter's unveiling of the statue was the inventor's 81-year-old widow, Elma (Pem) Farnsworth.

By 1933 there were 65 statues in Statuary Hall. The aesthetic appearance of the hall began to suffer from overcrowding, and the floor would not support the weight of any more of the heavy statues. So it was decided to keep the main portion of the collection in the hall and place the others in prominent locations of the Capitol.

The entire collection, although no longer in the same room, continues to be called National Statuary Hall. Today there are 38 statues in the Old House of Representatives, with the rest displayed in various parts of the Capitol building.

The diminutive 91-year-old man walked from his office on the second floor of the Smithsonian National Air and Space Museum and looked out over the huge Milestones of Flight Gallery, where many of the world's most historic flying machines are on permanent exhibit.

Charles Lindbergh's *Spirit of St. Louis* loomed above him. Suspended from the ceiling nearby was the Wright Brothers' 1903 *Flyer* of Kitty Hawk fame. Both are there because of this longtime friend of fliers and flying, Paul E. Garber.

Garber has had a hand in nearly every acquisition of the 385 historic airplanes in the Smithsonian Institution's collection. With 77 aircraft on display, the Air and Space Museum has the largest collection of historic airplanes and spacecraft anywhere in the world.

Since he went to work for the Smithsonian in 1920, Garber has been the driving force behind that collection. At 91, he's still at it. Five days a week, Garber continues to track down airplanes he considers vital to the collection and to oversee restorations.

In 1946, when Congress established the National Air Museum, Garber was named its first curator. Today he bears the title Historian Emeritus, National Air and Space Museum.

Garber's interest in flying goes back almost as far as flying itself. He boasts a personal acquaintance with a number of famous fliers, including Orville and Wilbur Wright.

When he was 9 years old, Garber watched Orville take off from Ft. Meyer, Va., for an hour-long demonstration flight. The plane he was flying—the Wright Brothers' 1909 two-seat *Military Flyer*—was the world's first military airplane. It's now part of the Smithsonian collection.

"Did you know that the Wright Brothers' 1903 *Flyer*, the first powered airplane ever to fly, was in England for 20 years, from 1928 to 1948?" asked Garber, gazing with pride at the fragile wood, fabric and wire flying machine that changed the world.

"Orville was upset because he thought he and Wilbur did not receive proper recognition for their historic flight, so he let the British have the airplane. I went to England and, with the help of the U.S. Navy, brought the 1903 *Flyer* back. It was dismantled and placed aboard a vessel for shipment to the Smithsonian, where it rightfully belonged."

Before he went to work for the Smithsonian, Garber worked for the Airmail Service with Charles Lindbergh. When 25-year-old "Lucky Lindy" took off for Paris on the first nonstop flight across the Atlantic in May of 1927, Garber cabled his friend.

"I knew everybody in the world would be after the *Spirit of St. Louis*," he recalled "I wired Lindbergh that the Smithsonian wanted the airplane when he was finished with it. After Lindbergh flew all over the United States, Mexico and South America immediately following the Atlantic flight, he called me one day from an airfield in the Midwest. He said, 'Paul, I'm flying the *Spirit* to Washington. You can have it.'"

Garber recalled the time years later when Lindbergh phoned to ask if he could come over and "sit in the *Spirit*." At the time, the plane was on exhibit, hanging from the ceiling of the Arts and Industry Building.

"It was near closing time when Lindbergh arrived," Garber said. "I suggested he wait until all the visitors left the museum. Then I got a tall double ladder, and he climbed it.

"I knew he wanted to be alone with his thoughts, so I went off and sat in a corner. Here was Lindbergh in his airplane and I with him, alone. What a moving experience. After about a half-hour, he leaned out the cockpit and called down, 'Hey, Paul, will you hold on to the ladder for me? I'm ready to come down.' He thanked me for taking good care of his airplane, and we went out to dinner together."

Garber strolled over to the red Lockheed Vega in the Air and Space Museum. This is the airplane Amelia Earhart flew across the Atlantic five years after Lindbergh's flight. She was the first woman to make the trip alone.

"Amelia was a good friend," said Garber. "She gave me the Vega for the Smithsonian collection. I talked to her before she left on her around-the-world flight with Fred Noonan in 1937. They were going to give the Smithsonian that airplane when they completed the flight.

"When their plane vanished near Howland Island in the South Pacific, I went out and bought four roses and put two on the propeller and two on the nose of the Vega."

The sprightly nonagenarian has been personally acquainted with all of this nation's and many of the world's top aviators.

"I love this place," Garber said, looking out over the museum. "Sometimes I can't believe that I've seen all this happen in my lifetime. My work is far from finished. There are still planes out there I'd like to get my hands on. Right now I'm trying to track down a 1927 Loening Amphibian...."

In addition to the 77 restored historic planes in the National Air and Space Museum, the collection includes 56 more restored airplanes and 154 others awaiting restoration at the Smithsonian's Paul E. Garber Preservation, Restoration and Storage Facility in nearby Suitland, Md. Another 71 restored aircraft are on loan from the collection to aviation museums throughout the United States and abroad.

It was in 1980 that Suitland's Silver Hill Museum was renamed in honor of Garber's 60th anniversary with the Smithsonian. One of the 24 buildings at the 25-acre complex holds one of the world's most complete archives of historical aircraft.

Other Garber buildings house airplanes and airplane parts. There are always several aircraft in the midst of restoration. Fifteen full-time mechanics restore airplanes with the help of volunteers, many of them retired aerospace workers. Paul Garber keeps his hand in the restoration work by spending a day there each week.

Historic airplanes now in restoration include the B-29 Superfortress *Enola Gay*, the airplane that ushered in the Nuclear Age when it dropped the first atomic bomb on Hiroshima on Aug. 6, 1945.

A Sopwith Snipe, the first fighter used by the British Royal Air Force, is also being restored here. So is a German World War II Aerado 234, the world's first operational jet bomber, and a Hawker Hurricane, the airplane that bore the brunt of Britain's defense against the Luftwaffe's aerial armada.

George Genotti, 72, has been part of the *Enola Gay* restoration team since 1984. That restoration was nearing completion.

Genotti, a former aviation mechanic for Eastern Airlines and North American Aviation, was busy removing dust from a piston in one of the *Enola Gay*'s four engines. "We restore each plane using original parts whenever possible, to the point where the plane could fly," he said. "We are preserving them for posterity's sake. We want them to last for at least another 300 to 400 years."

The restoration process involves cleaning every part of the aircraft, chemically treating its surfaces to remove and neutralize corrosion and coating surfaces for protection. Replaced parts are marked so that future researchers will know they are not original.

Among the photographs and memorabilia hanging from the walls in Garber's office is a letter from President Ronald Reagan, who saluted Garber for dedicating his life to the preservation of our nation's treasures of aviation.

"Your foresight and hard work help make the Air and Space Museum possible," the President wrote. "Thanks to you, the museum has under its roof the most impressive collection of historic airplanes and spacecraft in the world."

The interview with Paul Garber took place in May of 1990. He died at the age of 93 on Sept. 23, 1992.

FOUR

VIRGINIA

Arlington National Cemetery

T HIS BURIAL PLACE of history and heroes, of men and women who fought in all of America's wars, was crowded on Memorial Day with those who came to honor the more than 210,000 interred at Arlington National Cemetery.

President Bill Clinton straightened the red, white and blue ribbons on a huge wreath, then placed it on the Tomb of the Unknowns. He bowed his head and prayed.

A handful of those making the Memorial Day pilgrimage were men in their 90s. They trudged up a steep hill to pay homage to Pulitzer Prize-winning General of the Armies John J. (Black Jack) Pershing.

These men, who served under Pershing during World War I, gathered as they do each Memorial and Veterans days at the three-foot-high government-issue white Vermont-marble headstone that marks his grave.

Graves of men and women who sacrificed their lives in the service of their country—and burial sites of veterans who served in wars of this country—were visited on this Memorial Day by relatives and friends.

Everywhere you looked across the lush, green rolling hills of the 612-acre cemetery were rows of white headstones. Interspersed among the glistening marble markers were other monuments and memorials.

There is no facet of American history overlooked in this hallowed graveyard. Here rest the remains of those who served in the Revolutionary War, the War of 1812, the Mexican and Civil wars, the Indian campaigns, the Spanish–American War, the Philippine Insurrection, World Wars I and II and the Korean, Vietnam and Gulf wars.

Here are the graves of two Presidents, William Howard Taft and John Fitzgerald Kennedy, of Supreme Court justices and members of the U.S. Congress and Cabinet.

Headstones with gold lettering mark the final resting places of more than 300 Medal of Honor recipients.

One section of the cemetery marks the graves of more than 3,800 former slaves with headstones designated "civilian" or "citizen."

A total of 4,725 unknowns from America's wars are buried at the cemetery. A massive sarcophagus holds the remains of 2,111 unknowns of the Civil War. Their scattered bones were collected from battlefields strewn with Union and Confederate soldiers.

One grave, in a section set aside for Union soldiers, has a pointed headstone signifying a Confederate burial. The unknown soldier was found wearing a Confederate jacket and Union trousers.

The grave of Gen. Philip Kearny, who lost his left arm in the Mexican War and his life in the Civil War, is marked with a life-size statue of the general on his horse.

On June 14, 1914, President Woodrow Wilson dedicated the 32-foot-tall Confederate Monument. A larger-than-life-size statue of a woman holding a laurel wreath and facing the South crowns the gift from the United Daughters of the Confederacy.

When the monument was dedicated, Union and Confederate veterans placed wreaths on graves of their former enemies to symbolize reconciliation.

The towering mast of the battleship *Maine* is here. It was raised from Havana Harbor after the ship was sunk in a prelude to the Spanish–American War. Headstones for the graves of 229 men who went down with the ship lie in the shadows of the mast. The etched memorial bears the long-ago slogan, "Remember the *Maine!*"

Chaplains' Hill has graves for the 134 chaplains of various faiths killed in five wars. Chaplains' Monument on the hill commemorates 23 who lost their lives in World War I. One of the chaplains is Maj. Charles J. Watters, killed during an assault on Hill 875 near Dak To in Vietnam.

The snow-white statue of a nurse stands on a hill above the graves of hundreds of nurses who served the armed forces. Nearby are 2,700 cenotaphs in memory of airmen and sailors whose bodies have never been found.

There is a Rough Riders monument, a Seabees memorial and the Pyramid Memorial to Coast Guards killed at sea. Nine astronauts are buried in Arlington National Cemetery. The Challenger Memorial displays busts of those aboard the ill-fated shuttle mission.

A memorial to the Screaming Eagles, the 101st Army Airborne Division, commemorates the 248 soldiers killed in the plane crash at Gander, Newfoundland, in December of 1985.

There is a memorial to the 161 servicemen killed in the Marine barracks at Beirut International Airport Oct. 23, 1983. Nearby is the grave of seaman Robert Stephen, killed by terrorists during the TWA hijacking June 15, 1985, and a cedar tree as a living memorial to all victims of terrorists throughout the world.

Many of America's best-known heroes found their final resting place at Arlington: "Hap" Arnold, Omar Bradley, Roger Chaffee, Claire Chennault, George Crook, "Wild Bill" Donovan, Gus Grissom, "Bull" Halsey, George C. Marshall, Audie Murphy, Francis Gary Powers, Hyman Rickover, Philip Henry Sherman, Walter Bedell Smith and Jonathan Wainwright—to name but a few.

Ira Hayes, the Pima Indian of Iwo Jima flag-raising fame, is here. So are Daniel "Chappie" James, the first black four-star general; Robert E. Peary, the first person to reach the North Pole; civil rights leader Medgar Evers, and Chief Justice Earl Warren.

As are heavyweight champion Joe Louis, actor Lee Marvin and ABC correspondent Frank Reynolds. Actress Constance Bennett is buried with her husband, Air Force Brig. Gen. John Coulter.

Arlington National Cemetery has more visitors than any cemetery in America, more than 4 million a year. New burials average 15 a day, and at this rate the cemetery will be full by the year 2020.

Because space is limited, burials are restricted to a few categories. These include those who die on active duty, veterans having at least 20 years' service and holders of the nation's highest military decorations.

Any veteran with an honorary discharge, however, if cremated, can be interred in the cemetery's columbarium. It opened in April of 1990 with room for 100,000 remains.

Prior to its establishment in 1864, Arlington National Cemetery was the estate of Gen. Robert E. Lee and his wife Mary Anna Randolph Custis. They lived for 30 years in Arlington House, or, as it is also known, the Custis–Lee Mansion. The stately columned home was completed in 1817 by George Washington Parke Custis, grandson of Martha Washington and her first husband.

When Lee resigned his commission and went over to the Confederate side, the home and estate were confiscated by the federal government and the grounds became the national cemetery. Arlington House is open to the public and administered by the National Park Service.

John F. Kennedy visited the Custis–Lee Mansion during his presidency. Commenting on its beauty, serenity and setting—high on a hill visible from many places in the capital—he remarked: "I could stay here forever."

Eleven days before his assassination, Kennedy placed a wreath at the Tomb of the Unknowns on Veterans Day 1963.

His grave is 300 feet down the hill below the Custis–Lee Mansion, on a direct line with the Lincoln Memorial across the Memorial Bridge spanning the Potomac. Jacqueline Kennedy lit the eternal flame at President Kennedy's grave on the day of his funeral. She is now buried beside him.

A simple white wooden cross nearby marks the grave of the President's brother, Sen. Robert F. Kennedy, who died June 6, 1968, after being shot by Sirhan Sirhan at the Ambassador Hotel in Los Angeles.

The rows of simple white markers and the stirring memorials and monuments of Arlington National Cemetery trace a moving panorama of American history, a panorama that spans the birth of the nation to the present day.

The guard at the Tomb of the Unknowns walks 21 steps, the length of the black mat. Rigid and straight, he carries an M-14 rifle on his shoulder.

He turns and faces the tomb for 21 seconds. He turns again. He pauses 21 seconds. Then he takes 21 steps to the other end of the walkway. The rifle always rests on the shoulder away from the tomb.

The number of steps taken and the number of seconds paused in the ritual symbolize the 21-gun salute, the highest honor that can be bestowed.

Inside the sarcophagus rests an unknown soldier from World War I, placed there when President Warren G. Harding led the nation in dedicating the Tomb of the Unknown Soldier on Nov. 11, 1921. Now buried immediately outside the tomb are unknowns from World War II and the Korean and Vietnam wars. They symbolize all who gave their lives as the supreme sacrifice.

Sculpted on the east side of the 50-ton tomb facing the nation's capital are the figures representing peace, victory and valor. On the west side of the tomb, an inscription reads: "Here Rests in Honored Glory an American Soldier Known But to God."

Thirty young men, members of the elite 3rd Infantry Regiment—the Old Guard, the oldest active infantry unit in the Army—guard Arlington National Cemetery's Tomb of the Unknown Soldier, now more commonly known as the Tomb of the Unknowns. An individual guard repeats the ritual procedure for a half-hour between March 1 and Oct. 1; for an hour the rest of the year. Then the guard is relieved.

"It is, of course, a great honor to be a Tomb Guard, an experience I will remember with tremendous pride as long as I live," said Pfc. John Porter, 19, of Westminster, Calif. He was between sentry duty in the Tomb Guard quarters in the basement of the Memorial Amphitheater immediately behind the tomb.

At least a dozen wreath-laying ceremonies take place at the tomb each day. When the ceremony occurs, a bugler from the U.S. Army Band plays taps. "That especially gets to you," Porter said.

"As a Tomb Guard, you think about all the unknowns all the time. You wonder who they were, what they were like, where they grew up and lived, how they died in battle."

Porter said that at night, when the Tomb Guard is all alone at the shrine to the fallen heroes, he does a lot of thinking as well. Even at 2 or 3 in the morning, on less rigidly formal night patrol around the perimeter of the monument, his thoughts often center on those men whose remains he is guarding.

According to Staff Sgt. Wayne King, who is in charge of one of the 10-man Tomb Guard units, the discipline, the physical training to be a Tomb Guard, are the toughest in the Army. There are three teams. Each guards the tomb for 24 hours, then has 48 hours off. The days when the men are not guarding the tomb, they are in training in the Catacombs, in the basement of the Memorial Amphitheater.

"It's not easy duty for these young men—18 and 19 years old," said King, a black soldier from Darlington, S.C. Average tour of duty for Tomb Guards is 18 months.

He explained that to be a Tomb Guard, one must be in the Old Guard, the 1,000-member 3rd U.S. Infantry Regiment based at Fort Meyer, adjacent to Arlington National Cemetery. The Old Guard is the President's own Honor Guard. They take part in ceremonies at the White House and at the Pentagon. They are guards of honor at state funerals and funerals at Arlington.

"It is extremely difficult to get into the Old Guard," said King. "Younger members of the Old Guard may volunteer for duty as Tomb Guards. The Tomb Guards are the best of the best."

In 1996, for the first time in the 75 years since the dedication of the Tomb of the Unknowns, women soldiers will be permitted to serve as Tomb Guards.

Tomb Guards until now had to be at least six feet tall.

"Our uniforms have to be spotless, perfectly pressed," said King, "our black leather shoes spit-polished shining. It is tiring walking guard duty so stiff and straight the way we do, especially toward the end of the day. Sometimes when we click our heels together we hurt our ankles. Then we stand so still our knees are locked in place.

"We keep our eyes straight ahead, but we can see people. Sometimes little kids come under the chains, and that is the only time we speak and change our pattern. We go to port arms and announce: 'It is requested parents keep their children outside the chains.'"

Tomb Guard Porter noted that the parents of Tomb Guards must both be born in America. "The Army goes through our school records. Teachers, neighbors, friends and relatives are contacted to check out our character. If we were expelled from school, did drugs or had speeding tickets adding up to more than $150, we cannot be Tomb Guards."

During summer, when the changing of the guard occurs every half-hour, a Tomb Guard will walk the mat eight different times during the course of a day. In winter, when the guard changes every hour, four times.

Because they are on duty 24 hours, Tomb Guards sleep in short stints between guard duty in their quarters at the Memorial Amphitheater.

Tomb Guards wear white gloves, blue jackets and blue pants designed after Cavalry uniforms. A gold band runs up and down their pant legs.

The U.S. Army Band is part of the Old Guard. Buglers and trumpet players from the Army Band play taps at each wreath-laying ceremony.

"I have been coming down here off and on for the entire 16 years I have been in the Army," said Sgt. Dave Detwiler, 37, of Altoona, Pa. He plays lead trumpet with the band and plays taps at wreath-laying ceremonies. "I am proud of it. It is an honor for me to work with the Tomb Guards."

Tomb Guard Pvt. K. Todd Wilber, 19, of Warrentown, Va., said that ever since the age of 5 he hoped to become a sentry at the Tomb of the Unknowns. "I have been coming to Arlington National Cemetery ever since I can remember," he said. As a child, he visited the grave of his grandfather who is buried here.

"When I saw the Tomb Guards the first time," he said, "I knew that I wanted to hold vigil some day over the unknown soldiers who went to war and died for our country. This is the greatest contribution I believe I can make to my country, next to going to war."

FIVE

NEW JERSEY

Before Hollywood There Was New Jersey

F ILM HISTORIAN Thomas F. Hanlon stood outside a weather-beaten white clapboard printing plant in Fort Lee, N.J.

"You'd never know it today," he said, "but that, my friend, was the old Universal Studios before World War I, when Fort Lee was the movie capital of the world."

The turn-of-the-century building is the only one still standing from that magical era. Yet few people are aware of its historical significance.

Fort Lee, population 32,000, is a bedroom community for New York City. It connects to the Bronx by the George Washington Bridge over the Hudson River. Hanlon, who has lived in Fort Lee most of his life, produced the 45-minute documentary *Before Hollywood There Was a Fort Lee.*

"Hundreds of films were produced in Fort Lee from 1903 to 1927," Hanlon noted, "most during its heyday, 1908 to 1917.

"But Fort Lee has been forgotten. Hardly anybody in New Jersey, New York, Hollywood or anywhere else outside this town realizes its importance in the history of motion pictures. Everybody thinks it all happened in Hollywood."

There were seven major film studios in Fort Lee. Twenty-one other film companies shot on location here.

D.W. Griffith directed several films in Fort Lee, including his first, *The Adventures of Dolly*, in 1908. Fort Lee was the location of Mary Pickford's first film, *The Lonely Villa* in 1909, as well as several of her other pictures.

The Barrymores, Dorothy and Lillian Gish, Mae Marsh, Tom Mix, Charlie Chaplin, Will Rogers and other famous pre-World War I actors and actresses starred in films produced in Fort Lee.

It was here that Theda Bara made her vamp movies and where the *Perils of Pauline* serials were filmed. Biograph's first slapstick comedy, *Curtain Pole* starring Mack Sennett, was shot in Fort Lee. The Keystone Kops started here.

Blown-up stills from movies hang on the walls of the Fort Lee Public Library. The library has 1,000 stills and 30 prints of films made here. Every month it screens a film produced in Fort Lee. A couple of times a year it features Tom Hanlon's documentary on the early days of moviemaking.

Why Fort Lee?

Librarian Rita Altomara of the Fort Lee Public Library had the answers right at hand. "First," she said, "filmmaking itself began in New Jersey. Then, Fort Lee had everything the filmmakers needed for backdrops—fields, rolling hills, the Palisades on the Hudson, the river itself, woods, farms, a small-town setting—and it was close to Broadway where the actors came from."

Altomara wrote the 200-page illustrated book *Hollywood on the Palisades,* published in 1983. It lists 917 films made in Fort Lee, including casts and credits.

"There were many more films made here than those I've listed," she said. "But that was all I managed to find in the archives and memorabilia stored at the Fort Lee Library, from periodicals of that time and in my research at the New York Public Library, Museum of Modern Art and other sources."

The reason only a few Fort Lee films still exist, the librarian explained, is because they were printed on extremely flammable silver-nitrate film. Most were lost in studio fires or reprocessed to recover the valuable silver.

"The sad thing about Fort Lee is that no one visiting the town would ever know it had been a filmmaking center unless they happened to come to the library," Altomara said. "There are no signs proclaiming 'America's First Film Capital,' no historic landmarks, no streets named D.W. Griffith or

Pauline White or Mack Sennett, no local film festivals."

But Fort Lee *was* America's first film capital. And it rests not far from where the world of make-believe on the silver screen truly began.

Twenty-five miles southwest of Fort Lee, in West Orange, the National Park Service oversees the Edison National Historic Site, once the huge red-brick research laboratory complex of Thomas A. Edison.

It was in West Orange in 1888 that Edison, with the help of his assistant William K.L. Dickson and others, began his experiments with motion pictures.

On Oct. 8, 1888, Edison wrote the U.S. Patent Office: "I am experimenting upon an instrument which does for the eye what the phonograph does for the ear, which is the recording and reproduction of things in motion."

On Edison's return from a trip to Europe in 1889, Dickson met him at the lab where the movie experiments were going on in accordance with Edison's instructions. Dickson dimmed the lights and cranked the first image ever flashed on a screen. It was footage of Dickson lifting his hat from his head, welcoming Edison home.

"Good morning, Mr. Edison," said Dickson's animated image on the wall. "Glad to see you back. I hope you are satisfied with the Kineto-phonograph."

The first motion pictures were talkies, not silents. They were produced 38 years before Al Jolson appeared in *The Jazz Singer*, a film often credited as the first with sound.

Edison had difficulties synchronizing the sound system between a phonograph (another Edison invention) and a projector. So, after the inventor's initial work with talkies, he concentrated on making silent films.

The earliest film in the Library of Congress archives shows Edison's walrus-mustached lab assistant John Ott sneezing in 1889.

In 1893, Edison built the first motion-picture studio: a 50- by 18-foot tar-paper shack mounted on rollers that ran on a circular track. He called it the Black Maria because it resembled the police paddy wagon known by that name.

The roof of Edison's studio opened with pulleys to provide natural light—electric bulbs weren't strong enough then. To maintain adequate lighting during the filmmaking, workers pushed the studio around the track in line with the sun's progress.

Edison made hundreds of one- and two-reel movies in the Black Maria, but very few survive.

Originals of many of his motion-picture cameras, however, are on exhibit at the Edison Historic Site along with projectors and other movie equipment as well as many of his other inventions. The exhibit includes a 1954 replica of the Black Maria.

The early films ran 60, 90 and 120 seconds. They were viewed by one person at a time for a nickel each at Edison Kinetoscope Peep Shows.

Long lines gathered on lower Broadway in New York on April 14, 1894, to marvel at Edison's latest invention. It wasn't long before huge crowds were viewing the movies in peep shows from coast to coast.

Two years later, on April 23, 1896, in a music hall on Herald Square, an auditorium full of people sat and watched several of Edison's motion pictures on a big screen. There were movies of ballet dancers, boxing matches, waves crashing on a beach.

A new form of entertainment had arrived. The world would never be the same.

Because Edison had the patents, he had a corner on the film industry for several years, manufacturing motion-picture machines and producing the films.

His 14-minute movie *The Great Train Robbery*, directed by Edwin S. Porter and released in 1903, is considered the classic prototype of the motion-picture play. It's shown daily at the historic site.

In 1912, the Edison Talking Picture Co. began distributing talkies through much of the world. Among the exhibits at the historic site are original theater show cards with still photographs from early talkies. "They laugh," the show cards proclaim. "They talk. They sing. The only genuine talking pictures."

"But there were a lot of bugs," said Edward J. Pershey, curator at the Edison National Historic Site. The synchronization of the phonograph and the projector did not always mesh. Technical problems plagued the system.

Finally, there was a disastrous fire in 1914 in Edison's film-processing plant. Although the motion-picture division was Edison's major money-maker for a number of years, by 1916 the inventor quit the movie business.

In the small town of Nutley, N.J., midway between Fort Lee and West Orange, lives Robert E. Lee. He is founder-president of the Essex Film Club, which started in 1939 and claims to be the oldest film club in the United States.

Like Thomas F. Hanlon, Lee too is a noted film historian. A former radio station owner and announcer, he was a film editor for many years. He has his own 50-seat movie theater behind his home.

Among his collection of 400 feature films and 1,500 shorts are eight Edison originals. During a visit to Lee's personal theater, he showed a 1913 Edison talking picture entitled *Nursery Favorites*. In it, costumed singers perform nursery songs—in a film made 14 years before Jolson's *Jazz Singer*. The sound, synchronization and quality of the 1913 talky are surprisingly good.

Lee spent a year visiting schools and libraries throughout the state, commissioned by the New Jersey Department of Education to lecture on the beginnings of moviemaking in the United States.

"It is amazing how many people here in New Jersey still do not know that this is where the motion picture originated," Lee said with a sigh.

Why did the moviemakers abandon New Jersey and head for California? "There are many reasons," he replied. "One was to get out from under Edison's efforts to keep a stranglehold on the industry. Another was that the climate was so much better for filmmaking in Southern California.

"Then, when World War I came along, the government did not consider movies essential. The film companies could not get enough coal to heat their huge studios. That really helped chase them West. New Jersey folded its tent, and the rest is history."

SIX

NEW YORK

Seneca Falls, Cradle of Women's Rights

SENECA FALLS, the small central-New York town on the north shore of Cayuga Lake, is the birthplace of the women's rights movement. That's why the Women's Rights National Historic Park and the National Women's Hall of Fame are here.

"Few are aware that the first women's rights convention in the world took place in Seneca Falls," noted Judy Hart, the National Park Service's liaison with Congress. "It was held July 19 and 20, 1848."

It was Hart who suggested a national historic park to preserve and protect the sites associated with the 1848 convention and to spread the word about the ensuing struggle for women's rights and equality.

Hart did the principal work in promoting the idea through Congress. She got it off the ground in March of 1981 as the park's first superintendent.

The women's rights movement began inconspicuously with five women at a tea party on July 9, 1848.

Four of the women were Quakers, active in temperance and abolition work: Lucretia Mott, her sister Martha Wright, Mary Ann McClintock and Jane Hunt. The fifth woman was Elizabeth Cady Stanton, mother of seven children. She later became known as the founder and philosopher of the women's rights movement.

Stanton, whose husband Henry was an abolitionist leader, first met Mott in 1840 at the World Anti-Slavery Convention in London. There the two women discussed women's rights and equality and vowed to meet again to formulate a plan to do something about the issues.

But it wasn't until eight years later that they saw each other again, this time at the tea party where they and the other three women began expressing anger and discontent about women's lot in life. They decided to have a women's rights convention and agreed to meet at McClintock's house a week later to plan the event.

At the McClintock home, the five women sat around a mahogany table and drafted a document called the Declaration of Sentiments, which served as a framework for their convention.

Stanton, principal architect of the Declaration of Sentiments, was 33 at the time—the same age as Thomas Jefferson when he wrote the Declaration of Independence. It was her idea to model the Declaration of Sentiments after the Declaration of Independence.

"We hold these truths to be self-evident: that all men and women are created equal," read the Declaration of Sentiments, with the words *and women* added.

The Declaration of Sentiments stated that "the history of mankind is a history of repeated injuries and usurpations on the part of man toward woman, having its direct object the establishment of an absolute tyranny over her.

"Because women do feel themselves aggrieved, oppressed and fraudulently deprived of their most sacred rights, we insist they have immediate admission to all the rights and privileges which belong to them as citizens of the United States."

The document spelled out grievances of woman against man, including:

"He has never permitted her to exercise her inalienable right to the elective franchise.

"He has compelled her to submit to laws, in the formation of which she had no voice.

"He has oppressed her on all sides. He has made her, if married, in the eye of the law, civilly dead.

"He has taken from her all right in property, even to the wages she earns.

"He has monopolized nearly all the profitable employment, and from those she is permitted to follow, she receives but a scanty remuneration.

"He has denied her the facilities for obtaining a thorough education—all colleges being closed against her."

The *Seneca Courier* carried an announcement that a women's rights convention would be held at the Weslayan Methodist Church on July 19 and 20, 1848, only nine days after the five women first sat around a table drinking tea and airing their grievances.

More than 300 men and women showed up at the church. Stanton, a housewife who had never given a speech in her life, courageously stood up and read the Declaration of Sentiments. Genteel women at that time did not speak in public.

"Mrs. Stanton had been filled with increasing terror," wrote Miriam Gurko in *The Ladies of Seneca Falls,* her book about the birth of the women's rights movement. "It was a combination of stage fright at the prospect of making her first public speech, and consternation at having initiated this unprecedented action by women.

"A housewife in any period might have quailed at such a formidable undertaking; for a woman in 1848 it was outrageously rash and untraditional, which made it practically earth-shaking."

At the convention, they passed resolutions proposing women's right to vote, their right to equal pay, their right to control their own money and their right to receive equal treatment under the law. The declaration and resolutions were signed by 68 women and 32 men.

The suffrage movement was under way.

When Judy Hart came to Seneca Falls, population 7,000, to launch the Women's Rights National Historic Park in 1981, her first office was in a vacant room at the local radio station.

"Funding that first year was $5,000," she recalled. "The park consisted of me, my secondhand typewriter and a couple of temporary exhibits."

Park headquarters remained in cramped facilities until 1993, when the turn-of-the-century Old Seneca Falls Town Hall was completely renovated and dedicated as the Women's Rights Visitors Center.

Upon entering the new Visitors Center, people are greeted by life-size statues of 20 of the principal figures involved in launching the women's rights movement. The statues were created by sculptor Lloyd Lillie.

The Visitors Center is filled with exhibits pertaining to the history of the women's rights struggle. It tells the story of the suffrage movement beginning with the tea party in Seneca Falls in 1848 and the women's rights convention that same year. A 25-minute documentary film reenacts the convention and charts its aftermath.

Harvard School of Design students Ann Marshall and Ray Kinoshita won $15,000 for their winning entry in a nationwide contest to design Declaration Park adjacent to the Visitors Center.

The centerpiece of Declaration Park is the roof and two walls of the 1830 Weslayan Methodist Church, all that's left of the site of the first women's rights convention. The park also features a 140-foot-long water wall. The water flows over a huge reproduction of the Declaration of Sentiments and the names of the women and men who signed the declaration and convention resolutions.

In the education center of the Women's Rights National Historic Park, a 19th-Century print shop recalls the women's movement newspaper published in Seneca Falls between 1849 and 1854 by Amelia Bloomer, a temperance, women's rights and women's dress-reform activist. Bloomers are named after her.

The Mary Ann McClintock home, where the Declaration of Sentiments was drafted, is owned by the U.S. Park Service but not yet open to the public. The Elizabeth Cady Stanton home, donated by the Elizabeth Cady Stanton Foundation, is open for visits. The Jane Hunt home, where the tea party took place that started it all, is privately owned. The Park Service hopes to acquire it at a future date.

A block from the Women's Rights National Historic Park is the National Women's Hall of Fame.

In 1969, two dozen Seneca Falls women met over tea, just like the five original feminists, to formulate plans for the Hall of Fame. In 1973, they inducted the first group of 20 women who made outstanding contributions to this nation's history.

By 1995, the total of 132 women honored included Marian Anderson, Susan B. Anthony, Clara Barton, Pearl Buck, Rachel Carson, Willa Cather, Jacqueline Cochran, Emily Dickinson, Amelia Earhart, Helen Hayes, Helen Keller, Billie Jean King, Margaret Mead, Annie Oakley, Georgia O'Keefe, Sally Ride, Eleanor Roosevelt, Margaret Sanger, Harriet Beecher Stowe,

Sojourner Truth, Oprah Winfrey, Sarah Winnemucca and "Babe" Didrikson Zaharias. The five Seneca Falls women who launched the women's rights movement are there as well.

An illustrated biography of each inductee is featured on a large panel in the Hall of Fame.

Since 1979, the town has celebrated Convention Days every second weekend in July to mark the anniversary of that historic meeting. Events include a women's rights parade, lectures on the suffrage movement and a play that reenacts the women's rights convention of 1848.

Another big holiday in Seneca Falls comes in August with the anniversary of the passage of the 19th Amendment. The day's numerous events focus on the historic occasion that gave women the right to vote.

Thanks to the Women's Rights National Historic Park and the National Women's Hall of Fame, more and more Americans each year are learning about the feminists of Seneca Falls, their Declaration of Sentiments and the history of the women's rights movement.

SEVEN

CONNECTICUT

Mystic Seaport's Maritime Marvel

FOR THOSE WHO would go down to the sea in ships, Mystic Seaport is the place to drop anchor.

The 17-acre, 66-year-old maritime museum welcomes visitors to Mystic, Conn. It preserves tall ships, including the last of the wooden whalers; the largest collection of historic small craft in America (more than 400); a working 19th-Century shipyard, and 60 waterfront buildings of that era.

Boats dating back to 1824 are stacked like books on library shelves in the museum's large warehouse. Each has a placard telling its history and unique features. Here is a restored 1824 rope-making factory, functioning as it did in the beginning; an 1836 sail loft, and an 1874 lifesaving station with rescue boat and gear of that day.

Other 19th-Century waterfront businesses—all restored and operating the old-fashioned way—include a ship's chandlery, a hoop shop for fashioning wooden mast hoops and a cooperage for crafting casks and barrels.

At Mystic Seaport, the clock has been turned back to a time when the sea and the ships that sailed the sea dominated New England life.

In 1988, the U.S. Postal Service chose Mystic Seaport to represent Connecticut in its commemorative stamp series. Featured on the 22-cent stamp was the 1841 wooden whaling ship *Charles W. Morgan*, a National Historic Landmark.

In 1929, three Mystic residents joined forces after agreeing on the urgent need to preserve surviving maritime artifacts. The three who spawned Mystic Seaport were Carl Cutler, author of *Greyhounds of the Sea,* published in 1930 and to this day the definitive work on American clipper ships; Dr. Charles K. Stillman, descendant of local shipbuilders, and Edward E. Bradley, a successful businessman who had gone to sea as a boy.

The purpose of Mystic Seaport since its inception has been to collect, preserve and exhibit artifacts and skills related to maritime history and its influence on American life.

Mystic, site of shipbuilding since the 1600s, is an ideal location for a maritime museum of this magnitude. At the height of the 19th-Century shipbuilding industry, a greater tonnage of top-of-the-line vessels was produced here than at any port of its size in America. Ship and boat yards lined six miles of the Mystic River.

The past springs to life at Mystic in the form of vessels like the *Charles W. Morgan,* last of the wooden whaling ships. She sailed the seven seas for 80 years.

The *Morgan's* 40-month maiden voyage began Sept. 6, 1841. The ship rounded Cape Horn, cruised the Pacific and did not return to New Bedford until her holds were filled with oil and whalebone to be processed into candles, lamp oil, cosmetics, buggy whips, parasols, corset stays and much more.

The *Morgan* made 37 voyages, some lasting as long as five years. When her whaling days ended in 1921, Col. E.H.R. Green, son of multimillionaire Hetty Green, preserved the ship on his estate. In 1941, the *Morgan* came to Mystic.

Another tall ship docked here is the square-rigger *Joseph Conrad*, a training ship launched in Denmark in 1882. Since 1949, thousands of boys and girls, ages 12 to 17, have lived aboard the *Conrad* while learning about sailing ships and the sea.

Other historic vessels in use include the 1908 *Sabino,* one of the last coal-fired ferryboats in the United States. The *Sabino* once served the islands off Portland, Me. Today it zips up and down the Mystic River, tooting its quaint horn and carrying passengers.

Among the thousands of daily visitors to Mystic Seaport each summer are graduate students enrolled in American maritime history classes. During the school year, Williams College offers an undergraduate maritime program.

Mystic Seaport Museum has one of the most comprehensive maritime history libraries in the United States. It boasts more than 350,000 manuscripts, 56,000 ships' plans and charts and a collection of hundreds of ships' logs.

At the Preservation Shipyard, modern shipwrights and craftsmen use traditional tools and techniques to restore and maintain the tall ships, pleasure boats, fishing boats, yachts and other craft from the past.

The museum's huge small-craft storage facility is filled with historic boats like Connecticut river drags, Kingston lobster boats, double-ended Hamptons, oyster boats, Bay of Fundy shads and Gloucester fishing schooners.

Many boats were donated by their owners. The yacht *Barracuda*, for example, came from the family of a man who vowed in 1932 that if Franklin D. Roosevelt were elected President, he would never sail his boat again. He disliked FDR with a passion. The boat never sailed after the election. It remained in the man's boathouse until his death, when his family gave the *Barracuda* to Mystic Seaport.

An iceboat on exhibit was found in the basement of a bank, where it had been stored and forgotten for nearly a century. The four-cylinder *Panhard I*, a torpedo-shaped auto boat built in 1904 and exhibited at the 1905 New York boat show, is here. So is an Eskimo walrus-skin boat from Umiak, Alaska.

Some of the boats were rescued from boneyards, some from the briny deep.

Max Hamlin, owner of the 57-foot racing sloop *Gesture,* was visiting Mystic Seaport far from his home in Newport Beach, Calif. He spent hours soaking up the color and romance of the place.

"I love it here," he said. Hamlin's sentiments are echoed by all who love to go down to the sea in boats: "A boat person just couldn't ask for anything more."

EIGHT

RHODE ISLAND

How Small Is It?

R HODE ISLAND IS so small—48 miles north to south, 37 miles east to west—that no one is ever more than an hour away from any point in the state.

It's so small that it has a single bus system crisscrossing it, so small that the governor is routinely invited to christenings and bar mitzvahs, so small that every high school freshman must come to Providence, the state's capital, to meet the governor and the chief justice.

Many counties in other states are larger than tiny Rhode Island.

Alaska is 485 times its size, Texas 220 times. California could fit 130 Rhode Islands within its border.

Despite its small size and high population density, nearly two-thirds of the state is open space. With a population of 1 million, Rhode Island has more people than eight other states.

Miles and miles of country roads meander through woods and meadows, past hundreds of ponds and farms and through a rural countryside dotted with villages, Grange halls and old-fashioned general stores.

Centuries-old stone fences separate farms, and 200-year-old windmills still grind corn to make johnnycakes. Adamsville has a monument to a chicken, the Rhode Island Red, featured on a U.S. postage stamp issued in 1982.

Rhode Island is the only state that has a statewide mass-transit system, the Rhode Island Public Transit Authority. RIPTA buses crisscross the state from Watch Hill to Woonsocket, from Wallum Lake to Sakonnet.

There is a single state health department—no local, city or county health departments. There is one prison for the entire state and one landfill dump. There are, however, 43 departments of education.

Rural or not, every inch of the state lies within the borders of one of the 39 cities and towns that make up Rhode Island. And within many of the towns are villages.

Rhode Island has five counties. But there are no county officials, except county sheriffs who carry no guns and do not fight crime as sheriffs do in other states. They provide court security, serve writs and transport prisoners.

"Rhode Islanders are fiercely loyal and proud of 'Little Rhody,' " said Joseph Garrahy, governor during the 1970s and '80s. "We're proud of its history, heritage and, yes, its smallness."

Famed 19th-Century historian George Bancroft wrote that "more ideas adopted nationally emanated from little Rhode Island than from all of the other American states."

Rhode Island was the first haven for religious freedom in the New World. It was here that America's first law against slavery was enacted in 1652, some 211 years before the Emancipation Proclamation. Rhode Island declared its independence from Great Britain two months before the 12 other colonies.

"What Rhode Island may lack in size, it doesn't lack in pride and enthusiasm," said the former governor. "We're the state with the longest name—State of Rhode Island and Providence Plantations—and the shortest motto—Hope."

Garrahy's parents came to Rhode Island from Ireland in the late 1920s. Before becoming governor in 1977, Garrahy was lieutenant governor for six years and a senator for six years before that.

"My mother worked as a cleaning woman in the Capitol," Garrahy recalled. "When I was elected lieutenant governor, I suggest it might be a good idea if she quit her job.

" 'Why?' she asked.

"I told her, 'Ma, I don't think it's right for the lieutenant governor to have his mother cleaning his office.' Reluctantly, she quit.

"Being governor of Rhode Island is different because the state is so small. The governor is invited to attend practically every christening, bar mitzvah and wedding in the state; the functions of just about every organization; the ethnic picnics, small-town political rallies—you name it."

To make sure every young person in the state has an opportunity to meet government officials, each year all high school freshmen spend four days in Providence. Each student personally meets the governor, members of the General Assembly and the judiciary, other state officials and members of the press.

Len Panaggio of Newport, a lifelong Rhode Island resident, calls his state one of America's best-kept secrets. "Being small has many advantages," he said. "There is a closeness among the people of this state unmatched anywhere in the United States."

Rhode Island is sprinkled with tiny villages bearing colorful, hard-to-pronounce names, the legacy of five Indian tribes that lived here—the Narragansetts, Niantics, Nipmucks, Pequots and Wampanoags.

Michael Pellam stood in front of the Grange Hall in tiny Quonochontaug, a coastal village. He shrugged his shoulders sheepishly. "Only those of us who live here can pronounce the name of our village," he said, "and even we have a hard time.

"You hear the name of the town pronounced a dozen different ways by locals. Strangers don't even try."

Pellam, owner of Michael's Grocery and Michael's Garage, said he didn't name his businesses Quonochontaug Grocery or Quonochontaug Garage "because it's too much of a mouthful for one person to handle." Residents here call the place Quany and themselves Quanies.

Quonochontaug means black fish.

Quonochontaug boasts the oldest farmhouse in Rhode Island. It was erected in 1710. Three British sailors killed during the War of 1812 are buried behind the farmhouse. British vessels fired hot cannonballs at Quonochontaug to set houses on fire and terrorize the farmers.

Down the road from Quonochontaug in Weekapaug, at the Weekapaug Dairy on Passapapaug Road, nobody was home except the cows.

Posted on the door and window of the dairy's retail store were stickers that read: "Never Mind the Dog, Beware of Owner"; "Milk Drinkers Are More Passionate," and "This place Guarded by Shotgun 3 Nights a Week. You Guess Which 3 Nights."

Usquepaug, population 35, is famous throughout New England for its 270-year-old gristmill and its annual Johnnycake Festival. *Usquepaug* is an Indian word meaning whiskey.

Johnnycakes, also known as jonny or journey cakes, are a Rhode Island specialty made of white-cap Indian flint corn. The cornmeal cakes, fried on a griddle until the crust is crispy, take the place of potatoes for many Rhode Islanders at breakfast, lunch and dinner. There is a Society for the Propagation of Johnnycakes in Rhode Island.

Two of Rhode Island's eight cities bear Indian names—Pawtucket and Woonsocket. Among the villages with tongue-twisting Indian names are: Apponaug, Canonchet, Chepiwanoxet, Conimicut, Matunuck, Meshanticut, Misquamicut, Moosup, Nausauket, Ninigret, Pettaquamscutt, Quidnick, Sakonnet, Scituate, Shawomet, Watchaug, Winnapaug and Yawgoo.

The Brown and Hopkins Country Store, located in the village of Chepachet, is filled with original 19th-Century grocery items. Founded in 1809, it is reputedly the oldest continuously operated general store in America. Carol and Paul Wilcox are the 21st owners of the establishment.

Corona Magner, 60, lives in Pascoag and works as a postal clerk in Chepachet. "I have no idea what either name means," she confessed. "But that's not so strange. These names are something we live with all our lives. To us they don't seem that unusual."

The Common Burying Ground in Newport is considered the finest collection of Colonial tombstones in America.

It is one of 2,400 historic graveyards in Rhode Island, where some of the old cemeteries are in backyards, some in woods, others on farms, in towns, in the hearts of cities.

Edwin Wilmot Connelly, Rhode Island's cemetery director, keeps a watchful eye on the old burying grounds. He parked his car on Farewell Street at Newport's Common Burying Ground and walked into the centuries-old cemetery, his eyes dancing with excitement. "What treasures," he exclaimed.

Connelly darted from one lichen-covered 17th-Century slate tombstone to another, pointing out elaborate old-style lettering, winged cherubs and other primitive etchings and lively epitaphs.

"This is folk culture," he said, "the earliest form of American primitive art. History is all over this place. The stories these dead could tell, and the stories we could tell them...."

NINE

MASSACHUSETTS

Gloucester, America's Premier Fishing Port

J UST IMAGINE, 10,000 men of Gloucester lost at sea," mused author-historian Joseph E. Garland as he looked out across Gloucester Harbor and the Atlantic Ocean from the back porch of his home.

"This is the greatest fishing port in the history of the Western Hemisphere, also the one with the most tragedies." The rugged 68-year-old former fisherman and newspaper reporter has written 15 books, many about the men of Gloucester and their defiant battle with the sea.

A Fishermen's Memorial stands on Gloucester's waterfront. Sculpted by Leonard Craske and dedicated to the 10,000 Gloucester men who lost their lives while fishing, the statue of a helmsman in slicker, boots and hat bears the inscription "They That Go Down To The Sea In Ships."

It was here on the North Massachusetts coast, in 1623, that a handful of British fishermen established the New World's first viable commercial enterprises. They shipped their bountiful catches back across the Atlantic. Fishing was the mainstay of the Massachusetts Bay Colony, and Gloucester was its capital. Cod was America's first currency.

Fishing has been the town's lifeblood for nearly 400 years. A century ago, about 7,000 fishermen shipped out on 400 huge schooners to fish the North Atlantic and the Grand Banks. Today, 500 fishermen set out from Gloucester in about 140 smaller boats.

"We still lose men who go down to sea and never come back," said Garland, whose family has lived in Gloucester since Colonial times.

"Seven years ago, two brothers were fishing in a small boat in Gloucester Harbor, 200 to 300 yards from this back porch where my wife and I were having lunch. A squall came up and the boat capsized. One brother made it, the other drowned; and we were powerless to do anything about it."

In the days of the big fishing schooners, the numbers of losses were truly awesome. From 1870 to 1874, for example, 129 boats went to the cruel depths, carrying 877 fishermen with them.

"Among the endless legends of man's struggle with the sea, none is more magnificently moving than that of the fishermen from Gloucester," wrote Sterling Hayden in his forward to Garland's book *Down to the Sea: The Fishing Schooners of Gloucester*. Before Hayden became an actor, he fished out of Gloucester.

Garland said that fishing the Atlantic from Gloucester is "dangerous as hell—the storms, the terrible seas, the privations and suffering. The community's fishing casualties have far exceeded those from any wars or natural disasters."

Garland, who may have written more than anyone about Gloucester fishermen, cited Rudyard Kipling's 1897 book *Captains Courageous* as the best ever written about the subject. Kipling's book inspired the 1937 MGM movie of the same name that won Spencer Tracy an Oscar for his portrayal of Gloucester Portuguese fisherman Manuel Fidelo.

The film poignantly captures the perilous life of Gloucester men fishing under sail. It ends with the all-too-common loss at sea.

Portuguese have played a major role in Gloucester fishing since the 1830s. On a pedestal between the two towers of Our Lady of Good Voyage—the church of the Portuguese fishermen—a 10-foot statue of the Virgin Mary cradles the figure of a Gloucester fishing schooner carved in Oporto, Portugal.

Following the migration of Portuguese fishermen from the Azores to

Gloucester came Bluenose fishermen from Nova Scotia and Newfoundland, Irish fishermen from Galway Bay, Italian fishermen from Sicily.

Through the years, many of Gloucester's men of the sea have exemplified the ability to survive. "Howard Blackburn, the greatest of the dory men, is one of them," noted Garland. His book *Long Voyager* traces the life of Blackburn, describing him as a "giant figure in the most griping of Gloucester's uncounted sagas of death and survival at sea."

In 1883, while Blackburn and his dory mate fished for halibut off Nova Scotia, a blizzard separated them from their schooner. The dory mate froze to death.

When Blackburn's gloves washed overboard and he realized his hands would soon freeze, he curled them in place around the oars so they would stiffen in the shape of his grasp.

"Blackburn rowed for five days with his frozen hands," Garland said, "without food or water, with his dead dory mate in the boat beside him. He rowed 60 miles until he finally reached land.

"He lost all his fingers, half of each thumb and most of his toes. Yet, years later, in 1889, he sailed his sloop alone from Gloucester to England. Two years after that, he sailed alone from Gloucester to Portugal in 39 days—a record that stood for 38 years.

"Blackburn's defiance was: 'You bastard, sea. You licked me once. I'm going to outlick you on my terms.' Blackburn twice conquered the Atlantic *with no goddamn fingers.*"

The whole town of Gloucester, population 27,000, is a shrine to fishermen. The First Baptist Church is shaped like the bow of a ship. Fishing boats clutter the harbor. Lobster traps pile high on St. Peter's Square.

Recently, at Our Lady of Good Voyage, the priest began his Sunday sermon, "We have come to Praise God..." A parishioner cried out: "—and to catch fish."

TEN

VERMONT

To Be a Real Vermonter, You've Got to Earn It

T HE THREE-STORY, yellow, weathered, century-old general store was stirring with activity one cold, snowy mid-April Saturday morning in East Burke, Vt., population 200.

Dairy farmers, maple syrup makers, old-timers and others were buying groceries, picking up mail at the back-of-the-store post office and exchanging greetings and the latest tidbits about local happenings.

Kids darted in and out, reaching into large jars on a bottom shelf filled with Whoppers and other penny candy. Yes, *penny candy*—candy that sell just about everywhere else in America for a nickel or a dime a shot.

"I'll bet almost everyone in East Burke is a native Vermonter," said a stranger to Delin McPhee, 25, manning the cash register.

"Nope," she replied. "Even East Burke has Flatlanders. To be considered a real Vermonter in this part of the state, your great-grandfather had to be born here."

Dairy farmer Albert Gorham, 65, standing at the counter waiting to pay for his purchase, nodded his head in agreement. "Yup," he said. "You've got to earn it."

By definition and tradition you must be born in Vermont to call yourself a Vermonter. If you lived in Vermont all your life—60, 70, 80, 90 years—but were born somewhere else, you don't dare call yourself a Vermonter. You're a Flatlander.

It's an important distinction. Vermonters pay attention to such things.

Vermont is a mountainous state—hence the term Flatlander.

Flatlanders have migrated to Vermont in greater numbers during the last 30 years, from New York, from other New England states, from across the nation. They come to escape the fast lane, to seek the simple life.

Today there are nearly as many Flatlanders as native Vermonters. Old-time Vermonters fear that outsiders may buy out the small state. They fear losing their identity. They know that the majority of their political leaders are Flatlanders, originally from other states.

In East Burke, you can be a third-generation Vermonter, as Delin McPhee said, and still be considered a Flatlander, someone "from away." That's how it is in the Northeast Kingdom (Caledonia, Essex and Orleans counties), Vermont's most isolated, most rural section of this predominantly rural state.

"We can tell a real Vermonter right away," McPhee insisted. "Way a person talks. Way a person acts. Flatlanders are more forward. They're just different in every way. We real Vermonters are born with something in us that's special. We can sense that unique quality in other Vermonters."

A sign in the East Burke General Store window told of a sugar-on-snow party at the local Methodist church. Spring snowstorms often occur in Northern Vermont through late April. The parties take place in the higher reaches if the snow has melted at lower elevations.

Sugar-on-snow dates back to Colonial days. It means pouring freshly made hot maple syrup onto snow. When the syrup hits, it takes on the consistency of taffy. Then it's picked up and wrapped around a dinner fork and eaten.

Traditionalists eat homemade doughnuts and dill pickles with the chilled syrup—the sour pickles to contrast with the sweetness of the syrup.

Vermont cherishes its small-town traditions, its woods and wild animals—moose, bear, deer—its lakes and mountains and little hamlets like East Burke. The state's biggest town—call it a city, if you like—is Burlington (population 40,000) on Lake Champlain.

Montpelier, the capital, has a population of 8,247. The entire state claims a population of 562,758. Only Wyoming has fewer people.

"Vermonters are the salt of the earth," said John MacDonald, 40, shopping at the East Burke General Store. "People here laugh at little things. Folks in urban areas need a whole lot of big things. Not here."

Carol Wahl, 42, a stained-glass artist, moved to East Burke 12 years ago from Western Pennsylvania. She told how Vermonters do business by handshake.

"Someone tells you something, you can rely on it," she said. "People here don't have locks on their doors. The sense of being a good neighbor is very strong, people doing for other people.

"It's turn back the clock, especially here in the Northeast Kingdom where many old-fashioned practices persist—horses for plowing, horses for logging. People here shun clothes dryers. They hang their clothes out to dry in all kinds of weather."

Vermonters are hardy, shrewd, frugal, self-reliant people of few words. You hear "yup" and "nope" and little else as Vermonters size up strangers, suspicious of their motives.

As for frugal: Scudder Parker's 13 household efficiency tips, listed in *The Vermont Chef Cookbook,* published by a women's organization in St. Johnsbury, include:

"When you throw wash clothes into the hamper, use them first to do a quick damp mopping in the dusty corners of the bathroom." And "always leave the bathroom and kitchen sink hot water in until it gets cold. Think of all that heat gain in your bathroom and kitchen."

Ethan Allen, George Dewey, Calvin Coolidge and Dwight Dwinell head the roster of Vermont's legendary heroes. Allen tops the list. He was the farmer-statesman who, in 1775, led Vermont's Green Mountain Boys in capturing Fort Ticonderoga from the British. It was the first offensive action of the Revolutionary War.

Allen was a leader in establishing the Independent Republic of Vermont. The republic lasted 14 years, from 1777 until Vermont became the 14th state in 1791. It minted its own coins, had its own postal service and carried on diplomatic relations with foreign powers. Allen wrote Vermont's constitution, which included the prohibition of slavery and provided for universal manhood suffrage without owning property.

A four-ton marble statue of Ethan Allen stands on the Vermont Capitol steps. On the lawn rest two Spanish navy guns captured at the Battle of Manila in 1898. Adm. George Dewey, a native Vermonter, commanded the fleet in the battle.

Vice President Calvin Coolidge was asleep at his father's home in Plymouth, Vt., when President Warren Harding died Aug. 3, 1923. Coolidge's father, a notary public, awakened him in the middle of the night and administered the oath of the 30th President by lamplight in the dining room. Then the two men went back to sleep.

It was Calvin Coolidge who said: "If liberty and freedom ever disappeared from the United States, they could be rediscovered in Vermont."

Who was Dwight Dwinell?

He was the 86-year-old Vermonter who carved the 14-foot pine statue of Ceres, the Roman goddess of agriculture, that stands atop a six-foot pedestal on the Capitol's gold dome.

"When I was a kid, you could tell what town people were from just by the way they talked," mused Vermonter Everett Drinkwine, 60, a woodsman. "Their accent was different, one town to the next. Television, cars and Flatlanders moving in here from other states have changed all that.

"I'm a Vermonter first, a U.S. citizen second. Eight grades in a one-room Vermont school is as good as a high school education anywhere else. Glad I didn't get any more learning. Might of made me a different person. I like the way I am."

Drinkwine described Flatlanders as "a strange lot. They didn't like it where they come from. Now they try to make Vermont a carbon copy of where they lived before. They want paved roads. Many of our roads ain't paved. It's the Flatlanders that did away with many of our one-room schools."

Practically every town, village and hamlet in the 150-mile-long, 40- to 90-mile-wide state has a general store. The biggest is Willey's at Greensboro, a wide spot on a winding two-lane country road six miles north of Hardwick. In the middle of nowhere.

Customers come for miles to shop under the tin ceiling at Willey's. It's huge—groceries, hardware, clothing, sporting goods, auto supplies, you name it. Over the years, the store has grown by connecting walls to the town's old post office, to two other stores, to two residences and an icehouse. Now it's all under one roof, and it's all Willey's General Store.

"I'm the last of the Willeys," said Phyllis Willey Hurst, 60, who owns and operates the emporium with her husband Ernie and 33 employees in the summer, 20 the rest of the year. "My grandfather bought the store in 1900. We handle everything that's basic. I was born upstairs in the store and never left."

More than 100 covered bridges, most of them still in use, dot the state. You also find mute evidence of the Vermonters' sense of humor. Like the "Milk—The Udder Cola" sign on a dairy barn at Morrisville. Like the mailbox on a pole 30 feet above the ground outside an Alburg farmhouse with the sign "Air Mail."

Every town and village has a white frame Protestant church with towering steeple, the hallmark of Vermont. United Methodist Rev. Dawn Robbins, 27, heads congregations in Burke Hollow, West Burke and East Haven. One of her three churches is the Burke Hollow historic Meeting House built by four denominations in 1825 and still used by all four—Universalist, Congregationalist, Baptist and Methodist.

"Vermonters are very protective about their church and their state," said the youthful minister. "Even young people are tied to the past and place a lot of stock in tradition.

"Imagine my situation. Here I am a Flatlander six months from Massachusetts, a woman and under 30. My congregations sit back, waiting and watching. Some of the young people have accepted me. Most of the older ones are hesitant. That's the way Vermonters are—skeptical of outsiders."

Together with the general store and school, the church serves as a cornerstone of the community. "We have a very active youth group," the reverend said. "There is nothing else for the kids to do. People here won't travel eight or nine miles to the next town to do something. They want to do whatever in their own backyard."

Arthur Dubois, 29, co-owns a bookstore in St. Johnsbury, population 8,000. He is one of only 1,130 black citizens in Vermont. African-Americans make up only two-tenths of 1% of Vermont's population, fewer than in any other state. Dubois came from New York. "It's a much easier life here," he said. "Sure, there is subtle racism here; but there is blatant racism in New York.

"Vermonters in general are very accepting. They leave you alone. They are likable people. I find it comfortable living here. Vermonters in general judge you on your worth as a human being, not on the color of your skin."

Jim Armosky of South Ryegate, a writer-illustrator of children's books, described Vermont as "a little smaller than other places in every way. You can embrace it. The mountains are smaller. You can observe a whole valley. It is a perfect combination of living beside and working with nature."

Former Gov. Richard Snelling once said: "The rest of the world would be better off if it understood some of the things that we understand in Vermont, if it prized some of the things we prize in Vermont."

Albert Gorham, the 65-year-old dairy farmer at the East Burke store, gave an example: "If you stub your toe here in Vermont, you don't turn around and sue somebody."

ELEVEN

NEW HAMPSHIRE

Give Thanks for Sarah Josepha Hale

ARAH JOSEPHA HALE from Newport, a small New Hampshire village, gave us both Thanksgiving Day as a national holiday and the popular children's poem "Mary Had a Little Lamb."

It was Hale—editor, poet, novelist and one of the most influential women in 19th-Century America—who convinced Abraham Lincoln that Thanksgiving should be an official holiday.

For 36 years, from 1827 to 1863, Hale wrote letters to members of Congress, to governors and to Presidents urging that Thanksgiving be an annual celebration. She campaigned in editorials written for *American Ladies' Magazine* and later for *Godey's Lady's Book.*

Many states followed her suggestion, setting aside a special day for Thanksgiving each November.

Finally, during the height of the Civil War, President Lincoln issued a proclamation declaring Thanksgiving a national holiday. It has been celebrated ever since.

Thanksgiving originated with the Pilgrims in 1621 when William Bradford, governor of Plymouth Colony, called for a day of prayer and thanksgiving. It became a tradition in New England following the annual harvest of crops, but was not observed in the rest of the nation until Lincoln issued his proclamation in 1863.

Hale's contribution to the November turkey feast and family reunion has been pretty well forgotten. Her name is unknown to most Americans. Yet she was one of the foremost pioneers of women's rights in this country.

She wrote *Northwood*, one of the first novels of consequence by an American woman. Published in 1827, it was one of the first books dealing with slavery in the United States. It appeared 25 years before Harriet Beecher Stowe's *Uncle Tom's Cabin*.

The year *Northwood* was published, Hale became editor of *American Ladies' Magazine*, a position she held for nine years. For the next 41 years she edited *Godey's Lady's Book*. Both magazines circulated nationally. *Godey's*, published in Philadelphia from 1830 to 1898, had more than 500,000 subscribers and employed 150 women just to hand-tint its famous fashion plates.

In both magazines Hale championed women's causes, including better working conditions and higher wages. She encouraged women to get into the medical profession at a time when there were no women doctors.

Hale deplored the fact that girls were prohibited from going to school. She waged vigorous campaigns for female education at a time when the vast majority of women were illiterate.

In the 1985 biography *Sarah Josepha Hale, a New England Pioneer,* author Sherbrooke Roger quotes one of Hale's editorials from the August 1837 edition of *Godey's*:

"We cannot learn, neither can we teach. Give us the facilities for education enjoyed by the other sex, so we will be able to find out what our capabilities are."

At the age of 88, Hale published her 36-volume *Woman's Record, Sketches of Distinguished Women*. It profiled more than 2,000 outstanding women from ancient times through the late 1800s. When she was 90, in her final editorial for *Godey's*, she penned a farewell "to my countrywomen." She died a year later in 1879.

Sarah Josepha Buell was born in Newport, a New Hampshire mill town, on Oct. 24, 1788. She was educated by her mother, Martha Buell, because only boys went to school at that time. Despite the fact that she never went to school, the young woman became a teacher in a private school in Newport when she was 18. It was there one day that a pet lamb followed one of her students, a girl named Mary, to school.

The lamb went right into the classroom, "for everywhere that Mary went, the lamb was sure to go." In 1830, "Mary Had a Little Lamb" appeared in *Poems for Our Children*, a book of poetry by Sarah Josepha Hale. Her marriage to Newport attorney David Hale produced five children and lasted nine years until his death from pneumonia in 1822. Widowed at 34, she never remarried.

Hale's memory lives on in Newport, population 6,500, where each year a bronze medal bearing her name and portrait is presented in recognition of "distinguished work in the field of letters."

A virtual Who's Who of the literary world has received the Sarah Josepha Hale Award, beginning in 1956 with the first recipient, poet Robert Frost. Other winners: John P. Marquand, Archibald MacLeish, Dorothy Canfield Fisher, John Hersey, Ogden Nash, Elizabeth Yates, Louis Untermeyer, John Kenneth Galbraith, Norman Cousins, Henry Steele Commager, Roger Tory Peterson, Barbara Tuchman and Stephen Jay Gould.

One of the stipulations is that the recipient must appear in person to receive the medal and speak at Newport's century-old Richards Free Library, which sponsors the prize.

Only one person named to receive the award turned it down, in 1963, the 100th anniversary of Lincoln's Thanksgiving Day Proclamation.

It was John Fitzgerald Kennedy who reluctantly declined the prize that year, due to a previous engagement for Nov. 22. Like many who received the award, he was a Pulitzer Prize-winning author. President Kennedy was shot and killed in Dallas on the day John Hersey won the Sarah Josepha Hale Award in his place.

TWELVE

MAINE

Islanders of Maine, a Hardy Bunch

IT WAS EARLY MORNING and 5 degrees above zero. Robert Quinn, 43, the Eagle Island mailman, piloted his 38-foot lobster boat, *The Last Straw,* through the choppy surf across Maine's East Penobscot Bay.

Windows in the wheelhouse were thick with frost. Icicles draped the weather-beaten craft. A stick held the window open in front of Quinn so he could see his way across the angry, frothing sea.

Freezing spray repeatedly struck his face. His cold, numb cheeks were beet red. Fierce gusts made the wind-chill factor 10 degrees below.

It was a three-mile, 45-minute run from Sunset, a tiny town on Deer Isle, to Eagle Island, a 1^1/4-mile-long, half-mile-wide island settled in 1825 by his great-great-grandparents Samuel and Lucy Quinn.

From mid-September to mid-June, Eagle Island is the only stop for Quinn, who makes the mail run on Tuesdays and Fridays. In summer, he carries the mail across East Penobscot Bay six days a week to several families vacationing in cottages on Eagle, Bear, Barred and Great Spruce Head islands. It's a contract route that earns him $256 a month.

No one lives on Bear, Barred and Great Spruce Head nine months of the year. If they did, Quinn would deliver them mail. He has had the mail run for 12 years. His father had it for 30 years before him. A mail boat has served the islands since 1904. Quinn fishes and does carpentry work when not delivering mail.

When Quinn left Sunset for Eagle Island, he climbed down an icy ladder from the dock to his skiff and shoveled a foot of snow out of it. He rowed over to *The Last Straw*, so named because his last boat sunk, "and if I lose this one, that's it."

As he rounded Northeast Head and entered the calmer waters of the island's lee side, he spotted Adam Broome, 27, snowshoeing to the dock through glistening powder two to three feet deep.

It was low tide, and the sea was 15 feet below the dock. Quinn gingerly made his way up the icy ladder carrying a sack of groceries in his mailbag.

Broome and his wife Alison, 26, and their children Tom, 3, and Maisie, 11 months, are the only people on Eagle Island nine months of the year.

On Quinn's twice-weekly mail run in winter, he also brings groceries and supplies to the Broomes.

Adam migrated to Maine from England when he was 19 years old. "There wasn't much work in the U.K.," he said. In Maine he played guitar and sang in a five-man band, Attitude Problem.

After he married Alison, they ran a classified ad in *Folk*, a weekly newspaper, seeking a position as island caretakers. Maine has nearly 2,000 islands off its rocky coast. Eagle Island needed a caretaker.

"We came out four years ago and have been here ever since," Alison said. "We are not paid to be caretakers. However, we do get to live in this marvelous old house rent free."

The island has no electricity, no phones, no indoor plumbing. The Broomes heat the vintage-1845 house and cook with a century-old wood stove. It's a turn-back-the-clock existence.

Every time she does her laundry in an old ringer-washer, Alison has to hand-carry 20 gallons of water for one load, empty it, then replace it with 20 more gallons to rinse.

"We like the solitude," Adam said. "We're kept busy—Alison with the children, cooking and chores. I have a lot to do around the house, fetching water from the well in buckets, filling the lanterns with kerosene, chopping and splitting wood, keeping the fire going.

"We do an awful lot of reading. We read every day to Tom and Maisie."

The couple seldom watch their five-inch, black-and-white battery-powered television.

"We write a lot of letters," Alison said. "I'm from a big family. I miss my family. I miss interacting with people. The island is so remote. But I'm like Adam. I like the solitude and quiet.

"Being out here alone makes you realize how much you can do without in the world. I appreciate things so much more not being able to run to a store."

Adam does carpentry work during the winter in the nine summer cottages on the island. Last year he earned $4,500. He and his wife have a garden in summer. Alison puts up string beans and tomatoes. She makes jams, jellies and pies from wild strawberries, raspberries and rhubarb. She bakes bread.

Over the winter they keep their homegrown potatoes, carrots, onions, beets and green peppers in the cellar along with apples harvested from trees on the island.

They had a dozen chickens and a duck. A wild mink ate them.

During their nine months alone each year, the Broomes have never left the island except when the children were born. Alison went to the mainland on the mail boat a week before the birth of each child. "I had to make sure I wouldn't be stuck on Eagle Island due to high seas when my time came," she said.

They don't have a boat. If an emergency occurred, they would call for help over their citizens-band radio.

The island is heavily forested with spruce except for the Big Field, a large meadow next to their home.

For 100 years, the island was the private domain of the Quinn family. Lucy and Sam Quinn had 13 children, and many of them married off-island spouses and lived out their lives on Eagle Island. Now there is only one home on the island owned by the Quinns, the two-story house the caretakers live in.

A cemetery in the center of the island has 50 graves, most of them Quinns. The mottled headstone inscription for a Quinn woman who died in 1867 reads:

> *A seat by the fireside is vacant*
> *A dear form so loved is now gone*
> *Yet, one from our number is taken*
> *Whose place can be filled by none.*

The Quinns were lobster fishermen, boat builders and farmers on the 263-acre island. There was a one-room school from 1870 to 1942. Each year it had 5 to 13 pupils, nearly all Quinns.

A teacher in the beginning earned $3 a week. The salary increased to $5.12 a week in 1900, to $12 a week in 1924, $21.72 a week in 1930. The Eagle Island Lighthouse was manned by keepers from 1838 to 1959.

For three months a year, the Broomes have as many as 40 men, women and children as neighbors. Then, come Labor Day or a few days after, the vacationing families who own the island's nine summer cottages locked them up, and the Broomes have the island all to themselves.

"We know every inch of Eagle Island," Alison said. "We hike a great deal in summer and cross-country ski in winter. We really love it here, but know we cannot say forever. When Tom is of school age we will have to leave."

"They're special," mused mailman Quinn as he rode back to Sunset on *The Last Straw*. "Not many people could live alone cut off from the world, without electricity and modern conveniences, all by themselves in long, miserable Maine winters as they do."

Seventh grader Jemma Rauscher trudged through the deep snow along the shores of Isle au Haut, looking through her binoculars at loons.

"Listen to those big birds," she said. "They make the funniest sounds: a wail, a laugh, a yodel and a toot."

Jemma, 13, was doing a report on loons for her class. She is one of eight students in the one-room school on this 3-by-6-mile island, population 55.

She isn't an islander; she's a city girl.

"I never heard of Isle au Haut until my parents rented a house out here last August," Jemma said. "I loved the island so much, I asked if I could stay and go to school here. My parents let me. It's a great experience."

Her father Andrew, 40, is an anesthesiologist in Cooperstown, N.Y., where Jemma attended a school with more than 300 students.

"Can you imagine what it's like for me to be on this island," she exclaimed with wide-eyed amazement, "to know everybody that lives here, to be in a school where there are just eight of us?"

There are no telephones, no sidewalks, no traffic lights or stop signs on Isle au Haut. There is a post office and a tiny general store. The 1906 Town Hall is closed all winter because it costs too much to heat. Jemma lives with Lisa Turner, 22, who runs the store.

Nearly all the men on the island are fishermen who catch lobster, scallops and mussels.

"We love this island because we are so far away from everything, because we can live a quiet life," explained Belvia MacDonald, 45, Isle au Haut's mayor.

"Nobody ever gets a traffic ticket. We have no jail. Nobody has ever been arrested that I know of in the 27 years I have lived here. We have no bad apples.

"We have a constable to take care of any problems. He's a fisherman appointed to the job, paid $100 a year and $6 an hour whenever he's needed—which isn't very often."

When someone dies on the island, the body is taken by boat to a mortician six miles away on the mainland. Then it's returned for burial in the island cemetery. Some of the graveyard's lichen-mottled headstones date back to the early 1800s.

Every Wednesday is Social Day for the women. They gather to knit, crochet, sew and visit.

Doreen Carlson, 30, in her second year of teaching here, is from Northampton, Mass. She and her husband Bob, 33, a lobsterman, pay $75 a month to live in the schoolteacher's house. She earns $16,500 a year.

"You can walk everywhere," Carlson said. "You don't need a car. The pace is so slow. The people are so friendly."

The island's link to the mainland is a daily mail boat, the *Miss Lizzie,* named for Lizzie Rich, 95. She retired eight years ago after working 65 years for the island post office, much of the time as postmaster.

According to Philip Conkling, 38, founder and executive director of the Island Institute headquartered at Rockland, there are nearly 2,000 islands off the coast of Maine—900 of them occupied at least part of the year.

The most remote island—22 miles off Rockland—is Matinicus, $1^{1}/_{2}$ miles long and three-quarters of a mile wide. Like Isle au Haut, Matinicus has a year-round population of 55, mainly lobstermen and their families.

A mail boat sails to Matinicus Island once a month from the mainland, providing mail, food, supplies and transportation.

Island Institute has 1,200 members, mostly islanders, who pay annual dues of $25. The institute was established to make year-round and summer residents, scientists, governmental agencies and recreational users aware of the natural resources and human elements of the islands.

Members receive an annual magazine, which serves as a forum and a celebration of island life. The institute sponsors conferences pertaining to island concerns and also publishes a quarterly newsletter.

In Casco Bay off Portland, Maine's largest city, lie the Calendar Islands, so called because early settlers thought surely there must be at least one island in the archipelago for every day of the year. There are actually about 250 in the group.

Nine of the inhabited Calendar Islands are within Portland city limits. Cliff Island, 1 mile wide and 3^1/2 miles long, lies the farthest out at 13 miles.

Six of the islands are served all year by the ferryboats of Casco Bay Lines, a transportation company owned by islanders. High school children on the islands ride the ferryboats back and forth to school in Portland. Workers who live on the islands also commute.

"This water might seem rough to you, but it's not rough to us," said Capt. Nick Mavodones, 26, piloting the 65-foot ferryboat *Abnaki* on an early morning run. The boat is named after the prehistoric "People of the Canoe" Indians.

There are times when the ferryboats break channels through the ice to get to and from the islands, when seals sit on the ice barking at passing ferryboats.

The boats brave blizzards, stormy seas and zero-visibility fog. Maine islanders are a hardy bunch.

"There's not enough dynamite to get me off the island," said Jeff Sawyer, 35, a marine electronics technician and one of the 60 year-round residents of Cliff Island.

"You have to like it to ride this boat every day regardless of weather," said Roberta Dyer, 49, who works for Blue Cross and is one of 350 year-round residents of 2- by 5-mile Great Chebeague Island.

For Robert Jordan, 44, a professor of economics at the University of Southern Maine in Portland, life with 59 other year-round residents on 1 ^{1}/2- by 3^1/2-mile Long Island, including his wife and two children, is everything he could ask for.

"We have no electricity," Jordan said, "no television by choice. We built our own house. We cook on and receive our heat from a wood stove. Our lights are kerosene lanterns. We could live in the city with all the modern conveniences, but we wouldn't trade our lifestyle on an isolated Maine island for all the money in China."

THIRTEEN

PENNSYLVANIA

America's First Public Library

EDWIN WOLF II, librarian emeritus of the oldest public library in America, pulled a small book with a faded yellow cover off a stack and opened it.

In the smooth, round handwriting of a teen-ager at the top of the title page of *Logic; Or, The Art Of Thinking,* a 16-year-old had written his name—"B. Franklin."

It is the earliest signature of Benjamin Franklin known to exist.

When Franklin was 25 in 1731, he launched the first public library in America. The Library Company of Philadelphia continues to operate to this day. Its first location was in a home on Pewter Platter Alley.

In his autobiography, Franklin describes reading *Logic; Or, The Art Of Thinking.* He mentions giving the book to the Library Company in 1733. When he donated it, in front of his signature he wrote, "Given by...."

Today the library has one of the nation's largest collections of books from the 17th and 18th centuries. Of the 450,000 books, 160,000 manuscripts and 50,000 prints in its collection, half were published in the 1700s and first half of the 1800s.

Franklin's library served as the library for the Continental Congress, for the 55 delegates who wrote the Constitution in Philadelphia in 1787 and for the nation's first Congress. It held most of the accumulated wisdom published up to that time. The Library Company was then in Carpenter's Hall across from Independence Hall.

When the Revolution began, the library had more than 5,000 volumes, books still on the shelves today in its latest quarters, an eight-story modern building at 1314 Locust St. in the heart of Philadelphia.

"Several hundred books and pamphlets on our shelves belonged to Franklin," noted Wolf, the Library Company librarian from 1952 to 1984. He brought the historic institution out of bankruptcy into a vigorous new era.

The Library Company was the largest public library in America from Franklin's time through the mid-19th Century.

In 1727, at the age of 21, Franklin organized Junto, a discussion group also known as the Leather Apron Club. Its members met to debate politics and philosophy and to exchange knowledge.

When Franklin wrote his autobiography, he began: "My first project of a public nature, was a subscription library." Fifty members of Junto pooled their resources to launch the library and ordered a well-rounded collection of books from London. There were no bookstores in America then.

Their first shipment contained 141 volumes, including Palladio's *Architecture,* Bailey's *Dictionarium,* Boerhaave's *Chemistry,* Drake's *Anatomy,* Ellis' *Practical Farmer,* Defoe's *Complete English Tradesman,* Plutarch's *Lives,* Pope's *Homer,* Dryden's *Virgil,* Milton's *Paradise Lost* and Rapin-Thoyras' *History of England.*

A letter about the library published in the spring of 1740 appeared in Franklin's *Pennsylvania Gazette,* one of the colonies' leading newspapers. The writer commented:

"I am but a poor ordinary Mechanick of this city, obligated to work hard for the maintenance of myself, my wife and several small children. When my daily labour is over, instead of going to the Alehouse, I amuse myself with the books of The Library Company."

Forty years after Franklin founded the nation's first public library, he wrote: "This was the mother of all American subscription libraries now so numerous.

"These libraries have improved the general conversation of the Americans, made the common tradesmen and farmers as intelligent as most gentlemen from other countries, and perhaps contribute in some degree to the stand so generally made throughout the colonies in defence of their privileges."

Although the library was established by members paying a fee and annual dues, it was open to the public "to make available substantial and comprehensive book resources for all the citizenry of Philadelphia."

Today the library has 969 shareholders, but it's still open to everyone.

The Library Company of Philadelphia fell upon hard times during the Great Depression and went bankrupt in 1941. The Philadelphia Public Library administered the rich historic collections from 1941 to 1955.

During that time, rare-book dealer Edwin Wolf II was asked to take an inventory of the vast holdings. After he accepted the appointment as librarian in 1952, he turned the negative financial situation around and set the library in a new direction. The Library Company ended its relationship with the public library in 1955 and was on its own again.

From 1879 to 1966 the collections occupied a huge Parthenon-like structure, whose massive Doric columns faced a four-acre site in South Philadelphia. Insiders called it "the Great Pile." In his will, wealthy eccentric James Rush, a physician who died in 1869, left $1 million to erect the building.

He attached many codicils to his bequest. He and his wife, Phoebe Anne Rush, were to be buried in the library. The chairs were to be austere, without upholstery. No poetry, biographies of unknown persons or daily newspapers were to be permitted.

The Library Company sold the building and the four acres to the city in 1966. When the move was made to the library's present location, the remains of Dr. Rush and his wife were reburied in the courtyard of the new building under their original tombstones.

"There was always this rumor that Phoebe Rush was buried in 1857 wearing a fantastic collection of jewelry," Wolf recalled. "We opened her coffin when the move was made. No jewelry."

In addition to its endowments, fund drives and memberships, an important source of income for the Library Company has been a four-story downtown garage that it owns. The library receives no public funding.

Today the Library Company of Philadelphia is a research library, not a lending library as it was in the past. In addition to its books, it preserves many historic treasures, works of art, 18th-Century furniture and memorabilia from prominent Colonial families. Benjamin Franklin's hand-cranked static electricity machine, for example, is here.

But for scholars, authors, historians and graduate students, the real treasures are the books from the 18th and 19th centuries. Those who use the library come from all over the nation and from many different parts of the world.

Rebecca Larson came from Santa Barbara, Calif., to do research for a Harvard Ph.D. dissertation about 18th-Century Quaker women who were traveling ministers.

Larson spent weeks pouring through journals written during the 1700s. "These were women, many with husbands and children, who felt they had a divine call to leave their families for months, sometimes years, and travel throughout the colonies preaching the word of God," she explained.

"Some of the women traveled by ship to the British Isles to preach as they wandered the countryside there. Others came from the British Isles to America to preach here. I'm the first person since the early, middle and late 1700s to run my fingers through these pages and read many of these journals. It's an amazing story. For me, the Library Company of Philadelphia is a gold mine."

It is a gold mine for anyone doing research on any subject pertaining to the 18th and early 19th centuries.

FOURTEEN

WEST VIRGINIA

Life in the Hills and Hollers

SYLVIA O'BRION, 76, sat beside an oil lamp and wood-burning stove in her clapboard cabin on the subzero night, strumming her banjo and singing: "This is my home, where the bobcats holler and the wild deer roam."

She has lived in the primitive dwelling without running water or electricity on the slopes of Dead Fall Mountain her entire life. She shuns modern conveniences. She lives alone in one of the isolated pockets beyond the power lines in West Virginia.

The hardy, fiercely independent mountain woman has never had a radio or TV. She chops wood to cook her food and heat her home. She uses an outhouse, even in the dead of winter. Her nearest neighbors are on the other side of the mountain, a mile and a half away by footpath.

"I have never been sick," said the banjo woman of Dead Fall Run. "Never been in a doctor's office. Never took a dose of medicine.

"Oh, I could move and git indoor plumbin' and electricity if I wanted. But I'm set in my ways. I like the old-time way of livin'. I'm afraid of electricity. I don't understand it." Her banjo is made from a 1935 Buick transmission.

West Virginia is America's Mountain State. The entire state is Appalachian Mountains. Wave after wave of mountains. Like a sea. Most of the state's 1.8 million people live in narrow valleys called hollers.

Get out of the cities and towns and into the remote hills and hollers where the roads dead-end, and it's a step back in time.

Here live descendants of pioneer families who came from Scotland, Ireland, England and Wales in the 17th and 18th centuries. More people in the mountains of West Virginia have ties to the traditions, speech and way of life of early America than anywhere else in the nation.

Scattered through the hills and hollers are a few stubborn mountaineers like Sylvia O'Brion, who hang on to the past by choice.

Wylene (Gini) Dial, associate professor at the University of West Virginia's Appalachian Center, has been collecting words, phrases and sayings of her state's hill people for 30 years. She has published a dictionary and written numerous articles on the subject.

"The people of many West Virginia rural areas have been so isolated from the mainstream of American life for generations that Chaucerian and Elizabethan forms of speech are still in everyday use," she said.

"Outsiders think their speech is strange, even downright uncultured. That is because they don't realize what they are hearing is antique English from the days of the first Queen Elizabeth, the speech the highest educated used at that time.

"*Whar, thar* and *dar* are Scotch pronunciations brought here when the hollers were first settled. 'Blinked milk,' an expression in common use today, for example, is a term for sour milk. It goes back to the 1600s when people believed in witches and the power of the evil eye."

For outsiders, listening to the hill people of West Virginia often requires an interpreter. *Reckon we better git on into the house; it's right airish out,* translates: "Let's go into the house; it's cold outside."

"It is only as recently as 30 years," Dial noted, "with the incursion of radio, television and roads, that the colorful language in the backcountry hollers has begun to level out. I hope West Virginians never lose the color of their language. They are the best talkers God ever put on earth. I'd hate to see all of America become like a herd of sheep, all sounding like

TV announcers."

The massive road-building projects throughout the state in the 1960s and early '70s reduced the isolation and afforded today's easy access to most rural areas. Until the roads were finally pushed through, many in the state never ventured out of their remote villages.

Giant mushroom-like satellite TV dishes are sprinkled throughout the hills and hollers of West Virginia—like the one outside Dulcie Nicholson's two-story white 1875 farmhouse near a tiny town called Pickle Street.

"I got that thing two yars ago. Bought it for a thousand dollars," said Nicholson, an 88-year-old widow who has four cows and grows "tabaccer." "Got it from a man comin' door-to-door. He sold it to me, set it up, and it's been a-workin' right smart ever since. Had a TV afore, but never got me a picture. Now, on my honor, I git the world right *cheer* [here]."

West Virginia is soup beans, corn pone, biscuits and country gravy, plain American fare.

It's Friday Nights in Boulder, a mountain valley village populated by 17 families. Friday Nights at the Boulder Mercantile has been a tradition for 81 years, ever since the tongue-in-groove frame store was erected.

Villagers gather around the potbellied stove in the country store each Friday night to play the card game Rook and pass the news. Womenfolk bring "covered dishes" for a potluck.

"None of us knows what the others will bring," said Patricia George, owner of the store with her husband Hertsel. "One night we ended up with all pies. That's the fun of it."

"It sure beats settin' and watchin' TV," insisted lifelong coal miner Cecil Anderson, 76.

Shelves at Boulder Mercantile are jammed with canned goods, dry cereals, household items, chicken feed, sheep dip and hog worm powder. Boxes of home remedies left over from bygone days—like Save-the-Baby, a medicinal tonic for croup, coughs and congestion—gather dust in the country store.

Widow Bonnie Collins, 68, travels the state spinning yarns before PTAs, women's clubs, church socials, service clubs and colleges. Storytellers are a West Virginia tradition going back to the mid 1700s, to the time of Timmy Corn, the tallest tall-tale teller of them all.

"My stories all have a grain of truth," Collins said. "They're about kinfolk and neighbors. I also keep alive the old tales handed down by my daddy, my granddaddy and several granddaddies before them, all right fine storytellers."

Collins, known far and wide as "Mountain Mama," measures 5-foot-2 and tips the scale at more than 200 pounds. "The reason I'm so fat," she explained "is they pay me in meals and ball-point pens."

Collins, like Sylvia O'Brion, lives in a log cabin in an isolated holler. But unlike O'Brion, she has all the modern conveniences. "I don't wash clothes on a board like I used ta," she said, laughing. Her stories are about people living in the hills today and those who lived there in the past, stories about mountaineers like Charlie Spurgeon, the local undertaker.

"Charlie Spurgeon is the only man I can truthfully say is after my body," Collins said. "If I can bring some happiness to everyone I see, then I will not have lived in vain when Charlie comes for me."

She lives in a tiny hamlet called Ashley, "up yonder" from the only place in America, maybe the world, where someone actually made a mountain out of a molehill.

In 1949, the 30 families living in Mole Hill, W.Va., changed the name of the post office and the town from Mole Hill to Mountain.

West Virginia is sprinkled with quaint hamlets with equally quaint names, such as Roane County's Looneyville, population 500. "This is the only Looneyville in the United States," said Ruth Vineyard, Looneyville postmaster. "Go ahead and laugh. Strangers to these parts always do.

"We got our name in the mid 1700s when a Looney family from the British Isle of Man settled here. Today there are Looneys all over West Virginia, descendants of those first settlers. Some have fun with the name. Just to get the Looneyville postmark, one man ships all his Christmas cards up here to send out to his old World War II Army buddies."

There are scores of West Virginia hamlets with quaint names, names like Bergoo, Big Isaac, Cucumber, Cyclone, Czar, Droop, Duck, Ida May, Left Hand, Mud, Myrtle, Pie, Pinch, Quick, Tad, Three Churches, Tornado, Twilight, War. The derivation of each is fascinating. Left Hand, for example, got its name because it stands on the left-hand side of Left Hand Creek.

Until 1985, West Virginia had Romance. Not anymore. At least not a Romance, W.Va., post office. It vanished after more than a century. Postmaster Belva Lanham, 70, quit after 30 years. Her eyesight failed her. No one else on the clay road leading to a dozen farms wanted to be postmaster, so the government closed the post office. The office in Belva's tin-roofed hog farm wash house was the only public structure in the Jackson County holler.

Odd, W.Va., got its name in the early 1800s because the residents thought it was such an odd place, it ought to be called Odd. Texie Letha

Baldwin, 77, and her sister Thelma Cole, 71, have lived up Tommy Run (*run* in West Virginia means creek) in Odd all their lives. Their home is "hard fast against" Johnny Sneed Mountain, named after their great-great-great-grandfather, who settled in Odd in the late 1700s.

Thelma taught school at the Odd Elementary School across from the Odd cemetery for years. She also taught in the next holler at the Long Wanted School, so named because the people waited so long to get it.

"Sure, we live in these isolated hollers and old-fashioned homes like my log cabin," said Bonnie Collins. "People think we're a bunch of hillbillies, all ignorant and uneducated. But that's not true. There isn't a holler in the state out of reach of a school bus today. I'm proud to be a West Virginian."

St. Albans poet Muriel Miller Dressler says: "I don't apologize to anyone for my background or heritage. When I hit the mountains I breathe a little sigh, and say: 'Thank you, Lord! I'm home.'"

In the $14-million West Virginia Cultural Center on the state Capitol grounds at Charleston, historian Ken Sullivan edits *Goldenseal*, *West Virginia Traditional Life*, a quarterly published by the State Department of Culture and History.

Goldenseal captures the flavor of mountain life in West Virginia with stories of West Virginians today and of those in living memory.

The quarterly contains stories, for example, about hog-killing day at Aunt Dorie's; about Moatsville midwife Opal Freeman, who delivered hundreds of babies in the hills and hollers; about Arthurdale, the first of more than 100 experimental resettlement homestead projects initiated by Eleanor Roosevelt in the Great Depression.

The West Virginia Cultural Center is a focal point and repository of the state's rich cultural resources. On display are quilts, woodwork, arts and crafts by West Virginia artisans created in the style and manner of the past.

Folk festivals held throughout the year at the Cultural Center draw on the talents of the fiddlers, storytellers, clog dancers, dulcimer players, old-time songsters and others from the far reaches of the mountains of West Virginia.

The festivals attract the likes of Basil Blake, 71, Brag Run dulcimer maker. For the past half-century, Blake—who said he prefers groundhog meat over chicken—has handcrafted more than 800 dulcimers. First brought to this nation by the original English settlers, the three-stringed wooden musical instrument is plucked with a quill while held in the lap of a player.

Another institution, Salem College in Salem, W.Va., takes an academic approach to the state's rich cultural resources. Students earn a four-year bachelor's degree in 18th-Century West Virginia trades and skills. They come to Salem College from all over the nation to live and study in 20 log cabins dating back as early as 1790, all from the surrounding countryside and lived in until Professor John H. Randolph moved them to the college campus in 1975.

College students learn 18th-Century spinning, weaving, blacksmithing, woodworking, fireplace cooking in iron pots, quilting, trapping and pioneer medicine. Knowledge in these folkways can be highly valuable for students planning to work in outdoor museums.

Salem College graduates are historical interpreters at Williamsburg, Jamestown and other national and state parks across America.

For years Jim Comstock published the weekly *West Virginia Hillbilly*. When the *Saturday Review* called his paper sophisticated, Comstock demanded a retraction.

And when the Legislature passed a law requiring high schools to teach a course on West Virginia but did not implement it, Comstock took it upon himself to be "the great implementer." He presented the county superintendent of schools in each of the state's 55 counties with a 106-book library on the state's history as source material for the mandated course.

"All I asked was if the books were found to be of value I be sent a check for what the mini-libraries cost me," Comstock explained. All the counties send him a check.

Comstock spent 20 years in his spare time preparing a 51-volume Encyclopedia of West Virginia, published in 1976. In Comstock's words, it is "crammed with everything anyone would ever want to know about the Mountain State. It has the entire cast of characters, from Morgan Morgan, the first permanent settler, through the Bicentennial Year. It tells what brought them here in the beginning and why they have stayed the way they have so long.

"Who we are and why we are that way," said Comstock, "is best described by our state's motto—*Montani Semper Liberi*—Mountaineers Are Always Free."

FIFTEEN

NORTH CAROLINA

Outer Bankers—Descendants of Shipwrecked Colonists

A S THE NORTH CAROLINA state ferry set sail from Ocracoke Island heading for Beaufort, Annie Lou Gaskins looked to shore and sighed, "I love this island so much. I start getting homesick the minute the ferryboat leaves the dock and heads toward the mainland."

She stood on the stern of the ferry with her husband Earl as the boat began its voyage across Pamlico Sound. Both their families have lived on 16-mile-long, half- to 2-mile-wide Ocracoke Island since the 1700s.

They are descendants of British immigrants on their way to the Colonies who shipwrecked on Ocracoke and never left. Their speech, mannerisms and customs are a throwback to 18th-Century Britain.

Annie Lou and Earl Gaskins had boarded the ferry with other Ocracokers for the two-hour, 15-minute, 23-mile sail from their Outer Banks home to spend the day shopping in Beaufort.

The narrow band of sandy islands called the Outer Banks stretches along the entire length of North Carolina's 320-mile coast, from Carova on the Virginia state line to Calabash at the South Carolina border.

Averaging only 20 feet above sea level, some of the islands are as close as 200 yards from the mainland. Others, like Hatteras, are as far as 30 miles out to sea. The islands average half a mile to a mile in width.

Dramatic change has come to the North Carolina islands in the last few decades. During World War II, Outer Bankers for the most part were isolated and cut off from mainstream America.

Islanders seldom, if ever, visited the mainland. They lived in tiny remote villages. Outer Bankers fished. They manned Coast Guard lighthouses and search-and-rescue stations dotting the long, narrow island chain—like famed candy-cane-striped Cape Hatteras Lighthouse, built in 1870 (at 208 feet, the nation's tallest), and Chicamacomico Lifesaving Station at Rodanthe, dating back to 1874.

After World War II, islanders began building roads; prior to that they drove their vehicles on beaches. Bridges were constructed linking the Outer Banks to the mainland. Private and state ferry systems were inaugurated. In the last 20 years, developers have had a field day.

Several islands are now solid condos, mile after mile of unpainted beach homes built on stilts for hurricane protection. A 125-mile stretch, however, has been spared development and set aside as national seashore. Cape Hatteras National Seashore, 70 miles long, was dedicated in 1958. Cape Lookout, 55 miles long, was established as America's bicentennial national seashore in 1976.

Within Cape Hatteras National Seashore are eight old Outer Banks fishing villages. These include Ocracoke, population 626, where most residents—like Annie Lou and Earl Gaskins—trace their ancestry on the island to before the Revolutionary War.

Isolated pockets of old-line Outer Bankers, with their quaint Elizabethan speech, can still be found in a number of fishing villages on other islands up and down the coast.

"Our forefathers were yeoman-class people, the lower class who escaped from England to seek a better life in the Colonies," explained Walter C. Willis, 64, chief engineer on the Ocracoke Ferry. Willis is a very common name among Outer Bankers.

"When I was a boy, my great-grandmother told me how her people washed ashore on a beach at Portsmouth Island in the early 1700s. My daddy was born in 1883 at Diamond City, then a thriving whaling town on Portsmouth Island. By the turn of the century, the town was gone. Hurricanes drove the people off the island and destroyed Diamond City.

"A few years ago, a hurricane came through and uprooted all the graves at Diamond City. A bunch of us went to the island, collected the bones and skeletons and reburied them."

Hurricanes often sweep through and create new inlets in the Outer Banks and close existing ones. Sand hills are always shifting. Wind and sea are forever changing the shape and character of the Outer Banks.

"Good God, Ocracokers have a strange way of speaking," said U.S. Coast Guard Bo's'ns Mate 2nd Ernest Rackliff, 30, of Rockland, Me., stationed at Ocracoke Island. "If you've not been here long, you can't catch what they're saying."

On the other hand, Rackliff's Maine accent seems equally strange to Ocracokers.

It takes a hardy sort to live year-round on these islands. Nor'easters blow something fierce—60 to 90 miles an hour in winter. And breakers can flood an island in a really bad storm.

Rackliff and other Coast Guardsmen at Ocracoke are kept busy in winter rescuing mariners in distress. Waters of the Outer Banks, called the Graveyard of the Atlantic, are littered with the skeletons of more than 600 ships lost in treacherous seas.

During World War II, the Outer Banks picked up another nickname—Torpedo Junction—because of the heavy loss of Allied merchant ships and tankers sunk by Nazi U-boats.

Coast Guardsmen on Ocracoke have an unusual chore. Each day they raise and lower the British Flag over a tiny island cemetery. The graveyard is deeded by the United States to the British government.

The British Cemetery on Ocracoke has only four graves, the final resting place of four British sailors washed ashore after their trawler *Bedfordshire* was sunk by a German sub May 11, 1942. Each May 11, Royal Navy officers come to Ocracoke for a memorial service. A plaque on the cemetery's white picket fence carries poet Rupert Brooke's verse:

> *If I should die, think only this of me;*
> *That there's some corner of a foreign field*
> *That is forever England....*

How did Ocracoke get its peculiar name?

"In the early days someone heard a rooster," Earl Gaskins answered over the raucous bleating of blackhead gulls trailing in the ferry's wake. "He said this was the island where 'o-cock-crow.' It stuck. 'O-cock-crow' became Ocracoke."

Ocracoke is the island where in 1718 British navy officer Robert Maynard beheaded the infamous Edward (Blackbeard) Teach. He hung the pirate's head from his ship's rigging for all to see and threw the body overboard. Legend has it that Blackbeard's headless body swam seven times around the British man-of-war before sinking.

Gaskins was in the Coast Guard, as were his father and grandfather, a time-honored Outer Banks tradition. He was also in the Army during the Korean War. "My mates in the Army had a hard time understanding me speak," he said with a laugh. "They thought I was a Limey. They thought I was in the wrong Army."

Part of the charm of the Outer Banks is that old-time families to this day bury their loved ones in their yards. What happens when the house is sold?

In the village of Duck on Bodie Island, retired schoolteacher Charles P. Wheless, 68, bought his house in 1969. It came with six graves, the most recent burial, 1961. Tombstones on his lawn bear the names of the deceased, birth and death dates, and epitaphs like "Asleep in Jesus" and "Gone But Not Forgotten."

"By law I can never disturb the tombstones in any way," Wheless explained, "nor, of course, the coffins, without permission from the relatives."

Many Outer Bankers are laid to rest in the Old Burying Grounds at Beaufort, a graveyard dating back to the early 1700s. The cemetery's 18th-Century graves face east because the occupants wanted to be facing the sun when they arose on Judgment Morn. A young British girl who died on a ship en route to the Colonies was preserved and buried in a keg of rum. A British Navy office was buried standing up. The epitaph on his lichen-mottled tomb reads:

> Resting neath a foreign ground,
> Here stands a sailor of Mad George's crown.
> Name unknown and all alone,
> Standing in the Rebel's ground.

For 300 years, fishing has been the mainstay of Outer Bankers. Hundreds of island boats fish in Pamlico, Albemarle, Currituck, Crotan, Core and other sounds separating the islands from the mainland, as well as in the rich waters of the Atlantic.

"Fishing has always been decent to Outer Bankers," said gill-netter "Bluewater Bob" Standing, 45, at Hatteras Village. "New York controls our market. Fish is trucked from the islands daily to Fulton's Fish Market in the Big Apple."

Shrimpers, scallopers, oystermen, lobstermen, clammers and crabbers ply the waters up and down the coast. Fishermen catch flounder, mullet, shad, herring, bluefish, spot, snapper, croaker, perch, king mackerel, trout, wahoo and much, much more.

Some Outer Bankers go down to sea in big 75- and 80-footers, others in sharpies, skiffs and smaller boats. And some, like Robert Willis, 53, of Gloucester, never leave the beach. They wade up to their waists in bays and dig into the sandy bottom, clamming.

Willis spends four hours a day tossing as many as 1,000 clams into his No. 3 washtub, which floats inside an inner tube. "I've been doing this since I was knee-high to a grasshopper," Willis said between digs. "I get 8 cents a clam. That's $80 on a good day. I've only dug 250 so far today. That's only $20 worth. But I'm just getting my feet wet."

At Davis, half of the 400 residents are named Davis and trace their ancestry to an English sailor shipwrecked there in 1713. "We have 40 shrimp boats here." said Grady Davis, 40, one of the Davis shrimpers. "We shrimp at night. You can't catch the type of shrimp we have during daylight hours."

In Hatteras Village, lifelong fisherman Ernal Foster, 75, has a building full of nets he has been using since the 1920s—shrimp nets, bluefish nets, all kinds of nets, many obsolete. "See those cotton nets?" Foster said. "Nobody uses cotton anymore. Times have changed.

"The Outer Bank way of life, our Elizabethan speech is fast disappearing. Our culture is dying, being replaced by yuppies, condos and miniature golf courses.

"People are buying property on these islands like crazy. They come from Virginia, Maryland, Pennsylvania, New York, Ohio. They're paving up our islands. A person can hardly breathe.

"We had something precious here once. It will be gone forever in another generation. Outer Bankers are being swallowed up by outsiders."

One group of 37 Outer Bankers on Bodie Island at Carova lives on a remote stretch of sand without roads. They reach their homes by driving on the beach, the highway of nearly all Outer Bankers until pavement came during the 1950s and '60s.

"We like it here because of the way it is," said resident Judy White. "No roads. Quiet. Isolated. Sand and sea. Wild Spanish mustangs." The mustangs run free—descendants of horses running free in the Outer Banks for 300 years.

Four hundred years ago, the Outer Banks became the site of America's first colony when Sir Walter Raleigh established a settlement on Roanoke Island. Virginia Dare was born here in 1587.

And it was on the sand dunes of Kitty Hawk, at Kill Devil Hills, Dec. 17, 1903, on a North Carolina Outer Bank, that Orville and Wilbur Wright accomplished man's first powered flight—another proud first for Outer Bankers who live in this special corner of America.

SIXTEEN

SOUTH CAROLINA

Charleston: City of Firsts

HISTORIC CHARLESTON, S.C., founded in 1670, is truly a city
of firsts.

It was here at Fort Sumter where the first shots of the Civil War
were fired.

The first decisive victory of the Revolutionary War took place in Charleston.

The world's first successful submarine attack occurred in Charleston Harbor.

Here rice and indigo were first planted in America.

Charleston had America's first theater and its first opera performance.

This is the home of the country's first fire insurance company, first chamber of
commerce, first museum, first municipal college, first passenger railroad service,
first historic district and much more.

"Everyone knows the Civil War began at Fort Sumter, but people know little more than that about this historic fortress," noted National Park Service ranger David Ruth as he greeted a boatload of arrivals to Fort Sumter National Monument, a 2¹/₂-acre island in Charleston Harbor.

"Most people don't realize that the North and South fought over this tiny strip of land for four years, throughout the entire length of the Civil War.

"Fort Sumter was the South's symbol of nationhood and had to be defended at all costs. It was a symbol of secession for the North and had to be taken at whatever the cost. For four years the Confederate defenders withstood attack in one of the most heroic defenses of a fortress in human history."

Maj. Robert Anderson and his 85 officers and men stationed at Fort Sumter knew the tiny island was in a precarious position when the South Carolina Legislature voted unanimously Dec. 20, 1860, to secede from the Union.

Confederate batteries ringed the shoreline of Charleston Harbor with cannons and mortars. On April 11, 1861, the Confederates demanded that Anderson and his men evacuate Fort Sumter. Anderson refused. The next day, at 4:30 a.m., a mortar shell exploded directly over the federal fort.

Within minutes, 43 Confederate cannons and mortars were blasting away at Fort Sumter. Capt. Abner Doubleday, second in command at the fort—the man who originated the rules for baseball in 1839 at Cooperstown, N.Y.—was the first to return fire for the North.

The bombardment and returning Union fire continued for two days. Anderson finally surrendered and lowered the America flag. Remarkably, only one man was killed in the engagement—and that by accident during the gun salute when the American flag was brought down.

From the day the federal forces left Fort Sumter, the North was determined to retake the island. But Charleston was a Confederate stronghold, and Fort Sumter was a key to the strategic harbor. The island fortress was rebuilt, strengthened and manned by 300 Confederate soldiers and as many as 200 slaves.

On April 5, 1863, a fleet of nine federal ironclads entered the harbor and sought to regain Fort Sumter but were repulsed. One ship was sunk, four were disabled.

By August of that year, federal troops captured Morris Island, across from and within firing range of Fort Sumter. That began nearly two years of constant shelling of the fort.

Ironically, as the walls of the fort were blasted apart, the rubble piled up 20 feet around the first-tier casemates, giving the defenders bomb-proof rooms.

Slaves worked day and night filling sandbags to patch holes in the walls for reinforcement. Sand and other supplies were barged to the island at night.

Throughout the four-year period, 56 Confederate defenders and about four times as many slaves were killed on the island.

Finally, in the last days of the war, the Confederates abandoned Fort Sumter. Anderson, now a general, returned to the island and on April 14, 1865, raised the same tattered flag he had lowered four years to the date. The flag is in a museum on the island.

Abraham Lincoln had planned to come to Fort Sumter for the flag raising but had second thoughts. Instead he stayed in Washington and went to Ford's Theatre. Ironically, one of the last shots of the war took the life of the President, only six days after Lee surrendered to Grant at Appomattox.

A replica of the *H.L. Hunley*, the first submarine ever to sink an enemy ship, stands outside the Charleston Museum—founded in 1773, the first museum established in America.

The world's first successful submarine attack occurred in Charleston Harbor on Feb. 17, 1864. The *H.L. Hunley*, a 25-foot-long, 4-foot-wide Confederate sub, sank the Union warship *Housatonic*.

Powered by eight men hand-cranking its propeller, the *Hunley* had a maximum speed of 4 m.p.h. Its torpedo, filled with 90 pounds of gun powder, was towed and pulled against the hull of the target ship.

Five Union sailors were killed when the torpedo blew up *Housatonic's* magazine. The rest of the crew were rescued. But the *Hunley* had worse luck. The Confederate sub sustained damage from the explosion it caused aboard the *Housatonic*. It sank and its entire eight-man crew perished.

Charleston is the home of America's first woman artist, Henrietta Johnson, who painted portraits of the city's leading men and women beginning in 1707. The South's first newspaper, the *South Carolina Gazette*, was edited and published from 1739 to 1744 by Elizabeth Timothy, America's first woman editor and publisher.

America's first theater, the Dock Street Theatre, opened in 1736 with the play *The Recruiting Officer*. Later that same year, the theater presented America's first opera performance.

In 1800, Planter's Hotel was erected on the site of America's first theater (whose fate was lost in obscurity). The hotel—birthplace of Planter's Punch—thrived for nearly a century and then fell into ruin until Harry Hopkins, President Franklin Roosevelt's secretary of commerce, reconstructed the Dock Street Theatre in 1936.

The Recruiting Officer reopened the theater just as it had launched it 200 years earlier at the same location. The Footlight Players, the city's oldest community theater group, operates and manages the city-owned theater.

Charleston was the home of the Friendly Society for the Mutual Insuring of Houses Against Fire, America's first fire insurance company. The company didn't last long. It went belly-up when the great fire of 1740 destroyed more than 300 buildings.

America's first chamber of commerce was organized in Charleston in 1773, the year Charleston Library Society founded America's first museum. Four signers of the Declaration of Independence were among the museum's earliest directors.

Hanging in America's first museum is an 1826 poster that proclaims: "An extensive collection of beasts, birds, reptiles, fishes and many curiosities among which are the head of a New Zealand chief, an Egyptian mummy and a great white bear from Greenland. Occasional performances by a band of musicians. Admittance 25 cents."

The College of Charleston, the first municipal college in America and the nation's oldest publicly supported college, opened its doors in 1770. In today's time-honored graduation ceremonies, women wear long Colonial gowns and men wear tuxedos.

America's first passenger railroad train, the *Best Friend,* started service from Charleston to Hamburg, S.C., in 1830 along 136 miles of track. It was the longest continuous railroad in the world at the time.

Charleston is America's "Porgy and Bess" town. The former tenements on Cabbage Row were the model for Catfish Row in author DuBose Heyward's novel *Porgy,* which George Gershwin turned into the popular folk opera *Porgy and Bess.* Cabbage Row got its name because its residents sold the vegetable from their windowsills.

Charleston, the city that gave the most popular dancing style of the 1920s its name—the twisting toes-in, heels-out dance step called the Charleston—is one of America's best preserved cities.

On Oct. 13, 1931, the Charleston City Council established the Charleston Old and Historic District with the nation's first zoning ordinance to preserve a city's architectural heritage.

Today there are more than 2,000 restored buildings, many with tiered porches called piazzas lining narrow alleys, cobblestone streets and walled courtyard gardens. These architectural treasures, dating from the 1600s to the Civil War, have been preserved and restored under the leadership of the Preservation Society of Charleston.

SEVENTEEN

GEORGIA

Berry College, Twice the Size of Manhattan

G EORGIA'S MOUNT BERRY is home of the largest college campus in America.
Twice the size of Manhattan, 28,000-acre Berry College's irregular-shaped boundaries run 15 miles in one direction, 12 in the other. Berry College is so big that visitors receive a tape to play on a 16-mile motor tour of the campus.

Some have driven its back roads for two days and never touched the same road twice.

Dotted with lakes, the entire campus is a wildlife sanctuary with more than 4,000 deer, hundreds of wild turkeys, fox, swans and a wealth of other birds and animals. Much of the campus is a forest preserve.

"Being president of Berry is like dying and going to heaven," said Gloria M. Shatto, who celebrated her 15th year as the school's president in 1995.

"They call this the Miracle of the Mountain. It's Georgia's best kept secret."

Located on the outskirts of the town of Rome, in the northwest corner of Georgia, Berry is a liberal arts school that's enormous in size and small in enrollment—1,800 students. Yet scholastically it consistently ranks among the top small liberal arts colleges in the nation. In an evaluation by *U.S. News and World Report,* for example, Berry placed fifth.

The average Scholastic Aptitude Test score for entering freshmen was 1,049—145 points above the national average and 201 points above the Georgia average.

Berry is one of about half a dozen work colleges in the country. Along with diplomas, 90% of the graduates receive certificates of work noting they worked at least 10 hours a week on campus, usually at a variety of jobs.

"Work has always been an integral part of the educational process at Berry," explained John Heneisen, Berry's dean of work. "We encourage, but do not force, students to work on campus in addition to their studies."

The college pays $2.2 million a year in wages to students who work at 120 different job classifications. Some are groundskeepers, carpenters, mechanics, electricians, painters and foresters. Others run a cable-TV company or a dairy with 200 cows, care for 750 head of beef or work as research assistants, secretaries or switchboard operators.

Still others handcraft clothing sold in a school gift shop, make and repair furniture for campus buildings, run the school cafeterias and residence halls and maintain the school's vehicles and farm equipment.

"Our young men and women come from affluent families, from welfare families and everything in between," Heneisen said. "Berry is a great leveler. Learning the value of work is for everyone."

Berry College traces its beginning to a Sunday afternoon in the spring of 1900. Martha Berry, the 34-year-old unmarried daughter of a wealthy plantation owner, sat alone reading in a log cabin near her Possum Trot home. Looking up from her book, she saw three mountain boys peering at her through a window.

"What are your names?" she asked as she invited them in. "Where do you live?"

"I'm Jed," said the oldest. "This is Adam and this is Least'un. When he come there were so many of us, Ma couldn't think of no more names, so we just call him Least'un." They lived nearby in Trapp Holler at the foot of Lavender Mountain.

Like nearly all the children in the area, they could neither read nor write.

At the time, there were no schools in this part of Georgia. Martha Berry read to them that afternoon.

The following Sunday the boys were back, their sisters and brothers in tow. On subsequent Sundays they showed up with their mother and father and soon with neighboring families. All wanted to be read to by the woman they called the "Sunday Lady of Possum Trot."

Berry opened a boarding school for boys in 1902, combining education with vocational training. The boys worked the plantation to earn their keep and education. Seven years later she started a girl's school.

In time the Berry schools became elementary and high schools, a junior college in 1926 and a four-year college in 1930. Berry's goal was to instill her students with a belief in the importance of work, their studies and faith in God. Eventually she gave the college her plantation and Oak Hill, her Greek revival antebellum mansion built in 1847.

Her students erected a log-cabin campus in the early years with structures for classrooms, dormitories, auditorium and faculty homes. The log cabins continue in use to this day.

In the 1930s, high school and college students fired their own bricks and built several Georgian-style buildings. These included a three-story science hall, gymnasium, residence halls, industrial shops, a large dairy complex and a 1,000-seat Christopher Wren-style church.

The schools were self-sufficient through the 1940s. Students grew crops, raised poultry, cared for beef and dairy herds and ran a cannery. They grew cotton and made their own fabric for clothing on looms. They harvested trees to construct and heat buildings. They built dams and reservoirs and erected a giant wheel and grist mill to grind corn and grain.

And, thanks to Martha Berry, all through the years they had one of the finest academic programs in the nation.

Hearing about Berry's remarkable school, Theodore Roosevelt came to visit. Andrew Carnegie was so impressed he started the Berry Endowment with a $50,000 gift. Other industrialists added to the fund.

Henry Ford became the largest benefactor. He and his wife Clara first visited the school in 1923. Though Ford disliked most institutions of higher learning and the things they taught, he liked Berry's emphasis on work and practical learning.

"I felt Martha Berry could make better use of some of my money than I could myself," said Ford, who gave nearly $5 million for campus improvements.

Ford brought stonemasons from Italy and constructed a complex of

Gothic buildings patterned after England's Oxford University, including residence and dining halls, classrooms, offices, auditorium and gymnasium. He also purchased additional land, built a large mountain reservoir and gave the school a fleet of tractors.

Good Housekeeping magazine called Martha Berry one of America's 12 greatest women. President Coolidge presented her with a medal. Two ships were named after her during World War II.

Martha Berry died on Feb. 27, 1942. She was buried on campus. Henry Ford was one of many notables at her funeral.

The high school and elementary schools were discontinued a number of years ago, except for the Berry College Laboratory School, a teachers' demonstration school for 110 kindergarten through fifth-grade students. Today Berry College consists of the original log cabin campus, the main campus, the Ford quadrangle and the mountain campus.

The mountain campus, formerly the high school, provides housing for 110 students on full four-year scholarships co-sponsored by Berry College and Truett Cathy's Chick-fil-A, a chain of fast-food outlets in 35 states.

Campus programs continue to be innovative. At the Rollins Beef Research Center at Berry's School of Agriculture, for example, a research program involves 40 water buffalo raised for beef, butchered on campus and sold in local supermarkets. Water buffalo tastes much like regular beef.

"The land is our endowment in addition to our $75-million endowment and trust funds," President Shatto explained. The school receives an income from regular timber harvest on campus, from a 200-acre rock quarry, from a large clay mine used for ceramic tile and from an industrial park.

Berry College's 19,000 alumni maintain strong ties to the school. Each May many return to the campus to spend a week repairing and upgrading log-cabin classrooms and dormitories.

Ed Kemp, a retired law enforcement officer now working as a realtor in Palm Springs, Calif., graduated in 1955. He paid for his tuition and room and board for four years by working at various jobs on campus, sometimes as a cowboy with the school's registered black Angus, other times bailing hay and mowing the pasture.

Kemp's two brothers and sister also graduated from Berry, as did two of his uncles. It was through his uncles that he learned about this most unusual school.

"Looking back," Kemp said, "other than the school's excellent academic program, I think what really affected my life because of the Berry experience is the sense of discipline and the work ethic instilled in students—for which I am extremely grateful."

Every four years since 1912, an international youth camp has been part of the Olympic Games. Berry College was selected as the 1996 site to host 500 young men and women from all over the world.

Joe Patterson, Berry's public relations director, stood at the Gate of Opportunity, the school's main entrance. A visitor asked him what Martha Berry would think of the place now.

"She would be astounded," he said, "and pleased as punch to see how the school has developed from a small cabin to one of the leading small colleges in America. I'm sure she would be absolutely delighted if she were to pop in today."

EIGHTEEN

FLORIDA

The Sanibel Stoop and
The Best Friend Ducks Ever Had

FLORIDA'S SANIBEL ISLAND is famous for seashells and shorebirds. Twenty miles southwest of Fort Myers on the Gulf Coast, the 14-mile-long, 2-mile-wide island connects to the mainland by a three-mile causeway.

First the seashells:

From dawn to dusk, all one sees dotting Sanibel's dazzling white beaches are the derrieres of men, women and children bent over picking up seashells. They call it the "Sanibel Stoop."

This island is a mecca for shell collectors. It's the seashell capital of America.

Ponce de Leon, Florida's discover, is said to be the first non-Indian to set foot on the island. He stopped by in 1513, on his search for the Fountain of Youth.

Spanish mariners who sailed to these shores in the 16th and 17th centuries called Sanibel the *Costa de Caracoles*—the "Coast of Seashells." Legend has it that Sanibel is named after Santa Isabelle, queen of Spain.

Every spring, the "Tiffany of seashell shows"—the four-day Sanibel Shell Fair—takes place at the Sanibel Community Center on Periwinkle Drive, a thoroughfare named, of course, after a seashell.

Thousands of shellers from all over the world come to the Sanibel Shell Fair.

"It's the oldest shell fair in the country so far as we know," said Dot Putnam, a fair director since 1972. The first official Sanibel Shell Fair was held in 1937.

But its roots go way back.

Professor R. Tucker Abbott, who to shellers is what Audubon is to birdwatchers, in his book *Kingdom of the Seashell* traced the origin of shell fairs to Sanibel. "Shell shows are an American innovation," he wrote, "begun informally in Florida at the turn of the century when enthusiastic shellers on Sanibel Island displayed their spoils on long tables set up on the verandah of the Island Inn."

Abbott is one of the founders of the Shell Museum and Educational Foundation, the group that erected the $1.25-million Bailey–Matthews Seashell Museum on an eight-acre site on Sanibel. Opened in 1995, it is America's only seashell museum and has more than 2 million seashells in its collection.

Visitors at the annual Sanibel Seashell Fair encounter an array of aquariums, the traditional "Live Shell Exhibit" by fifth graders from Sanibel Elementary School.

"These are egg cases of lightning whelks," explained Jenny Grondi, 10, pulling a long string of tan snail egg cases from her tank.

"Live angel wings," said Marty Traucht, 11, pointing to two seashells in his aquarium.

"This is the common five-arm sea star," said Angie Sicca, 10, leaning over her aquarium. "Most people call it a starfish, only it isn't a fish."

Teachers Mary McHarag and Alice Anders introduce the youngsters to local seashells and shore life throughout the school year. Then the boys and girls impart their knowledge to visitors at the shell fair.

Tiny coquinas, clam shells, alphabet cones, tulips, paper figs, horse conchs, fighting conchs, kings crowns, sea anemones, feather worms, sea slugs, lace murexes and nippy dogfish—all gathered from local shores—thrive in the tanks.

So does a rare Junonia, or Juno, Sanibel's most celebrated and sought-after shell. When anyone finds a Junonia, a ship's bell rings on the island to tell of the exciting discovery.

It happens several times each year.

Proceeds from the shell fair are used to maintain the Sanibel Community Center. Islanders donate thousands of shells for sale under the big Shell Tent.

Art Ford, 80, and his wife Kay, 77, spend months teaching and working with islanders who handcraft shell animals and contribute them to the seashell fair for sale.

Professional shellers from around the world, such as Yasuji Ando of Japan with his Japanese miniatures, exhibit collections at the show. Trophies are awarded for outstanding scientific collections, and prizes go for shell creations including paintings, necklaces, flowers and figures.

The shell fair is sponsored by the 410-member Sanibel–Captiva Shell Club and the Sanibel Community Assn. Sanibel and its 5-mile-long, half-mile-wide neighbor island Captiva boast the greatest numbers and varieties of seashells anywhere in the nation.

Sanibel may be the only place in the country where one can hire a professional seashell guide. The guides lead shellers to beaches with the greatest number of species.

Captiva and Sanibel bookstores have huge selections of seashell books. Both islands are dotted with stores with names like She Sells Sea Shells, which happens to specialize in selling seashells. On the other hand, Sea Shells of Sanibel is a big condominium complex....

It goes on and on. For anyone nuts about seashells, this is the closest place to heaven.

Now the shorebirds:

"Look at the roseate spoonbills coming right at us," shouted Doug Mackey, a U.S. Fish and Wildlife public-use manager. High atop a 20-foot tower, he pointed to two large, pink wading birds with huge spoon-shaped bills flying toward the observation platform.

The platform held a dozen visitors to the J.N. (Ding) Darling National Wildlife Refuge on Sanibel Island. The birds' flashy pass was just part of the spectacular display of nature that Mackey shares with guests at this refuge.

From their perch on the tower, the visitors overlooked tidal bays and tiny islands covered with dense forests of red mangrove trees tangled in a mass of above-water, above-ground roots.

The visitors saw spoonbills with shafts of sunlight shimmering through their wings. They viewed endangered prehistoric-looking wood storks; laughing gulls whose calls sounded like human laughter; blue-wing teals; glossy black anhingas, or water turkeys; double-crested cormorants; golden-slippered snowy egrets; white ibis; spindly legged sandpipers; yellow-billed great white egrets; blue herons, and numerous other bird species standing in the shallows feeding on fish or just flying by.

The powder-blue sky and sparkling azure waters at this 5,014-acre wildlife sanctuary were alive with thousands of birds.

Young pelicans bravely plunged their pouchy bills 20 to 30 times into the tidal bays before catching a fish. Nearby, adult pelicans succeeded at the same task on their first tries.

Donald Reed, a watercolor wildlife artist from Oregon, Ill., sat on a bank and recorded nature's fascinating show.

"I come here every couple of years to research birds in the wild," he explained. "This is the best place I know of for huge numbers of birds, for constantly changing varieties of birds. Half to three-quarters of all species of birds in America pass through here at some point during the year."

More than 800,000 people from all over the country come each year as well.

This, the most popular of more than 450 national wildlife refuges in America, is named after Jay Norwood (Ding) Darling, a newspaper political cartoonist.

Darling, who lived from 1876 to 1962, was a giant in the cause of conservation. Through his nationally syndicated cartoons, he alerted the nation to the urgent needs of preventing the extinction of wildlife and preserving precious natural resources decades before such causes became fashionable.

As father of the Migratory Bird Hunting and Conservation Act, Darling launched the program to establish a nationwide system of wildlife refuges, to rescue and set aside lands as migratory bird sanctuaries.

He is known as the best friend ducks ever had.

Ding Darling (his nickname was a contraction of his last name) was born in Norwood, Mich. He grew up in Iowa and went to work as a reporter-cartoonist for the *Sioux City Journal* in 1900.

In 1906, Darling was hired as the *Des Moines Register's* political cartoonist. By 1949, when he retired from the *Register*, he had drawn more than 15,000 daily cartoons.

He championed the cause of conservation from his first days as a cartoonist.

"I watched the prairie chicken disappear," he recalled in his later years, "watched the flight of migratory waterfowl dwindle from huge cloud-like formations to sporadic flights of remnants. It was the disappearance of all that wonderful wildlife I knew as a kid that got me started early on as a conservationist."

He never let up for 50 years, interspersing cartoons about saving the nation's natural resources with others on contemporary political matters.

He did a whole series of before-and-after cartoons showing how man has ravaged nature in his efforts to advance civilization.

The preservation of migratory waterfowl, he insisted, goes with "the management of water resources and the critical effect such management has upon human sustenance. Wild ducks, geese and shore birds are the delicate indicators of the prognosis for human existence, just as sure as God made little green apples."

Darling's cartoons appeared in 130 of America's leading newspapers. A 1934 poll of newspapers by *Editor and Publisher* magazine named him the outstanding cartoonist in the country.

In 1924, he won the second Pulitzer Prize ever awarded a cartoonist. He won that prestigious prize again in 1942.

In 1934, President Franklin D. Roosevelt named Darling chief of the Bureau of Biological Survey, forerunner of the U.S. Fish and Wildlife Service. He held the position for two years during a hiatus from his drawing board.

In the depths of the Great Depression, Darling was able to pry $20 million in federal appropriations for wildlife conservation from Congress.

In 1934, he designed the first duck stamp, which showed two mallards about to descend to the water. Ever since, every duck hunter must be in possession of a valid duck stamp. A new stamp is issued each year. The first stamp cost $1. Now they sell for $7.50. Proceeds from the stamps are earmarked for refuges.

In 1990, Jeannette Rudy of Nashville, Tenn., purchased the first duck stamp ever issued from another collector. Darling had signed his name across the stamp. The price was an undisclosed six-figure amount. Rudy had the stamp insured for $300,000.

Since the duck stamp program began in 1934, more than $400 million has been raised to buy and preserve more than 4 million wetland acres. Many of the more than 450 national wildlife refuges have been paid for either entirely or in part by duck stamp revenue.

Darling was the founder and first president of the National Wildlife Federation. A lake in Iowa, a lake in Canada, a species of flowering crab tree and several conservation club chapters across America have been named after him. He won the prestigious Audubon medal and many other national honors.

Sigma Delta Chi, now the Society of Professional Journalists, designated the Des Moines Register Building a historic site because that is where Darling worked as a cartoonist.

The visitor center of the J.N. (Ding) Darling National Wildlife Refuge displays several of the cartoonist's works. A gift shop sells reproductions of his wildlife cartoons in a book put out by the J.N. (Ding) Darling Foundation. It also sells David Lendt's award-winning biography *Ding—The Life of Jay Norwood Darling.*

Darling's studio, recreated in the visitor center, looks just as it did when he left it for the final time and is depicted in his last cartoon, "Bye Now— It's Been Wonderful Knowing You." The cartoon ran on the *Register's* front page the morning after he died, Feb. 12, 1962.

Darling's last cartoon showed the artist running out the studio door, hat in hand.

The studio replica includes his swivel chair, easel with final cartoon, brushes, half-filled coffee cup with spoon, the original duck stamp and several of his most famous cartoons on the walls.

It's appropriate that the wildlife refuge that carries Darling's name is here on the island of Sanibel in Florida, his winter home for many years.

And it's especially noteworthy that a newspaper cartoonist has had such a lasting effect on the protection and preservation of wildlife in America.

NINETEEN

ALABAMA

Tuskegee: University and National Park

TUSKEGEE UNIVERSITY, one of the nation's foremost African-American schools—the school made famous by Booker T. Washington and George Washington Carver—is not only a university, it's a national park as well.

Some 53 acres of the main campus and 23 historic buildings in the area—many still in use as classrooms, dormitories, school offices, a hospital, theater, museum and chapel—are jointly administered by the National Park Service and Tuskegee University.

In the heart of the 268-acre campus, not far from the university's striking chapel, are the graves of Booker T. Washington and George Washington Carver. They rest in that part of the school set aside by President Gerald Ford in 1974 as a national historic site.

Across from the graves stands Charles Keck's 1922 *Lifting the Veil* monument to Washington. It bears the inscription, "Booker T. Washington, 1856-1915. He lifted the veil of ignorance from his people and pointed the way to progress through education and industry."

Nearby is the red-brick George Washington Carver Museum, dedicated by Henry Ford in 1941 when the automaker came to Tuskegee to pay tribute to the aging professor-scientist. Carver died two years later.

The museum, now part of the Tuskegee National Historic Site, preserves and exhibits paintings, tools, handiwork and lab experiments produced by the famed scientist during his 40 years as a member of Tuskegee Institute's faculty.

Carver came to Tuskegee in 1896 to head the agricultural college and conduct his research and experiments with peanuts, sweet potatoes and other crops.

Thirty-minute films telling the story of the lives of both Carver and Washington are shown to visitors in the museum's theater.

In recent years, as part of the national historic site experience, an estimated 600,000 visitors a year have come from every state and many foreign countries to visit the school made famous by Booker T. Washington and George Washington Carver.

Visiting men, women and children mingle on campus with the 3,300 students from throughout the United States and overseas. Tuskegee is the only active university designated a national historic site.

It was Washington, a former slave, who founded Tuskegee Institute on July 4, 1881. He was only 22 at the time. The school operated as Tuskegee Institute until 1986, when its name was changed to Tuskegee University.

Washington answered the call to start a black teachers' school after Lewis Adams, a tinsmith and former slave, and George W. Campbell, a banker and former slave owner—an unlikely combination—persuaded the Alabama Legislature to establish the school in Tuskegee.

The Legislature appropriated $2,000 to launch Tuskegee Institute, making no provisions for land or buildings. That was left to Washington. Classes began in an abandoned plantation shanty with 30 young men and women, the school's first students.

Washington's objective was to turn out teachers who would go across the land and bring education to blacks. He succeeded beyond his greatest expectations.

To help pay for their education, students spent time each day growing crops and raising livestock. They became brick makers. They built the classrooms, dormitories and other school buildings from red bricks fired on campus.

By the time Washington died in 1915, Tuskegee had become an

internationally acclaimed institution. Along with modern campus buildings, nearly all of the original red brick structures are still in use today, many of them included in the national historic site.

The Oaks, Washington's 1899 home, is also part of the national historic site.

"Just the history itself of Tuskegee attracts many students—that and its preeminence in the academic world," said Ron Sample, a senior from San Bernardino, Calif., majoring in computer science. "As a black person I have a good feeling being here."

It was at Tuskegee during World War II that the Tuskegee Airmen, America's black fighter and bomber pilots, were trained. Chappie James, America's first African-American four-star Air Force general, was one of them.

Segregation was so entrenched in this country on the eve of World War II that black pilots were refused training at air bases throughout the United States.

An entire new airfield and $4-million training complex was built at Tuskegee Institute so that blacks could be quartered and trained separately from whites.

The black airmen went on to destroy 200 Nazi airplanes in aerial combat, damage 148 others, sink a German destroyer and wipe out hundreds of military vehicles when strafing convoys.

Members of the black air force came home with Distinguished Flying Crosses, Legions of Merit, Silver Stars, Purple Hearts, Bronze Stars—but they came home to an ungrateful nation.

"We put our life on the line," recalled Freddie Hutchins of Atlanta, one of the pilots. "Yet when we came back home after the war we were still called 'nigger' or 'boy.' That was a hard pill to swallow."

Of the 992 black cadets trained as Army Air Corps pilots at Tuskegee, 450 flew combat missions. The rest became members of four B-25 bomber squadrons based in the United States.

Sixty-six of the black pilots did not come back from overseas duty. They were killed in combat.

The Tuskegee Airmen were called the "Lonely Eagles"—airmen destined to fly alone.

They are national heroes—heroic for their fighting spirit and ability and for doing more to eliminate segregation in the armed forces than any other group of individuals.

The undergraduate instruction at Tuskegee University comes from seven major areas: the College of Arts and Sciences, School of Agriculture and Home Economics, School of Business, School of Education, School of Engineering and Architecture, School of Nursing and Allied Health and School of Veterinary Medicine.

There are 76 degrees offered, including 45 bachelor's, 26 master's, a doctor of veterinary medicine and four graduate degrees for educational specialists.

The veterinary school is one of only 27 in the nation. Founded in 1944, it has trained 72% of the African-American doctors of veterinary medicine in America. Its alumni number more than 1,300 veterinarians.

"Many of our students come here because their parents, grandparents and even great-grandparents went to school at Tuskegee," said John J. Johnson, director of public information. "Some are the first in their families to go beyond high school.

"Why go to a predominantly black school? They come here because of Tuskegee's academic excellence and prestige since the school started in 1881. They come because as blacks they have a better chance for leadership roles in a predominantly black school.

"They are more relaxed here, more comfortable than at a university or college where they're in a minority."

Napoleon Howard IV of Detroit said he enrolled at Tuskegee following the example of a couple of his high school teachers who graduated from the school and liked it very much.

"Also," he said, "I have a great-grandfather who went to school here and helped build some of the buildings.

"This is an old-fashioned place in a rural setting. I love it. The school is not only predominantly black, so is the town of Tuskegee and the surrounding countryside. The university is in Macon County, a county with an 85% black population."

The legacy of George Washington Carver and Booker T. Washington persists at this prestigious, predominantly black college, a school that is both a national park and a shrine of respect and achievement for black Americans.

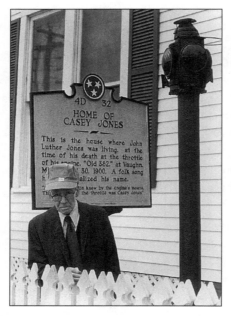

TENNESSEE

'Twas on the Illinois Central He Won His Fame

H E WAS KILLED April 30, 1900, and to this day just about every
American knows his name, the engineer who had his hand on the
throttle of the *Cannonball Special* that fateful day. He was the only
one who died in the crash. His name was Casey Jones.

> *Come all you rounders if you want to hear*
> *A story 'bout a brave engineer.*
> *Casey Jones was the rounder's name;*
> *'Twas on the Illinois Central he won his fame.*

"No, sir. Casey's fame hasn't died down whatsoever," said Blake White,
historian at the Casey Jones Museum in Jackson, Tenn. "It has been almost
a century since that train wreck, and the legend continues to grow.

"It's all because of the songs. The songs have kept it alive."

The ballad of Casey Jones—there are at least 150 different versions—has made the railroad engineer as much a part of American folklore as Johnny Appleseed and Paul Bunyon.

Jackson was Casey's hometown. The ill-fated engineer's home has been the Casey Jones Museum since 1956.

In 1980, Casey's house was moved from its original location at 211 W. Chester St. to Casey Jones Village on Casey Jones Lane where now, in addition to the Casey Jones Museum, there's a turn-of-the-century country store, a train store and a motel with some of the rooms in cabooses and rail cars.

Casey's museum-home is a national shrine for railroaders. It's filled with Casey Jones memorabilia, with bits and pieces from the days of steam.

"Many who come here," Blake said, "sometimes even railroaders, believe Casey Jones is a myth, that the train wreck never really happened, that there never was an engineer named Casey Jones."

Engineers, firemen, brakemen and conductors from all over the country, from all over the world, are named Casey. So are hundreds of men with the last name Jones, all because of Casey Jones—who really did exist.

He was born Jonathan Luther Jones in Missouri in 1863. His father was a schoolteacher, but Jonathan Luther and his four brothers all became railroad engineers.

The family moved to Cayce, Ky., when Jonathan Luther was a small boy. When he was 16, he came to Jackson to get a job as a telegrapher on the old Gulf, Mobile & Ohio line.

He moved into a boardinghouse for railroad men run by Annie Brady. When the gangly 6-foot, 4-inch youth arrived for dinner his first night, a brakeman named Bose Lashley asked him his name.

"Jonathan Luther Jones," he answered.

"Where you from?" inquired Lashley.

"Cayce, Kentucky."

"Well, sit down, Casey Jones, and make yourself at home."

It was Casey Jones until he died.

He went from telegrapher to brakeman to fireman to engineer.

When he was 22, he married the boardinghouse operator's daughter, Janie Brady, who was 16. They were married at St. Mary's Catholic Church in Jackson.

They had three children. In 1975, on the 75th anniversary of the famous train wreck, Casey's son Charlie was 86 and his daughter Helen Jones McKenzie was 81.

"Boy, there's a lot of history in this old house," Charlie Jones, a retired railroad pipe fitter, told the author in 1975 when visiting the house where he was born, Casey Jones' white cottage with white picket fence. Charlie pulled a railroad watch from his pocket and smiled.

"This is the watch my daddy had in his pocket the night he was killed," he said. "It still keeps good time."

"I was 11 when the *Cannonball Special* plowed into a caboose, a car full of corn, another full of hay and the fourth full of lumber."

> *On April 30, 1900, that rainy morn,*
> *Down in Mississippi near the town of Vaughn*
> *Sped the Cannonball Special only two minutes late,*
> *Traveling 70 miles an hour when they saw a freight.*

With obvious pride, Charlie Jones pointed out a whippoorwill calliope whistle, a carbon copy of the one his father had on Locomotive 382.

"I made that for the museum while I was still working for the I.C. as a pipe fitter," he said.

> *Casey pulled up that Reno hill;*
> *He tooted for the crossing with an awful shrill.*
> *The switchman knew by the engine's moan*
> *That the man at the throttle was Casey Jones.*

Charlie Jones walked out of the house he grew up in. A McQueen steam locomotive marked No. 382 was parked outside.

"It's not the original," he explained. "After the wreck, Old 382 was repaired at a cost of $1,396.25 and placed back in service for another 40 years."

Then, he said, somebody goofed.

"When diesels came out, No. 382 was cut up for scrap iron. Too bad we didn't get the original. This one's a similar model."

Casey Jones' youngest son died in 1938. His son Charlie died in 1977. His daughter Helen died in 1979.

Janie Jones, Casey's widow, never remarried. She wore black from the day the *Cannonball Special* crashed until she died in 1958 at the age of 92.

On display in the museum, established and operated by the city since 1956, is a wealth of Jones memorabilia: the original train order sheet showing Casey's final run; paintings of Casey and of the wreck; Casey's engineer's cap; a photo of Casey's engineers' graduating class; Casey's watch; Casey's marriage certificate, and much more.

There are scores of other old caps from engineers, brakemen, firemen and conductors. Early dining-car menus. Lanterns. Telegraph keys. Oil cans. Spikes.

On the 50th anniversary of the train wreck, April 30, 1950, the U.S. Post

Office issued a stamp to honor the railroad engineers of America. The stamp had Casey Jones' picture.

Visitors to the museum see a video of Casey's life and the story behind all the songs about the railroad engineer. The video and a cassette with different versions of songs about Casey are for sale at the museum gift shop. The shop also sells a tape made in 1951 of Sim Webb describing Casey's last run.

Webb, Casey's fireman, died in 1957 at age 83.

"There were no orders against our train," the black fireman recalled on the tape. "Our clearance card gave us the right over everything. We were 12 miles from the end of our 188-mile run from Memphis to Canton, Miss."

Need more coal there, fireman Sim;
Open that door and heave it in.
Give that shovel all you got,
And we'll reach Canton on the dot.
Fireman Sim, fire that hungry engine.
Fireman Sim, give her all you got.
Fireman Sim, fire that hungry engine
For we want to make Canton on the dot.

"Old 382 was pulling the nine-car *Cannonball Special* passenger train," Webb continued. "We came around the S curve just before Vaughn. There were two freight trains ahead on a siding waiting for us to go by, but four of the freight cars were sticking out on the main line. The air hose had burst on that freight train.

"I spotted it first from my side. I yelled to Casey, 'We're gonna hit!'

"Casey shouted to me, 'Jump, Sim, jump!'

"He shut off the throttle, applied the air brakes, pulled the reverse lever and sounded the whippoorwill. And I jumped.

"Casey never had a chance. He stayed at the controls sounding that whistle...."

The caboose of Number 83 was on the main line.
Casey's last words were "Jump, Sim, while you yet have time."
At 3:52 that morning came the fateful end.
Casey took his farewell trip to the promised land.

No one else was even seriously hurt in the wreck. Casey was found with an iron bolt through his neck. His body was under No. 382. The engine had turned over on its side.

"They didn't put the warning signals out," Webb recalled. "We saw no flares.

"We rounded the S curve at 70 miles an hour, and there were those four freight cars sticking out on the main line."

The man who spread Casey Jones' fame was a black engine wiper named Wallace Saunders, who wrote the original ballad when Jones was killed in the wreck.

"It has such a good beat, it spread like wildfire," said Casey's son Charlie. "It made my daddy a national hero overnight. And they're still singin' about the wreck, just as much as ever...."

> *Casey Jones, he died at the throttle,*
> *Casey Jones, with the whistle in his hand.*
> *Casey Jones, he died at the throttle,*
> *But we'll all see Casey in the promised land.*

TWENTY-ONE

KENTUCKY

Fort Knox, Monkey's Eyebrow and
A Home for Retired Dummies

FORT KNOX, funny-named towns and a haven for ventriloquist dummies are but a few of the fascinating places encountered in the green hills of Old Kentucky.

George B. Wright was the officer in charge of the U.S. Bullion Depository during a visit to Fort Knox.

Wright had a mind-boggling job. He was responsible for protecting Uncle Sam's $56.71-billion pile of gold.

At Fort Knox, 147.3 million ounces of America's gold are stored in a huge two-level steel and concrete vault embraced by the big military base.

"Don't worry," Wright insisted confidently, "the gold is safe. No one is going to storm the gold vault and walk away with any of America's treasure.

"This is the most secure facility you will find anywhere. Naturally, I would think that. We are ready to resist any and all attempts by an individual or groups to steal the gold."

Wright, predictably, would give no details about how his security force would fight off invaders. But he did say, "We are continually improving our security system to make certain we have the latest available sophisticated equipment and devices at our command within the depository.

"If added security should be needed, we have tanks and personnel carriers standing by and ready on the Army post surrounding the gold vault."

The gray stone building housing the vault is off-limits to everyone except its protectors.

Wright was, perhaps, the only executive in the country who had to leave the building where he worked—and even the building's grounds—to meet a visitor.

The U.S. Bullion Depository is reached by driving 30 miles southwest of Louisville on U.S. 31 to Bullion Boulevard on the Army base. The depository stands out like a sore thumb, surrounded by a nine-foot steel fence laced with live wires.

It is on 52 acres of lawn with no trees, shrubbery or anything else hiding it.

Past the turnoff from Bullion Boulevard onto Gold Vault Road, about a block's distance from the entrance gate, a speaker hung from a pole. A sign below proclaimed:

"HALT. State your business in loudspeaker. Do not enter."

That's as close to the gold as most people ever get.

"I'm sorry," Wright apologized at the gate, "but we must meet somewhere else. This may sound ridiculous, but I conduct all my face-to-face business two miles away in the post cafeteria or the officers' club. No one other than those working in the depository is permitted to visit me in my office."

There has been no movement of gold in or out of Fort Knox in several years. The gold just sits there, stacked floor to ceiling—446,000 gold bricks filling 28 compartments.

The gold is under constant guard. No one has ever attempted to break into the depository.

Guards don't open vault compartments and count the gold every day. The compartments are sealed, but there are peepholes to look through to check the gold.

Every summer a committee of 10 from the U.S. Bureau of the Mint inventories 10% of the gold, taking random chip samples from the bars to ascertain the gold's purity. Records are maintained of each bar, where it was cast and by whom. The end of the bar is stamped with the fineness of the gold. Each bar weighs 400 ounces.

The United States has been storing gold and silver as backing for its currency since 1790. The depository was built in 1936 when the government melted the gold coins that had been taken out of circulation. Of the 147.3-million ounces of gold at Fort Knox, 123-million ounces are in bars made from gold coins.

Currently, the United States has 264,601,798.2 ounces of gold in storage. America's gold is stored at Fort Knox, the U.S. Assay Office in New York, the San Francisco Mint, the Denver Mint, the Philadelphia Mint, West Point and the Federal Reserve Bank of New York.

The busiest time of day in the picturesque hamlet of Quicksand is 7:30 a.m. That's when Quicksanders gather around the potbellied stove in the old post office. They sit on chairs from the long-gone one-room Quicksand School and on gnarled benches, waiting for Postmaster Rosa Lea Davis to sort the mail.

Mail arrives early in this holler at the west end of the long, narrow one-way bridge crossing the Kentucky River. Quicksand has about 100 people. While many of them wait for the mail to be sorted, they exchange the latest gossip.

There's no quicksand in Quicksand, so far as anybody knows. But according to local legend—which sounds highly apocryphal—the town got its name after a 19th-Century tragedy.

"It happened before there was a bridge," said the postmaster, "when folks rode horses across the river. One day a local resident was returning home on his horse and the horse began to sink in the middle of the river. The horseman cried out for help. People ran to the river bank. But before they could get to him, the man and horse sank from sight, never to be seen again. And that's how this little place got its name."

The hills and hollers of Kentucky are sprinkled with hundreds of tiny communities like Quicksand, many with quaint names.

Colorful tales describe the derivation of such names as Shoulderblade, Sassafras, Dog Walk, Black Gnat, Hell for Certain, Kingdom Come, Moon, Falls of Rough, Preachersville, Mummie, Bright Shade, Summer Shade, Rabbit Hash, Rowdy, Skylight, Troublesome and Gravel Switch. There is an Add in Kentucky but no Subtract.

There are hamlets named after pioneer residents, like Charley, Phil, Idamay and Mazie. There are towns with just numbers for names, like Seventy Six and Eighty Eight.

At Happy, Ky., population 200, Margaret Stroul, 91, is caretaker of the Happy Bible Church. There's a Happy Store, a Happy Post Office and the R.W. Combs School where all the students are Happy kids.

In Goodluck, farmer Edgar Ford and his wife Gertie were visiting farmer Fim L. Fudge and his wife Florence on the Fudges' back porch when a stranger happened to pass.

"Everybody in Goodluck generally have good luck?" the stranger asked.

"Some does, some don't," Fim Fudge replied. "But I reckon there's more good luck in Goodluck than bad luck. Look at the four of us sittin' here. We're in our 70s, and we're still breathin'. Now, that's good luck, wouldn't you say?"

Opal Brown has lived in Ordinary, population 50, all her life. She was an Ordinary teacher at the one-room Ordinary School. "We're really not ordinary in Ordinary. We're all very special," she said, laughing.

Up the road from Ordinary is Newfoundland. You would expect people to pronounce the name of their town the same as the province in Canada. No way. Not in Kentucky. Here it's "New-fell-in."

"We have more fun with the name of our little community," said Ruth Ashford of Monkey's Eyebrow, a great place for goose hunting on the Ohio River in western Kentucky. "It always breaks people up when I am somewhere else and asked where I'm from.

"No one knows for sure why this place is called Monkey's Eyebrow. There's plenty of wildlife in these parts—deer, coyotes, wolves, muskrat and mink—but no monkeys."

Things are not ordinary in Ordinary, monkeys don't live in Monkey's Eyebrow, and life is far from dull in the hills and hollers of Old Kentucky.

Fort Mitchell, Ky., has a museum that presents a muted view of history, so to speak. The museum is Vent Haven. It's a museum not for your ordinary run of people, but for "vents." Vent is theatrical slang for ventriloquists. Ventriloquists come to Fort Mitchell from all over America, from all over the world.

More than 600 ventriloquist dummies sit side by side on folding chairs in the museum, staring straight ahead, waiting.

But there will be no more performances. Ventriloquists who owned the wood, papier-mâché, wood-plastic or plastic figures have died, retired or renounced them.

Their spirits live on at Vent Haven, the only museum in America dedicated exclusively to preserving the art of ventriloquism.

Vent Haven is the legacy of William Shakespeare Berger, wealthy president of a tile company and lifelong ventriloquist. He began collecting the dummies in 1916. Some of them date back to the 1850s.

Four floated ashore in a trunk from a ship wrecked off the coast of Texas. Ventriloquist Will B. Woods drowned in the accident in 1908.

Bunzli, a papier-mâché dummy, was found in the ruins of a house bombed by Allied planes in Germany during World War II. Ventriloquist Charlotte Bern-Keller and everyone in her family died in the bombing.

But Bunzli sits in his bow tie and tux on a folding chair, waiting.

Each July a ventriloquists' convention takes place at Vent Haven. In 1995, some 435 ventriloquists, several from foreign countries, attended the convention.

Berger, whose father was a Shakespearean actor, was president of the International Brotherhood of Ventriloquists for several years. The dummies were given to him, purchased by him or willed to him.

Dummies at one time filled every window of his two-story home. They stared out at the world until unnerved neighbors objected that the figures were watching them. In response to those complaints, Berger built Vent Haven to house the collection.

Berger had no heirs when he died in 1972 at age 94. He set up his estate as a trust fund to maintain and operate the museum as a center for ventriloquists and an archival repository for the art form. The will provided for a curator to live rent-free in his furnished home.

The collection includes more than 500 books about ventriloquism, some published as early as the 1700s. It also preserves several thousand photographs and original sketches of professional ventriloquists dating back to the 17th Century.

Edgar Bergen was a frequent visitor at Vent Haven before his death in 1978. To this day, whenever ventriloquists are anywhere near Fort Mitchell, they drop in.

TWENTY-TWO

OHIO

The Budget *Chronicles Amish Life*

*T*HE *BUDGET,* a nationally circulated weekly newspaper published since 1890 in Sugarcreek, a tiny Ohio hamlet, has more than 500 reporters—more contributing writers than the nation's largest dailies.

This is not your run-of-the-mill country weekly. Its scribes, as the paper's reporters are called, and its 21,000 subscribers are throwbacks to the 19th Century.

They are farmers who use horses to plow their fields and horse and buggy for transportation.

They're self-sufficient, erecting their own homes and barns, growing their own crops, raising their own livestock. They get along without automobiles, electricity, telephones, radios and television. They use wood cook stoves, iceboxes and out-houses. Kerosene lanterns are their source of light.

Readers of *The Budget,* a newspaper without headlines or photographs, wear old-fashioned clothing made in their homes. Their shirts, trousers and granny-style ankle-length dresses have no zippers or buttons. Hooks and eyes are used instead. Women and girls wear bonnets.

The Budget's subscribers are Amish, closely knit religious people whose simple way of life is a living museum of the past. An estimated 135,000 Amish are scattered across the United States in tiny settlements from Montana to Florida, from Texas to Upstate New York. The Amish have communities in 22 states and one Canadian province.

Since 1890, *The Budget* has been the sole communication link between Amish settlements throughout the country. Each Amish community has a scribe who files weekly or biweekly reports on the weather, births, weddings, deaths, accidents, illnesses, buggy wrecks, sightings of the first robin in spring and funny or odd happenings.

The reports—at least 350 per issue—are like letters from home. It's the way the Amish keep in touch with relatives and friends all over America, how they find out what's happening in the far-flung settlements.

Scribes file their copy in longhand on sheets of lined paper or any scrap paper such as the back of a calendar page or the back of a child's homework. They mail their community's latest news to *The Budget's* office at Sugarcreek, 100 miles south of Cleveland in east-central Ohio.

Sugarcreek lies at the heart of the state's Amish country, the largest concentration of Amish in the United States. Nearly 20,000 live in Holmes, Wayne, Coshocton and Tuscarawas counties—more Amish than in Pennsylvania's Lancaster County.

The Budget prints no news about local, state, national or international events or issues. The Amish aren't interested in what happens outside their own communities. They have turned their backs on the outside world. They don't read other newspapers, listen to the radio or watch television.

Crime stories are virtually nonexistent in *The Budget*. Crime seldom occurs in Amish settlements. Stories about politicians never appear. The Amish don't vote.

In a typical news item from the quaint 24- to 32-page newspaper, scribe Ida Kinsinger reported from Meyersdale, Pa.: "Katie Yoder's cough seems to be letting up. They put a rag in hot vinegar and applied that on the chest, then a flannel over it and then a plastic on top of that to hold in the heat. The first night they had that on she rested better."

From the Farmerstown, Ohio, meat house: "The stuffer we used to stuff the bologna broke. The lid popped up and we had 90 pounds of bologna mix all over the ceiling and all over the walls. One worker had meat in the face and ears and up the nose."

From E.S. Miller of Kingston, Wis.: "The proper thing is for a husband to hold the ladder while the wife cleans the gutter because if the wife held the ladder the husband could fall on her and hurt her."

From Shipshewana, Ind.: "When Nola Beechy untied her horse and got on the buggy she discovered one line had become unsnapped which greatly limited her maneuverability. The horse started off and the only choice she had was going around in circles. The horse kept going around in circles for several minutes until Mrs. Yutzy and Ora Eash came to Nola's rescue and got the horse stopped. After making the proper connections, the relieved lady, without injuries or damage, made her way home."

In Swanton, Md., Lydia Mae Kauffman had a bad case of pinkeye. Chicken pox was visiting the children of Withee, Wis. An albino red-tail hawk appeared at Limpytown, Ohio. "We feel extra busy the last three weeks since the flu found us," wrote the scribe from Altamont, Tenn. "Seems like there's always a nose to wipe or a dose of one thing or another to give to someone."

From Fredericksburg, Ohio: "The church was well attended yesterday but minister Loyd A. Yoder was not present due to a sore thumb. A knife hit him on the thumb while working at home in the shop, skinning it to the bone."

The Budget has been filled with news items like these week in and week out for more than a century.

The scribes are volunteers. They receive no compensation other than a free subscription to the paper and stamped envelopes to send in their reports. It is a distinct honor for an Amish to be a scribe. A subscription to The Budget costs $28 a year.

Several scribes—like Effie Troyer of Dover, Del., and John F. Glick of Gap, Pa.—have been sending in handwritten reports about their communities regularly for more than 50 years.

"We print the reports from our correspondents pretty much the way they write them—which often is in fractured English," noted George R. Smith, associate editor of the weekly paper. "But that's the charm of it.

"You know, English is a second language with the Amish. They speak Pennsylvania Dutch in their homes and at church. Their education ends at eighth grade because they don't want to learn too much about the world. They live the simple life on the farm."

Smith was 88 in 1995 and still coming to work every day. "Can't quit now," he said with a mischievous twinkle in his eyes. "I've been at it too long."

He has worked for The Budget 75 years, since he was 13 when his father Samuel Allan Smith bought the paper in 1920. In 1936, S.A. Smith quit publishing the paper to become postmaster of Sugarcreek. George Smith succeeded his father as publisher until he sold the paper in 1974. Then he stayed on to supervise the scribes, to edit and lay out the publication.

There are different groups of Amish, such as the Old Order, New Order, Swartzentruber Amish, Beachy Amish and Nebraska Amish. *The Budget* covers all groups as America's Amish paper.

The Budget's plant, a modern print shop, is not in keeping with the traditional Amish ways. George Smith, a Lutheran, and the 12 others who put out the paper are not Amish. That has been the case since the newspaper was first published in 1890.

Smith probably knows more Amish than any other living person. Each year the elderly editor makes trips to Amish communities throughout the country.

"Over the years I've seen some gradual changes in the people," Smith noted. "They would never ride in a car, for example. Today there are a number of non-Amish men and women who make a living hauling Amish in cars and vans to visit relatives, to attend weddings and funerals in other states.

"Another development is the creation of new communities in states where there have been no Amish in the past, in places like Wisconsin, Missouri, Kentucky, Tennessee and Texas. The Amish population doubles every 20 years. There is always a need for young people to find new land, so they move out from the traditional settlements."

Smith said the Amish, almost to a person, are totally honest and passive, not aggressive. "Scoundrels among them are extremely rare. I have tremendous respect and admiration for them and for their lifestyle."

A horse-and-buggy caravan crossed the Tuscarawas County countryside, heading for a huge Amish farm where a traditional Sunday evening sing was taking place. In the enormous basement of Mary and Eddie Miller's New Walnut Creek home, 125 of the faithful had gathered for a tasty potluck dinner of casserole, corn, potatoes, apple pie and water, no coffee or tea.

Later the women and girls in their plain clothes, wearing no makeup, of course, sat on roughhewn backless benches on one side of the basement. They faced bearded men and boys dressed in homemade vests, shirts and trousers—all blue in color—on the other side of the room on similar benches.

A minister preached in Pennsylvania Dutch. "There are only two ways in this life," he said. "One is wide, one is narrow."

Then the men and women, boys and girls, sang Amish hymns in Pennsylvania Dutch for two hours in the most beautiful voices imaginable.

TWENTY-THREE

INDIANA

The Apple Man

...And he ran with the rabbit and slept with the stream.
—VACHEL LINDSAY, "In Praise of Johnny Appleseed"

FORT WAYNE, IND., is the capital of Johnny Appleseed country. Yes, there really was a Johnny Appleseed. He planted thousands of apple trees across hundreds of miles of early America.

Sower of apple seeds, planter of apple orchards on the American frontier from the late 1790s through 1845, Johnny Appleseed was in and out of Fort Wayne the last 10 years of his life.

He died at age 70 on March 18, 1845, and is buried in Johnny Appleseed Park in Fort Wayne. Nearby, the block-long Johnny Appleseed Memorial Bridge spans the St. Joseph River.

Each summer a Johnny Appleseed Festival takes place at Johnny Appleseed Park, where huge quantities of elephant ears (a favorite Hoosier pastry) and apple cider are consumed. People dress in old-fashioned costumes, many wearing mush-pot hats.

"John Chapman, better remembered as Appleseed John or Johnny Appleseed, was a fascinating character, a true eccentric, one of the best-known American folk heroes," said Steven Fortriede, associate director of the Allen County Public Library and a lifelong resident of Fort Wayne.

"People are often surprised to learn Johnny Appleseed actually lived. Over the years many myths have emerged about his life. The mush-pot hat is one of them.

"I grew up on the Johnny Appleseed story, as does everyone else here. Fact and fiction blend when it comes to the apple man.

"True, he always wore weird garb, but nowhere in the bits and pieces of information we collected about his life is there any mention of a mush-pot hat, contrary to what Walt Disney and others would have us believe.

"He did, however, wear a funny-looking pasteboard hat with a huge brim to keep the sun from his eyes. He wore a coarse coffee sack for a shirt. He went barefoot sometimes and other times wore rags to protect his feet. He didn't wear shoes."

Fortriede wrote a 51-page pamphlet, "Johnny Appleseed: The Man Behind the Myth," published by Fort Wayne's Allen County Library.

The library, which also published six other pamphlets about the frontier nurseryman, has the best collection of Johnny Appleseed material in existence. The most definitive Chapman biography, Fortriede said, is Robert Price's *Johnny Appleseed—Man and Myth*, published in 1954 by Indiana University Press.

"Tales of Johnny Appleseed's extraordinary kindness to insects and animals portrayed in the Disney movie, in children's books, in novels and plays—such as putting out campfires to protect mosquitoes, remorse over killing a rattlesnake that bit him—are hogwash," said Fortriede. "Johnny was a gentle, forbearing sort, but he was no fool."

Chapman was born Sept. 26, 1774, at Leominster, Mass. His mother died when he was 2 years old. His father, Nathaniel Chapman, one of the original Minutemen, fought at Bunker Hill. Nothing else is known about Johnny's life until 1797, when at the age of 23 he showed up in northwestern Pennsylvania sowing apple seeds.

No one knows where he was educated or what motivated him to be an itinerant orchardist. "If I could find school records or other recorded information for that period of his life, I would write another pamphlet, perhaps a book," Fortriede said.

From 1797 to his death, Chapman's name appears on trading-post records, voting registration lists and in county recorders' archives that show when he homesteaded or purchased land. A small amount of correspondence exists as part of his original estate papers in the Allen County Public Library archives.

He traveled by foot, horseback and hollow-log canoe, always loaded with apple seeds in leather pouches. He gathered his seeds from cider presses. He planted orchards and sold and gave away seeds and seedlings. What money he earned he plowed back into land and into religious books by Emanuel Swedenborg, a Swedish scientist, mystic and spiritual leader. He distributed the religious books he bought.

"The American frontier in his time was western Pennsylvania, Ohio and Indiana," Fortriede said. "He was one jump ahead of the first settlers, clearing land, planting apple trees. He never married. He had an obsession to sow his seeds, plant his trees and to spread Swedenborg's teachings."

Chapman probably saw more of America than any other man of his day. He traveled hundreds of miles, leaving acres and acres of apple trees in his wake. No one who met him ever forgot him because of his dress, his demeanor. He was a small, wiry man with penetrating eyes, his contemporaries reported.

Johnny Appleseed touched the lives of pioneer families in much of western Pennsylvania, eastern Indiana and across the heart of Ohio. A monument in Ashland, Ohio, recalls that he ran 30 miles in 1812 to tell of an Indian massacre and to warn settlers that the Indians were heading their way.

"An awful lot of people in this part of mid-America claim Johnny Appleseed planted trees in their backyards," Fortriede said. He told of monuments and plaques in many little towns and crossroads in Ohio.

In Mansfield, Ohio, there is a Johnny Appleseed memorial put up by the local horticultural society in 1890, a Johnny Appleseed seat of honor in the public library and the Johnny Appleseed Middle School. The Johnny Appleseed Highway travels the apple man's pathway through the state.

At the same time he sowed his apple seeds, Chapman also was the best-known missionary of the small Swedenborgian congregation that started in London in 1788, some 16 years after the death of Emanuel Swedenborg.

The first Swedenborgian sermon in America was delivered in Baltimore in 1792.

"Every Swedenborgian in the world knows all about Johnny Appleseed," said the Rev. Harvey Tafel, senior minister of the Wayfarers' Chapel in California—the best known of the 35 Swedenborgian churches in North America. Perched on a picturesque Palos Verdes Peninsula bluff overlooking the Pacific Ocean, embraced by trees and lush gardens, the enchanting redwood-and-glass chapel is a popular wedding site for movie stars and Southern Californians.

To this day, the Swedenborgians remain a small congregation, with only 2,600 members in North America, a few thousand in Europe and a few thousand scattered elsewhere around the globe. The heaviest concentration of Swedenborgians is in South Africa, where it is an all-black church boasting 40,000 members.

Among films in all Swedenborgian church libraries is one titled *Johnny Appleseed, the Frontier Within*, produced by the Swedenborg Foundation and starring Joseph C. Davies as Johnny Appleseed and Lillian Gish as the movie's narrator. It is the church's portrait of its most famous missionary.

A granite marker at the site of John Chapman's birthplace reads: "He planted seeds that others might enjoy fruit." The grave in the Fort Wayne park that bears his name is marked by a granite boulder inscribed: "He lived for others."

TWENTY-FOUR

MICHIGAN

Henry Ford's Americana

HENRY FORD is best remembered for revolutionizing the automobile industry with his assembly-line method of mass production. But his passion for collecting Americana is another important part of his legacy.

Collecting was an obsession with Ford.

He collected everything he could lay his hands on pertaining to the development of the United States from Colonial times through the 20th Century—"to show how far and how fast we've come," he said.

Since 1929, Ford's collection of Americana—unparalleled in size, range and diversity—has been housed on 254 acres at Greenfield Village and the adjacent Henry Ford Museum in Dearborn, Mich., a suburb of Detroit.

Under one roof, the 14-acre museum holds thousands of everyday items that date from the nation's beginnings to the present. They include utensils, dinnerware, appliances, jewelry, furniture, tools, bicycles, agricultural implements, carriages, automobiles, streetcars and trains. They also include examples of the mammoth pieces of machinery from early foundries that turned America into an industrial giant.

The museum details the history of domestic life, from open-hearth cooking to the electric range. Displays of household inventions of the last 300 years include eggbeaters, hand-cranked washing machines, toasters, waffle irons, carpet sweepers, early radios and TVs.

A 60,000-square-foot wing of the museum holds the $6-million "Automobile in American Life" exhibit, devoted to the evolution of the automobile, its industry and its effect on 20th-Century America.

One hundred historic cars on spiraling ramps, graphics and assembly-line film footage dating back to the early 1900s chronical the development of motorized vehicles.

Included in the exhibit is the only 1896 Duryea motor wagon known to exist. Charles and Frank Duryea launched the American automobile industry over a century ago in Springfield, Mass., by producing 13 identical gasoline-powered vehicles.

Next to the Duryea is a 1865 Roper steam carriage, one of the earliest self-propelled road vehicles. Nearby is the *Tin Goose*, the Ford Trimotor airplane that Adm. Richard E. Byrd piloted in the first flight over the South Pole.

The invention of the car brought about numerous cultural exchanges. To illustrate, the museum traces the development of roadside businesses and entertainment to serve motorists.

Among the displays are Clovis Lamy's 1946 diner from Marlboro, Mass.; a 1930s Howard Johnson Simple Simon and the Pieman sign; a 1940 Texaco service station; a 1941 Ore-Mac $3-a-night tourist cabin from Irish Hills, Mich., and an early neon Holiday Inn sign.

New exhibits include the "African-American Family Life and Culture" section and "Motown Sound: The Music and the Story," a multimedia presentation opened in 1995 to show the effect of Motown music on the world.

Across from the museum, Greenfield Village is filled with historic homes and workshops. It has the New Haven, Conn., home of Noah Webster, where Webster lived the last 20 years of his life and wrote the dictionary. It has the home where Orville and Wilbur Wright were born.

Orville Wright gave Henry Ford the small Dayton, Ohio, Wright Brothers Bicycle Shop where he and his brother constructed the world's first flying machine. It's in Greenfield Village. So is Illinois' Logan County

Courthouse, where Abraham Lincoln practiced law. Inside the courthouse is the red Victorian rocking chair that Lincoln was seated in at Ford's Theatre on April 14, 1865, when he was shot and killed by John Wilkes Booth.

There's a steam-powered sawmill, a 19th-Century foundry, a tintype studio, tinsmith and cooper shops, a railroad roundhouse and a carriage repair shop.

Greenfield Village also has Thomas Edison's two-story clapboard invention factory. Originally located in Menlo Park, N.J., it was the world's first industrial research lab. Edison spent the most productive decade of his life working at the lab, which spawned 420 of his 1,093 patents.

Here as well is Sarah Jordan's boardinghouse. Old-fashioned incandescent bulbs still light it—the first dwelling to be fully illuminated by Edison's invention.

Thomas Edison was Henry Ford's greatest hero. The two men were close friends. To honor the inventor, Ford called his museum and village the Edison Institute. The complex was dedicated Oct. 21, 1929, the 50th anniversary of Edison's invention of the incandescent lamp. Edison was on hand for the opening. Several years after Ford's death, the name was changed to the Henry Ford Museum.

Initially, the museum and Greenfield Village were operated as part of a private school where, Ford said, "students would be able to go far beyond textbooks in their studies."

Monica Starrett, who works in the museum's interpretation department, studied at Edison Institute from kindergarten through high school. Her father was Alfred Lepine, secretary to Ford's son Edsel.

"Some of the students, like myself, were children of Ford employees," she recalled. "Others came from families whose parents worked elsewhere. It was a popular school with a long waiting list of students hoping to attend. The enrollment was always small, never more than 200."

Classes were held in nine historic Greenfield Village buildings, including the 19th-Century red Scotch Settlement School that Henry Ford attended as a youngster and the log cabin McGuffey School, birthplace of the first school textbook.

Ford visited classrooms on a regular basis, Starrett said. "There was always a lot of excitement when he came. We used the usual textbooks for classes, but whatever we studied there was always something in the museum or in the village that would relate to the subject matter.

"It was a wonderful hands-on way of learning. If we were studying about Colonial America, we would walk down the road to the original Colonial homes in the village. If we were studying inventors, we would spend time in Thomas Edison's Menlo Park laboratory. If we were studying English, we would hold classes in Noah Webster's home."

During the '30s and '40s when Starrett attended the school, the Henry Ford Museum and Greenfield Village were not open to the public. "I have no recollection of a lot of visitors here when I was in school," she said. The high school closed in 1952, the elementary school in 1969.

Nearly 50 years after Ford's death, collecting still goes on in the Henry Ford tradition. The Harvey Firestone farm, for example, including the tire man's birthplace and several farm buildings, was brought here from Ohio in 1981.

The farm animals at Harvey Firestone's place are extremely popular with children, especially those who live in the city. Chicken-hugging happens all the time. The merino sheep are bred to look as they did in the 1880s, with wrinkles in their wool.

Today Henry Ford's legacy of Americana is an independent nonprofit educational institution, not part of nor supported by the Ford Motor Co. or the Ford Foundation. It operates on a yearly budget of $25 million, one-third from entrance fees, one-third from sales of food and merchandise and one-third from endowments.

More than 1.3 million people visit the Henry Ford Museum and Green-field Village each year. They come from every state in America and from all over the world.

The mission of the Henry Ford Museum and Greenfield Village is to provide a unique educational experience based on authentic objects, stories and lives within the American tradition. Stressing ingenuity, resourcefulness and innovation, it hopes to inspire people to help shape a better future.

TWENTY-FIVE

WISCONSIN

America's Dairyland and
The Swiss Cheese Capital

D AIRYMEN, **women** and children from all 50 states, from Canada, Latin America, Europe, Asia, Africa, India, the Near East, Australia and New Zealand make pilgrimages to Fort Atkinson, Wis., each year.

They come to visit the most famous dairy farm on earth, to visit the shrine to the cow and to visit the offices of *Hoard's Dairyman,* a twice-monthly publication devoted to all facets of dairying—the bible of the dairy industry since 1885.

And they come to honor the memory of William Dempster Hoard (1836-1918), the father of modern dairying.

Wisconsin produces 14.6% of the nation's milk and 30% of its cheese. Wisconsin has more milk cows—1,494,000—and more dairy farms—29,000—than any other state.

"America's Dairyland," proclaim Wisconsin vehicle license plates. "Thanks to William D. Hoard," might well be added.

It was Hoard who campaigned to get Wisconsin farmers to convert from producing thin stands of failing wheat to dairying. He'd moved to the Midwest state from his native New York after serving as a soldier in the Civil War.

"I preach the gospel according to the cow," he said. In 1870 the "Apostle of the Dairy Cow" started a county weekly newspaper filled with editorials and articles promoting dairying. Fifteen years later he launched *Hoard's Dairyman*, the nation's first specialized agricultural magazine.

He pointed out that the shallow glaciated soils of Wisconsin were unsuitable for wheat production. He insisted the land was ideal for raising dairy herds.

In 1872 Hoard founded the Wisconsin Dairyman's Assn. A year later he secured a reduction in freight rates and leased the first railroad refrigeration car to ship Wisconsin cheese out of state to eastern markets.

In 1889 he financed and made the first cow census in the United States. It was through his efforts that the first dairy school in the nation was established in 1890 at the University of Wisconsin, where Hoard served as president of the board of regents. A statue to his memory stands at the entrance to the school's College of Agriculture.

During a term as Wisconsin governor in the 1890s, Hoard created the Wisconsin Dairy and Food Commission, the first state agency in America designed to ensure food purity.

In 1895 he began promoting the eradication of tuberculosis in cows. The move brought down the wrath of many farmers, who saw the slaughter of diseased herds as a loss from their own pockets. It was a campaign that lasted 45 years, and *Hoard's Dairyman* led the fight. Through the years, the magazine has led several campaigns to rid cows of crippling diseases.

In 1899 Hoard established the Hoard's Dairyman Farm, credited as the birthplace of modern dairying. He located it a mile from his publishing plant in downtown Fort Atkinson. To this day, the 550-acre farm is the best-known dairy farm in the world because of the attention devoted to it in the magazine.

It was here that Hoard pioneered many dairy practices now common. He demonstrated that alfalfa, not clover and traditional dairy feed, had far more protein value for cows. Today, thanks to Hoard, alfalfa is the greatest forage-producing plant in America.

The farm is listed on the National Registry of Historic Places. It is the home of North America's oldest continuously registered Guernsey herd—a herd consistently ranked among the nation's top milk producers.

Hoard's Dairyman, with a circulation of 125,000 in the United States and 103 foreign nations, is sent to the homes of 91% of all milk producers in this country. A subscription costs $14 a year.

It is affectionately known to dairy farmers as the "Big Cow Book." A cow always appears on the cover—sometimes only a speck in the pasture, but at least one cow is always there.

In each issue of *Hoard's Dairyman*—and on the walls of the magazine office, in the Dairy Shrine and on the farm—are W.D. Hoard sayings and slogans such as:

"The cow is the foster mother of the human race. The thoughts of men turn to this kindly and beneficent creature as one of the chief sustaining forces of human life."

"Notice to the help: The rule to be observed at all times toward the cattle, young and old, is that of patience and kindness. Remember this is the home of mothers. Treat each cow as a mother should be treated."

In the editorial room of *Hoard's Dairyman,* a sign proclaims: "THE NEXT ISSUE WILL BE OUR BEST."

"The biggest asset this magazine has is its credibility," said William D. Knox, 75, the publication's editor since 1949. "Every independent survey ever made reports our magazine having the highest credibility rating of any agricultural publication in the nation."

Knox is only the third editor since the magazine was founded in 1885. Hoard served as editor from 1885 until his death in 1918; Arthur J. Glover from 1918 until his death in 1949, and Knox since then.

Hoard's Dairyman publishes articles written by university professors, veterinarians, agricultural engineers and other dairying experts. The magazine has five editor-writers, including Knox. Each editor is responsible for his own area of expertise in the management and decision making at the magazine's dairy farm. The farm's 150 cows include 100 milking animals.

"We've struggled with our herd in good times and tough times, same as our readers," said Knox, whose turn-of-the-century rolltop desk is covered with miniature cows. Photos of prize-winning cows adorn the walls of his office.

Each editor is the product of a dairy farm, and each is a university graduate with a major in dairy science. The editors, recognized as industry authorities, are often called upon to address dairy meetings throughout the country.

Advice-seeking letters and phone calls come daily from across the land and overseas. "When farmers get stuck, they call or write us," said Eugene Meyer, 71, managing editor for years and overseer of the breeding program at the farm.

"The editors take the calls and provide them with the best available information."

There's something in the magazine for everyone on a farm: recipes and patterns for women, a youth page and articles covering all facets of dairy farming as well as ads for supplies and equipment.

Letters come in from farmers in their 90s, readers of the magazine since they first learned to read.

In 1993 a Japanese-language edition of *Hoard's Dairyman* was launched in Hokkaido, Japan. In 1994 a Spanish-language edition was started in Mexico City.

In cooperation with the magazine, experiments and research by scientists from the University of Wisconsin and other schools and institutions have gone on continuously at Hoard's Dairyman Farm since its establishment nearly a century ago.

The farm's heifer barn, built in 1976, served as the model for scores of similar barns now constructed throughout the country. Research includes experiments in solar and geothermal energy-saving systems.

When Knox came to work for *Hoard's Dairyman* in 1941, there were 2.4 million dairy farms in America—compared to about 149,900 in 1995. There were 25 million cows in the United States in 1941—compared to 9.525 million in 1995. The average herd held 19 cows in 1941, 64 in 1995.

For himself, Knox said, "The most dramatic change has been in upgrading the herds and getting three times the milk production per cow per day."

William Dempster Hoard is a household name to every man, woman and child living on a dairy farm in this country, a name little known to other Americans. Dairy producers by the thousands pour into Fort Atkinson, population 10,000, each year. But few others, even in Wisconsin, know about the town or realize its significance to dairy farmers.

In 1981 the Dairy Shrine—a $300,000 library, museum and hall of fame for the cow and the dairyman—was erected at Fort Atkinson.

Here tribute is paid to the cow. On display are photographs of every national grand championship of each dairy breed since 1906, when the awards began.

Each year the nation's outstanding dairy leader is selected by the Dairy Shrine's board of directors. The 12,000 members of the Dairy Shrine pay $50 for life memberships. There are no dues.

The Dairy Shrine Museum has superb collections of antique butter churns, milk jugs, milk bottles, milking stools, cheese kettles, curd knives and other dairy memorabilia.

There are more cows than people in Jefferson County, location of Fort Atkinson. A shrine seems only fitting.

"New Glarus is the most typical Swiss village on earth outside Switzerland," said Jean Holzer over a foamy stein of Feldschoesschen beer. He sat in the Chalet Landhaus country inn, in the snow-covered southern Wisconsin community of New Glarus.

Holzer ought to know. He spent 40 years in the Swiss diplomatic corps. With his home base in Chicago, he was Swiss consul general for 14 Midwestern states.

New Glarus, population 2,000, may be better known in Switzerland than any other place in America. Swiss children learn about New Glarus in their history classes.

"Small maps of the United States printed in Switzerland show a half-dozen cities: New York, Chicago, Seattle, San Francisco, Los Angeles, New Orleans—*and New Glarus*," said Holzer.

Swiss cheese, called *Emmenthaler* in Switzerland, got its start in the United States in a New Glarus cheese hut, or *kashutte*. The year was 1869. The cheesemaker was Niklaus Gerber. Swiss cheese, of course, is the one with the holes in the middle.

To this day, Green County, location of New Glarus, is the Swiss cheese capital of America. There are Swiss cheese factories on the outskirts of New Glarus, in Monroe 16 miles to the south and scattered throughout the county.

Strong bonds with Switzerland have persisted in New Glarus. It was founded Aug. 17, 1845, by 108 intrepid immigrants who traveled four months and more than 7,000 miles from their homes in Glarus Canton in Switzerland.

Every year groups of Swiss nationals make pilgrimages to New Glarus. Every year New Glarians make pilgrimages to the tiny Alpine nation in Central Europe.

The 150th anniversary of the founding of "America's Little Switzerland" by Swiss immigrants was marked by a big celebration in New Glarus Aug. 4 through 15, 1995.

Times were tough in Europe in the mid-1840s—extremely tough in the Swiss canton of Glarus. It was the only time in the history of Switzerland that the government sponsored a colony's emigration to another nation to help ease the economic woes.

It was called *Glarner Auswanderungsverein*—the Glarner Emigration Society.

Two scouts, Niklaus Durst and Fridolin Streiff, went ahead to find land in America for the colony. They made their way up the Mississippi River from St. Louis and found what they were looking for in the rolling hill country of southern Wisconsin. The land was ideal for raising crops and dairy herds. It had a good water supply. And it was cheap enough, $1.25 an acre.

A total of 193 men, women and children left Glarus Canton for the long voyage across the Atlantic and the subsequent journey to their new home in a promised land. Only 108 made it to New Glarus. The others settled elsewhere in the New World or died en route.

New Glarus' hardy, hard-working pioneers began their new life clearing land for crops, erecting log cabins and launching dairy herds.

The Swiss-Americans of New Glarus were among the few dairymen in Wisconsin when William D. Hoard embarked on his campaign to get farmers in the state to switch from wheat production to raising cows.

They spoke *Schweitzer Deutsch,* the Swiss-German dialect of the rural mile-high Alpine valley of their origin. Along with English, the dialect is spoken by the Swiss families of New Glarus to this day.

"When we visit Switzerland, people know immediately where we come from because of our dialect," said New Glarian Dennis Streiff.

"The Swiss are fascinated by the way we talk in a slow and singing fashion. Our dialect is a throwback to earlier times. It is a different dialect from the *Schweitzer Deutsch* spoken in Glarus Canton today."

Since its founding in 1845, there has been a steady trickle of Swiss citizens emigrating to New Glarus. Some remain in Green County for the rest of their lives. Some move to other parts of the nation.

Descendants of nearly all the original families continue to reside in or near New Glarus. They have family names like Aebli, Babler, Becker, Disch, Deurst, Figi, Hefty, Hosly, Klassy, Kundert, Legger, Schindler, Schmid, Stauffacher, Trumpi, Voegeli and Wild.

Many of the Swiss-American families live in sturdy farmhouses more than a century old. Doris Streiff, 64, and her husband Dean, 65, both fifth-generation Swiss, live in an 1882 farmhouse.

Streiff's great-grandfather was Fridolin Streiff, one of the two scouts sent ahead by the Swiss government to find land for the original colony. Dean Streiff's grandfather was the first baby born in the village.

For years children from Switzerland have lived with the Streiffs while attending school in New Glarus, part of an exchange program with students from New Glarus High School and students from Switzerland's Glarus Canton. The

Streiffs' daughter, Nancy, spent a winter working and going to school in Underwasser, Switzerland.

Many homes and nearly all the stores and public buildings in New Glarus are of Swiss chalet design. Several homes have *Schweitzer Deutsch* sayings painted by hand on the outside. On one chalet, the words translate: "This house is where we love to see you come and hate to see you leave. This house is mine and is not mine. I go out and you come in. Tell me, who will be the last one in?"

A glockenspiel tower stands in the middle of town. Adorning the buildings are emblems of Swiss cantons and murals painted by artists from Switzerland. The huge, Gothic Swiss United Church of Christ looms over all. In front of the church, built in 1900, rests a statue in memory of the village founders.

The Swiss connection is everywhere.The Upright Embroidery Factory manufactures Swiss laces and embroideries. The Roger Bright Band has been performing each year in New Glarus and in Switzerland since 1964.

The Edelweiss Stars, a group of two New Glarus men and four women who have been yodeling and singing together since l960, perform in Swiss clubs throughout the United States and in Switzerland as well.

Gift shops are filled with Swiss items replenished by proprietors during trips to Europe each year.

The Swiss Historical Museum occupies a square block. Its dozen historical structures include a replica of the 1849 log cabin Swiss church.

Townspeople have produced Friedrich Schiller's 1804 play *William Tell* in an outdoor amphitheater annually since 1938. They perform it twice in English and once in *Schweitzer Deutsch* every Labor Day weekend. The highlight of the production is Gessler the Tyrant's demand of William Tell: "Thou wilt shoot an apple off the boy's head."

There's an annual Heidi Festival in June. Volksfest, Swiss Independence Day, is celebrated the first Sunday of each August.

Busloads of Swiss vacationers come to New Glarus every summer.

"They would come and stay in hotels and motels in Madison, 25 miles north of here," said Hans Lenzinger, a ski instructor who emigrated from his home in Underwasser when he was 20.

In 1980, Lenzinger and three other local men built the 44-room Chalet Landhaus Swiss country inn so that visitors could stay in New Glarus. Like many of these Swiss visitors, Lenzinger said, "From the moment I read about New Glarus in my history class in school I planned to come here."

TWENTY-SIX

LOOK FOR THE LOON ON YOUR MINNESOTA TAX FORMS!

MINNESOTA

Looniest State in the Lower 48

I T WAS A RAINY MORNING at Lake Itasca, Minn., as the first rays of dawn sliced through occasional pockets in the clouds.

Birch and spruce branches swayed gently, brushed with puffs of light winds. Then it happened in all its weird, wonderful, haunting splendor: The plaintive cry of a loon.

First came the piercing yodel of a male loon asserting territorial dominance. Next a quavering, high-pitched, bizarre laugh—*a-haha-ho, a-haha-hoo, a-haha-hoo*—from another loon across the lake. Then a symphony of tremolos, wails, yodels and hoots, the eerie sounds of half a dozen of the big greenish-black, long-necked water birds.

Dawn had surfaced at Lake Itasca as it does over lakes all summer throughout Minnesota, land of 10,000 lakes. Loon magic was everywhere in the North Woods that misty morning, as it also was so often during the still of quiet nights.

The storied loon—three feet long, with a five-foot wingspan and checker-boarded with white streaks, spots and bars—is Minnesota's state bird.

Indian legend says the cry of the loon is that of a dead warrior refused entry into heaven. Crazy as a loon, goes the old saying—undoubtedly prompted by the bird's loud, uncanny and varied vocalization.

The loon is the symbol of the pristine wilderness of Minnesota, Wisconsin, Michigan and portions of New England.

There are more loons in Minnesota—about 10,000, as many loons as lakes—than in any other state except Alaska.

"Minnesotans have always had a love affair with the loon," said Minnesota State Park ranger-naturalist Ben Thoma. The wildlife biologist has studied loons on Minnesota lakes all his adult life. "Minnesotans take great pride in and are extremely protective of this amazing bird."

At this particular daybreak, Thoma was in his patrol boat checking the well-being of a pair of nesting loons on Y-shaped Lake Itasca.

His binoculars spotted one of the loons sitting on a matted sedge nest at the end of a fallen spruce tree that extended 40 feet out into the water. Several yards from the nest, signs on three posters protruding from the lake warned: "KEEP OUT. LOON NESTING."

"Loons are so skittish," Thoma said. "It's important that neither the male nor the female sitting on the nest be frightened away. A loon's egg is a fine feast for a predator."

When boats get too close to a loon nest, the bird flies away, abandoning the eggs. Crows, cranes, raccoons, skunks and other birds and animals hang around waiting for the parent to leave the nest unattended.

It's impossible to tell males from females from afar, according to Thoma. One parent always stays on the nest while the other is out diving for fish.

Thoma shut off the motor and rode quietly to a safe distance outside the posted area, where he observed the nesting loon. The loon lay low in the nest, its big red eyes fixed nervously on Thoma and his two companions in the boat.

Judy McIntyre, who has her Ph.D. in zoology from the University of Minnesota, is known throughout the ornithology world as the "Loon Lady." Since 1959 she has devoted herself to loon research in Minnesota, Canada, New York, New England and off the coast of Virginia.

McIntyre organized and hosted the first two North American conferences on common loons in 1977 and 1979. She has published three dozen scientific papers about the bird. Her book *Common Loon Spirit of the North* was published by the University of Minnesota in 1988.

McIntyre has spent a great deal of time studying the impact of recreational use of the lakes on the big bird. "Loons have had a hard time coping with the explosion of shoreline development and boats racing up and down and through areas where loons nest and raise chicks," she said.

Loons spend about seven months in Minnesota, then fly to the Atlantic Coast where they winter offshore, feeding on fish. They arrive in Minnesota in April and May, with the thawing of the lakes, and leave in late September and October.

"Loons mate for life," the ornithologist said. "They return to the same lakes each year. We know that by the yodels of the males, which are different and distinct, one from the other."

In 1971 McIntyre launched Minnesota's first loon watch—in which lake-area residents, fish-and-game wardens and park rangers counted the number of adults and young on the lakes. The watch caught on quickly and now occurs in all states that have loons.

Loons thrived on Northern California lakes until about the turn of this century. Now thousands of loons that summer in Alaska and British Columbia winter offshore along the coast of California.

But Californians do not know the loon, McIntyre said, because the loons do not come to shore, and the bird does not vocalize in winter when feeding off the coast.

Loons are found in great numbers on lakes all across Canada. The bird is the official emblem of the Canadian Wildlife Service. Its image appears on Canada's silver dollar, affectionately called the "Looney" by Canadians.

To help projects supporting non-game wildlife like loons, bluebirds and bald eagles, Minnesotans may fill out a line on their state income tax forms designating a deduction be made for the program.

Carrol Henderson, wildlife supervisor for the Minnesota Department of Natural Resources, explained that the donations support loon research, the annual loon census, the printing of 100,000 loon posters each year and "radio, television and newspaper notices warning people to please stay away from loon nests."

She said that one of the most cherished moments for a Minnesotan is to see a newborn jet-black ball of loon fluff riding on its parent's back during the first couple of weeks of its life.

"We Minnesotans," she added, "feel lucky just to *hear* a loon, the symbol of our lake wilderness."

TWENTY-SEVEN

IOWA

Mason City, the Music Man's Hometown

VISIT MASON CITY, Iowa, and it's easy to imagine Meredith Willson leading a marching band down Main Street playing "Seventy-Six Trombones."

Leading the big parade nearly every year at the North Iowa Band Festival in Mason City was a special treat for Willson during the 1950s, '60s and '70s.

Mason City, the north-central Iowa farm center, population 30,000, was the author-lyricist-composer's hometown, the real-life River City of the real-life Music Man.

Driving by Mason City's pool hall (that's P for pool and T for trouble) and by the old Carnegie Library, one can almost hear the *ra-da-da-da* of the 76 trombones, the 110 cornets and the thundering, thundering of the copper-bottom timpani.

Willson would be disappointed. They tore down the Cecil, the Mason

City movie house where he whiled away a lot of his youth.

He would be pleased, however, by the epitaph on his tombstone selected by his widow, Rosemary: "May the good Lord bless you and keep you."

Creator of the smash Broadway and film hit *The Music Man*, Willson died June 15, 1984. He was 82. He is buried in the family plot in Mason City.

"'May the good Lord bless you and keep you' was his mother's blessing to children as they left her Sunday-school class and the name of one of Meredith's songs," explained Rosemary Willson.

Meredith Willson's mother's name was Rosalie. She's the Rose in "Lida Rose," the song from *The Music Man*. Lida was Rosalie's sister, Meredith's favorite aunt.

Willson was born in Mason City, where he lived the first 17 years of his life. His father was the town baker. His grandfather was one of Mason City's first settlers.

His hometown provided Willson with the background and the characters for *The Music Man*.

"I didn't have to make up anything," he would later recall. "I simply remembered Mason City in Iowa as closely as I could the way it was when I was a boy growing up."

Willson played flute and piccolo at Mason City High School from 1915 to 1919. Upon graduation he joined the John Philip Sousa Band, later became a member of the New York Philharmonic and went on to direct several orchestras and compose music—from hit tunes to symphonies.

But he is best remembered for *The Music Man*, which opened on Broadway Dec. 19, 1957. The Warner Bros. film version starring Robert Preston and Shirley Jones premiered in Mason City on June 19, 1962.

Townspeople still talk about the movie premiere, held in conjunction with the annual North Iowa Band Festival. Willson led 121 bands through the streets of Mason City on that day.

Not surprisingly, Mason City High has one of the top high school music programs in the nation. The Mason City High School Band consistently ranks among the best in America.

"Mason City High has had an outstanding series of band directors dating back to the 1920s," noted Everett Johnson, executive secretary of the Iowa High School Music Assn. "Meredith Willson was a strong supporter of the high school band program all his adult life.

"The community, the kids, the school just don't dare to let that tradition ebb or die."

No other state has as many bands, per capita, as Iowa. Passed in the 1930s, the Iowa Band Law allows cities and towns to support municipal bands in annual budgets.

"Most communities of any size have a municipal band," said Johnson. "Every elementary, junior high, high school and college in the state has a band. Music is part of Iowa, part of the people's lives."

In 1928, famed conductor Walter Damrosch—who founded the New York Symphony Orchestra—declared: "Iowa is the most musical state in the union."

Gilbert L. Lettow, director of school bands (symphony, concert, marching and jazz) at Mason City High for 23 years, in 1995 told how Meredith Willson would walk into the school's music building unannounced while he was rehearsing the band.

"He would talk to the kids," he said. "He had a kind of enthusiasm that was absolutely fantastic. He never forgot his hometown, his high school."

When Willson's widow, who lives in Brentwood, Calif., learned the school needed 250 new band uniforms, she donated $27,000 toward the purchase. Throughout the '80s and '90s she contributed scholarships to Mason City High music majors.

Rosemary Willson was interviewed the day after she returned home from a trip to Beijing for the opening of *The Music Man* in the Chinese capital. She spoke fondly of her husband's strong ties to his hometown.

"We were forever flying to Mason City from our California home," she recalled. "We never missed the North Iowa Band Festival every June. At the drop of a hat Meredith would say, 'Honey, let's go home for a few days.' He loved Mason City and all his friends in his hometown."

She said *The Music Man* received excellent reviews in China. "I thought it was well done. I don't speak Chinese, but they laughed in all the right places. 'Shipoopi' was one number they really went wild about."

Gilbert Lettow not only directs the bands at Mason City High, he conducts the Mason City Municipal Band's summer concert programs and the North Iowa Concert Band's winter program. He is past president of the Iowa Bandmasters Assn.

"*The Music Man* lives on in Mason City," Lettow said. "We always play selections from the production at concerts—'Marian the Librarian,' 'Trouble in River City,' 'Goodnight, My Someone,' 'Lida Rose' and the others. 'Seventy-Six Trombones' is played more than any of the numbers. We play it at all the football games.

"It's synonymous with Mason City."

Kate Wilson, a senior in the Mason City High School Marching Band, was attending a practice session on school grounds ablaze with dandelions.

"Sure, Mason City is special," she said. "It's River City, *The Music Man*. We can all relate to that."

"Mr. Lettow is our Prof. Harold Hill," junior Kevin Enabnit added. "He isn't quite the con man Prof. Hill was, but he sure runs a super music department."

Many businesses in town use the name River City instead of Mason City, including River City Auto Body Shop, River City Bowling Alley, River City Glass Co. and River City Home Video.

When Carl Miller became mayor of Mason City in January, 1994, he declared he would do everything possible during his term of office to promote the legacy of Meredith Willson—"here in River City, U.S.A., America's whimsical city." The Mason City Foundation was established to accomplish that end.

Meredith Willson's boyhood home was purchased by the city, renovated, filled with Willson memorabilia and opened for public visitation in June, 1995. In the summer of 1995, the 1940 Meredith Willson Footbridge was reconstructed at a cost of $270,000.

"We're going to build a Meredith Willson Theater," vowed the mayor, "and a Meredith Willson Conservatory of Music."

"It never ceases to amaze me how the interest in Meredith Willson and *The Music Man* persists," said Madelyn Walls, a Mason City librarian for nearly half a century. "Out-of-towners are always stopping by the library asking where Meredith Willson lived. Every woman working in the library is called Marian the Librarian by people in town."

When Meredith Willson died, the local *Mason City Globe Gazette* newspaper changed its name for one day to the *River City Gazette*, in tribute to the town's favorite son.

Funeral services for Meredith Willson were held at the Mason City First Congregational Church on June 22, 1984.

"He was a small-town boy," Mayor Kenneth E. Kew said at the service. "He was Iowa stubborn. Each time I hear 'Seventy-Six Trombones' I get chills of pride.

"From this day forward, whenever I hear thunder rolling across the sky, like timpani and bass drums, I'll say to myself: There goes Meredith. He's leading another big parade."

TWENTY-EIGHT

ILLINOIS

Lincoln Country

WHEN DEVELOPERS WERE laying out lots to launch Lincoln, Ill., in 1853, they hired an attorney to draw up the legal papers. They didn't know what to call the place, so they named it after the attorney. It was the first thing, but far from the last, named in his honor.

Now, a century and a half after the founding of Lincoln, Ill., streets, buildings, schools, towns and cities in every state in America—and in many foreign countries—carry the name of the lawyer: Abraham Lincoln.

Lincoln's impact on the landscape, however, is far more evident in Illinois than anywhere else.

The 16th President lived in Illinois from the time he was 21 until the day before his 52nd birthday, when he left Springfield for the White House.

For several years Lincoln covered central Illinois by horseback—a favorite horse was Old Buck—as a circuit-riding attorney serving 14 county seats. Most of the old courthouses where he practiced still exist or have been recreated to honor the Great Emancipator's memory.

Lincoln crisscrossed the state not only as an attorney but during his political campaigns. Plaques, statues, monuments and buildings recall his appearances almost everywhere you go.

At the Vermilion County Museum in Danville, Ann Hillenburg was busy adjusting the pant legs on an Abraham Lincoln mannequin. The mannequin depicted Lincoln in stocking feet.

"Mr. Lincoln spent the night in this second-floor bedroom," she said. "It was the home of his friend, Dr. William Fithian, a legislator and horseback doctor. That's the bed Lincoln slept in Sept. 21, 1858, during his unsuccessful campaign for the Senate against Stephen A. Douglas."

Lincoln had walked from the Danville railroad station to Fithian's house and kicked off his boots in the bedroom. A crowd gathered outside the house to see him. His feet were so swollen he couldn't get his boots back on. So he made an appearance in his stocking feet on the balcony outside the bedroom.

On the town square of Clinton, a statue of Lincoln bears an inscription recalling the statement he made there during the campaign with Douglas: "You can fool all the people part of the time and part of the people all of the time, but you cannot fool all the people all the time."

There are more Lincoln statues in Illinois than in any other state, in town squares, outside courthouses, on school lawns, in parks. In Freeport a statue shows Lincoln debating. At Dixon he appears as a soldier during the Black Hawk War. In New Salem he reads a book while riding a horse. The famous Augustus Saint-Gaudens statue in Chicago's Lincoln Park shows him standing. Chicago's Grant Park statue shows him seated.

At Millikan University in Decatur, a statue shows Lincoln sitting on a tree stump, an ax by his side. The inscription reads, "At 21 I came to Illinois."

And, near Lawrenceville—on the western shores of the Wabash River, just over the Lincoln Memorial Bridge on the Lincoln Memorial Highway— stands Nellie V. Walker's 1931 monument to the Lincoln family. It shows them entering the state from Indiana for the first time on a cold, blustery winter day. The statue features a bigger-than-life-size figure of 21-year-old Abe leading the family in an ox-drawn covered wagon. An angel overhead guides their way.

It was while crossing the frozen Wabash River that the Lincoln family dog jumped out of the covered wagon and broke through the thin ice. Lincoln waded up to his waist in the chilling water to rescue the dog.

All summer long in New Salem State Park, 20 miles northwest of Springfield, Abraham Lincoln's life comes alive in the play *Your Obedient Servant, A. Lincoln*, written and produced by University of Illinois Theater Arts professor John Ahart.

The play takes place in a theater built by the Civilian Conservation Corps during the Great Depression. It rests 100 feet from the store and post office where young Lincoln worked as a clerk and postmaster from 1831 to 1837.

Today New Salem features 23 reconstructed log buildings that existed when Lincoln lived there, furnished as they were in the 1830s. A 30-foot-high portrait of Lincoln backs the theater stage where players reenact Lincoln's life amid the buzz of katydids and flickering of fireflies.

It was in New Salem that young Lincoln courted Ann Rutledge. In a cemetery at nearby Petersburg, not far from the grave of *Spoon River Anthology* author Edgar Lee Masters, a tombstone reads:

"I am Ann Rutledge who sleeps beneath these weeds. Beloved of Abraham Lincoln, wedded to him not through union, but through separation. Bloom forever O'Republic, from the dust of my bosom." She was born Jan. 7, 1813, and died Aug. 25, 1835.

The city limits signs of the state capital announce: "Springfield, Abraham Lincoln's Hometown." Springfield's many other reminders include a 30-foot-tall statue at the State Fairgrounds showing Lincoln as a rail-splitter, wielding an ax and wearing an open shirt, rugged trousers and boots.

At another location, Springfield's Oak Ridge Cemetery holds the massive Lincoln Tomb built in his honor with public donations. Nan Wynn manages the state historical site.

"Visiting the tomb where Lincoln, his wife Mary Todd Lincoln and three of their four boys are buried is an emotional experience for all who come here," she said.

"Many cry. I have cried when I've been alone in the tomb and thought of the family. The three boys—Eddie, Willie and Tad—all died so young. I can see Tad hitching up his goats to kitchen chairs in the White House...."

Only Robert Todd Lincoln lived to manhood. He died at the age of 82 and is buried in Arlington National Cemetery. The President's last direct descendant, Robert Todd Lincoln Beckwith, a great-grandson, died at 81 in Virginia in 1985.

More than 300,000 people visit Lincoln's Tomb each year. They come from throughout the world. A typical day saw wreaths placed near Lincoln's remains by groups from Hungary and Germany, from rural mail carriers and from the American Legion.

The nose on the large Gutzon Borglum bust of Lincoln outside the tomb, like the noses of busts and statues inside the tomb, shines from the thousands of visitors each year who rub it for good luck.

The Springfield home Abraham Lincoln and his family lived in for 17 years serves as the centerpiece of a four-block national historic site administered by the National Park Service.

A major $2.2-million renovation of the house was completed in the summer of 1988. The house is furnished just as it was when Lincoln left for Washington in 1861. The 65 original Lincoln pieces inside include the President's rocking chair.

Visitors to Springfield can still see the law office Lincoln shared with Billy Herndon, the federal courthouse where he appeared as an attorney in 200 cases, the Lincoln family pew in the First Presbyterian Church and the old Great Western Railway Depot where he bid farewell to his hometown friends and supporters.

"Here I lived a quarter of a century and have passed from a young to an old man," he said as he left for the White House. "Here my children have been born and one is buried. I now leave, not knowing when, or whether ever, I may return, with a task before me greater than that which rested upon Washington...."

The old statehouse, too, is preserved where Lincoln served as a representative, where he was laid in state following his assassination and where he delivered his famous speech: "A house divided against itself cannot stand. I believe this government cannot endure, permanently half slave and half free...."

One of the five original drafts of Lincoln's Gettysburg Address is on display in the old Capitol.

"Practically everything here is named for him," said Matt Mason, a printer for the weekly *Lincoln Courier* in Lincoln, population 15,000.

The community has two Lincoln Colleges. At one, a statue shows Lincoln with a book in his hand. The inscription reads, "I shall prepare myself. Some day my chance will come."

The town also has a Lincoln High School, Lincoln Junior High School, Lincoln Elementary School, Lincoln Development Center and Lincoln Correctional Center.

One monument is quite unusual—a statue of a slice of watermelon with the inscription: "Near this site Abraham Lincoln christened the town with the juice of a watermelon when the first lots were sold Aug. 27, 1853."

Lincoln's main street and many stores and businesses are named after the 16th President. There's the Abraham Lincoln Rail-splitters Park and the annual Lincoln Festival every September that features a reenactment of the watermelon christening.

It's easy to understand why the slogan "Land of Lincoln" appears on the Illinois license plate.

TWENTY-NINE

MISSOURI

Truman Territory

M ISSOURI GAVE AMERICA its 33rd President, Harry S. Truman.
For Missourians, in many ways Truman continues to be part of
their everyday lives.

Almost everywhere you go in the Show Me State, there's something
named after the colorful, down-to-earth man who was a dirt farmer until he
was 32 and wound up in the White House from 1945 to 1953.

Schools, streets and city, county, state and federal parks, buildings and
much, much more carry his name.

His birthday, May 8, is a state holiday each year in Missouri. And every
May 8th in Independence, his hometown, there's a big Harry Truman
Parade, a Harry Truman walk through his old neighborhood and a Harry
Truman 10K race.

It's a day when wreaths are placed on the graves of President Truman, who died at age 88 in 1972, and his wife Bess, who died at age 97 in 1982. They are buried side by side in the courtyard of the Harry S. Truman Library and Museum in Independence.

On May 21 and 22 each year in Grandview, 10 miles southwest of Independence, Harry's Hay Days are celebrated with an old-fashioned carnival, parade, arts and crafts show and pig roast. Grandview is where Truman operated a farm with a horse and plow for 13 years.

It's a wonder they haven't changed the name of Independence to Truman. There are two Truman hospitals in town, one named after Bess, the other after Harry. Truman High School is named after both of them. The main street in town? You guessed it: Truman Road.

The local Amtrak railroad station is the Harry S. Truman Station. Inside the depot, an exhibit of photographs depicts Truman's whistle-stop campaign by train in 1948. Other photos record the greeting by 10,000 local residents when he returned home following his presidency.

The railroad depot's ticket agent Edward Bird recalled Truman in the old days, when the former President was living back in Independence.

"He'd loaf around the waiting room," Bird said. "He was a fellow who could be anything to anyone. He'd come up to the ticket window and shoot the bull when he was waiting on the train. He wasn't the kind of man that would turn his face from you."

One of the biggest buildings in town is the Harry Truman Law Office. Truman wasn't a lawyer. He never went to college.

The Trumans' 19th-Century Victorian home, at 219 N. Delaware St., was the President's summer White House. The Trumans lived in the house from the time they were married in Independence in 1919 until they died, except when they were in Washington. Bess Truman bequeathed the home and everything in it to the American people.

The house is the essence of the Trumans' personalities. The simple kitchen—with its linoleum tacked to the floor by the former President to hold it in place when gaps occurred—is like grandmother's kitchen in small-town America. Truman was frugal. The floors squeak.

Truman's hat, coat and umbrella still hang on the rack at the side entrance to the house where he left them following his last early morning walk. He lived in the house for 20 years after he left the White House.

The former President erected an iron fence around his property after Bess observed a woman pulling tulips from the garden. The woman told the First Lady she wanted the flowers as a souvenir.

Their daughter Margaret was born in an upstairs bedroom in the house in 1924. Margaret's piano, a gift from her father on her eighth birthday, is there. All the official portraits of First Ladies hang in the White House except for Bess Truman's. Harry liked the picture so much he took it home with him.

The Trumans' home is a national historic site. National Park Service rangers provide guided tours.

Also in Independence, the Jackson County Courthouse courtroom is restored to just as it was when Truman presided there as a judge from 1926 to 1934. Outside the courthouse stands the life-size Gilbert Franklin statue of Truman dedicated by President Gerald R. Ford during the Bicentennial Year.

The Harry S. Truman Historic District in Independence includes the neighborhood of Victorian houses where the President took his daily walks, the church where he was married, the site of the high school he and Bess graduated from and other buildings associated with his life.

Six blocks from the Trumans' home, on a knoll overlooking Independence, stands the one-story Indiana limestone Harry S. Truman Library and Museum. The former President had an office in the library from the time it was dedicated in 1957 until his death.

Truman was 73 when he moved into the office. He walked to and from his home to the office, where he would spend six to eight hours each weekday. It was there he completed work on his two-volume memoirs, *Years of Decisions* and *Years of Trial and Hope.*

He used the office for five years until age forced him to curtail his activities. He spent hours in the office talking to foreign and national dignitaries, including presidents Dwight D. Eisenhower, John F. Kennedy, Lyndon B. Johnson, Herbert Hoover and Richard M. Nixon.

Kennedy came to visit the former President immediately after his own selection as 1960 Democratic presidential nominee. Johnson came in 1965 to sign the Medicare Act in honor of Truman. Johnson called him "the father of Medicare."

Jack Benny came to the library and museum and did a TV show featuring Truman.

Mary Jo Nick worked as a secretary for the former President the last two years he came to his library office on a daily basis.

"Mr. Truman was in the process of writing a book about presidents for high school students when I worked for him," she recalled. "It was a book he never finished. He became ill and never got back to it. He worked on his book, answered correspondence, but mainly he enjoyed meeting people. He addressed school groups in the museum auditorium. When boys and girls asked questions about the government, about history and about the presidency, he really liked that.

"Sometimes he would escort visitors on tours of the museum. It was a unique and wonderful experience for strangers coming to the museum—having the former President serve as their tour guide."

The library houses more than 13 million papers, including manuscripts and documents from more than 300 men and women associated with the President and his administration.

On file are documents containing the critical decisions and key programs of the Truman Administration from April 1945 to January 1953, including the Marshall Plan, the Truman Doctrine, the Point Four program, the Korean War, the recognition of Israel, the Berlin Airlift, the desegregation of the armed forces and the dropping of atomic bombs on Hiroshima and Nagasaki.

Displays in the museum include Truman's famous collection of Bibles and a reproduction of the President's office in the White House. Truman explains by tape recording the significance of the furnishings and objects on the President's desk.

Exhibits include the original Japanese instrument of surrender signed aboard the battleship *Missouri* in 1945 and the blue table on which the United Nations Charter was signed in San Francisco that year.

Interest in the Truman years continues to attract scholars from throughout the nation and all over the world.

"The die was cast for the world we live in today by many decisions Mr. Truman made," observed Benedick K. Zobrist, longtime director of the Truman Library and Museum. "You cannot deal with China, Russia, atomic energy, inflation and civil rights without going back to Harry Truman.

"It's amazing how many things in Missouri are named after this President. High schools all over the state, and in other states as well, of course. Missourians are proud of Harry Truman."

His mother always said, "Harry got his common sense on the farm, not in town." Today his birthplace, a humble frame farmhouse in Lamar, Mo., is a state park. His farmhouse at Grandview is a county park. The 1,440-acre Harry S. Truman State Park surrounds Harry S. Truman Lake, a huge reservoir in the central part of the state.

The Harry S. Truman State Office Building in Missouri's capital, Jefferson City, has offices for more than 2,300 state employees.

The 118,000-seat Harry S. Truman Sports Complex in Kansas City is home of the Royals baseball team and the Chiefs football team.

Not bad for a Middle American dirt farmer who used a horse and plow to work his farm for 13 years, then opened a haberdashery and after it failed became a politician. Truman served as a county judge, a U.S. senator, Franklin D. Roosevelt's vice president and, finally, the 33rd President.

THIRTY

ARKANSAS

Ozark Mountains Folkways

YOU STEP BACK IN TIME when you drive north from Little Rock over 130 miles of narrow, twisting mountain roads and through pungent piney woods to Mountain View, Ark. No main highways lead to the tiny hamlet in Stone County.

To recapture, preserve and perpetuate the rich heritage of mountain life as it existed from the early 1800s through World War II, Arkansas established the Ozark Folk Center, a most unusual state park. Here in Mountain View, from April through October, seven days a week, 50 local people demonstrate traditional family crafts.

"I learned how to make soap from my mama, who learned it from her granddaddy," explained Elsie Ward, 75. She was melting hog rinds into grease, pouring the grease, water and lye into a cast-iron kettle and boiling the mixture over an oak fire.

"Now, most folks you talk to nowadays have a bad idea about lye soap," she said. "That's wrong. Lye is one of the best soaps ever invented. It's good to take a bath and get rid of ticks and chiggers with this soap. It's good for poison ivy. I shampoo my hair with it. It takes the grease spots out of clothes and off floors."

As Elsie Ward finished off her last batch of lye soap for the day, Bill Sky and his daughters Tara and Laurie arrived at the Ozark Folk Center. They came to perform at the evening music show in the park's 1,000-seat auditorium.

The Skys were loaded down with instruments: fiddle, mandolin, auto-harp, washboard, frailin' banjo, guitar and bass fiddle. Laurie had her clog shoes to dance Irish jigs.

"The Ozark Folk Center is a living museum of American folk music," Bill Sky said. "Every night for seven months, from April through October, except Sundays, music is played and sung that has been handed down mouth to ear, generation to generation.

"The music predates country, predates bluegrass. It's the music Americans were singing in the 1600s, 1700s, 1800s and early 1900s. It was still sung and played by families here in the Ozark mountains as a regular thing until paved roads were pushed through in the 1950s and 1960s, breaking down the barriers of isolation."

Throughout the year special music workshops and programs are held at the Ozark Folk Center. In 1995, for example, there were autoharp work-shops, a clogging workshop, dulcimer jamboree, step dance weekend, the National Guitar Thumbpicking Competition, Arkansas State Old-Time Fid-dle Championships, Herb Harvest Fall Festival, a bluegrass fiddle champi-onship and much more.

The park turns the clock back to simpler times, when mountaineers were cut off from the outside world. Folks here were self-sufficient, raising their own crops, fashioning their own tools, making their own furniture and clothing and providing their own music for entertainment.

The wilderness of the Ozark mountains in northern Arkansas was first settled by Scotch, Irish and English immigrants 185 years ago. The pioneers made their way northward up a river they called Rackensack, now called the Arkansas.

"They were families moving westward from Kentucky and Tennessee and before that from the 13 Colonies," explained Bill McNeil, music folklorist at the Ozark Folk Center. "They came here seeking a better life."

The music they brought with them had traveled with their ancestors from the British Isles. Some songs, like "The Devil's Nine Questions," date as far back as the 1400s. Some of the old-time Ozark families still sing these songs.

"But this isolated heritage has been disappearing rapidly," McNeil said, "ever since the mountain boys went off to war in the 1940s and came back with different ideas, ever since pavement came to Stone County and the surrounding areas in the 1950s."

Local musicians for miles around come to the Ozark Folk Center night after night to perform the traditional music. They play dulcimers, fiddles, autoharps, guitars, doghouse bass fiddles and frailin' banjos. There are no electrical instruments, no new songs. McNeil records every performance for the park's archives, which include thousands of songs.

In the park's auditorium, 260-pound guitarist Bill Myers, 70, performed "Feed the Chickens" with guitarist Ida Copeland, 66, and her toothless, harmonica-playing husband Percy, 72. "I love the atmosphere of the Folk Center," Myers said after the set. "We're playing the old-time back-porch, front-porch music, trying to preserve the culture."

Finger-style guitar pickin' Art Flatt sang songs about the Spanish American War and a 1901 song about the assassination of President McKinley: "See what you have done, shot our President with a Johnny 41."

Bob and Melissa Atchison sang about Abraham Lincoln at Ford's Theatre: "All the people near him shouting, 'For God's sake, save that man.' Poor Lincoln was to say before he went to rest, 'Of all the actors in this town, I loved Booth the best.'"

Jim and Melva Adcock did a 19th-Century number: "The preacher went out a-huntin' and knowed he oughtn't do it. He came upon a bear. 'Oh, Lord, if you can't help me, please don't help that bear.'"

Kermit Taylor, a Stone County school-bus driver living in Happy Hollow, said the music is the kind he grew up with. "My family didn't own a radio until I came out of the Army in 1946," he said. "I brought a radio home with me from the war.

"My granddaddy was a jig dancer. We made our own music. We raised a little corn, fed a few hogs and turkeys, growed our own tobaccer. Our women smoked corncob pipes and dipped snuff. After 1946, '47 and '48, things started changing around here."

It was in 1972 that the $3-million Ozark Folk Center State Park was completed on 80 acres of wooded hillsides at the edge of Mountain View.

Crafts are demonstrated in 50 native stone and cedar buildings and the results sold in park stores. Daily demonstrations include bonnet making, spinning, weaving, quilting, gun smithery and old-time candy making. Artisans fashion primitive furniture, hooked rugs and baskets.

In the summer of 1995, classes in old-time crafts included corn shuckery. Doll making was the most popular shuckery class, in which students learned to make dolls in the manner pioneer children learned from the Indians.

There were classes in making apple-head dolls, Battenburg lace, lye soap, sorghum right from the cane field, white oak baskets and woven chair seats. A four-day class taught coopering.

Clarice Chitwood, 75, was weaving on a 19th-Century two-harness, two-foot treadle loom that had been handed down generation to generation. "We women made clothes for the family," she said. "We made bedding. People didn't have the luxuries we have today. We didn't know about them. You don't miss what you don't know. At least we always had plenty to eat, though we never had much money to speak of."

Julia Mae Case was making cornbread on a 1936 Community wood stove. She said that as a child she helped support the family by picking goose feathers for feather ticks and comforters.

Allene Grissette was making peach butter. She stirred a long wooden paddle in a copper kettle over an oak fire for two hours without stopping.

Dan Stewart was hand-crafting black muzzle-loading rifles, the type made between 1750 and 1830 and used by Davy Crockett and Daniel Boone.

"This is squirrel hunting season," he said as he put the finishing touches on a 32-caliber squirrel rifle with a 41-inch-long barrel. "Sometimes it sounds like a war going on around here.

"Yes, squirrel is a favorite dish in these hills. With dumplings, nothing's better."

To perpetuate the heritage of the Ozark hills, young people in apprenticeship programs understudy crafts practiced by older residents. Cheri Hessel learned spinning on a "walking wheel" with corn-husk bobbin from Ida Branscum, 82, who had been spinning since she was 9.

"In this part of the country, people were always resourceful," Hessel said as she spun thread from dryer lint combined with cotton. "They always made do with whatever was available.

"A dress made out of a flour sack, handed down to others as apparel, was later cut up and made into a quilt. When the quilt wore out, it was woven into a rug."

Gazelle Mode, 60, said she learned how to quilt as a necessity when she was a child. "Everybody always says, 'You must have patience to quilt.' My hillbilly philosophy is it doesn't take patience to do things you enjoy. It takes patience to do things you do not enjoy."

Musicians, craftsmen and women come to the park from little towns throughout Stone County, from Mountain View, Fifty Six, Timbo, Marcella, St. James, Alco, Onia, Fox, Pleasant Grove and Rushing.

"This is the only one of 43 Arkansas state parks that is self-supporting," said staff member John Thomas. The park operates on a $2-million annual budget. It includes an attractive 60-room lodge and a restaurant featuring 19th-Century dishes. The entrance fee is $6.50 to the crafts center, $7 to the nightly musical programs.

The apprenticeship programs, vital for the preservation of the dying crafts, are supported by the statewide Womens Committee of 100. A representative serves on the committee from each of Arkansas' 75 counties. And 25 women at large stage fund-raising events throughout the state to raise money for apprenticeships.

The Ozark Folk Center is making it possible for future generations to forge a direct link to history. Today's visitors experience the rich legacy of music and crafts that grew out of life in the isolated Ozark mountains of northern Arkansas.

THIRTY-ONE

MISSISSIPPI

Astronaut and Cameraman Ronald E. McNair

I N THE BIGGER-THAN-LIFE-SIZE PORTRAIT by Mississippi artist Marshall Bouldin III, astronaut Ronald E. McNair grasps a large camera with fish-eye lens as he floats weightlessly in the spaceship *Challenger.*

The painting of McNair, one of seven astronauts killed when the *Challenger* blew up shortly after launch Jan. 28, 1986, is the centerpiece of the Ronald E. McNair Space Theater in Jackson, Miss. The theater is part of Davis Planetarium, the largest planetarium in the Southeast.

McNair, killed in his second flight in the same space capsule, never lived in Mississippi. He became an adopted son of the state.

The black astronaut visited Jackson numerous times during the last two years of his life. An outgoing, friendly person, he became something of a local hero. He rode in the Jackson parade that honored him.

It was the making of a unique film that first brought McNair to Jackson.

The award-winning half-hour documentary, *The Space Shuttle: An American Odyssey*, was produced by Richard Knapp, director of the Davis Planetarium, and staff members Don Warren, cinematographer, and Lenard Jenkins, production coordinator.

McNair, the world's first orbital cinematographer, was the film's chief cameraman. McNair's spectacular footage for the documentary was filmed during his first spaceflight aboard the *Challenger* in February, 1984.

He and astronaut Bruce McCandless, second cameraman aboard the flight, were inducted into the prestigious American Society of Cinematography for their camera work. The documentary won the gold medal at the 1985 International Film and TV Festival in New York.

It was Knapp, the planetarium's director, who proposed the idea for the space movie to NASA. "We were in the right place at the right time and had the right kind of an organization for NASA to work with—non-commercial," he recalled. "NASA said yes and cooperated all the way."

The Space Shuttle: An American Odyssey premiered Jan. 10, 1985, in the 60-foot-diameter domed theater now named after McNair. It has been shown there ever since, and at 13 other planetariums across the nation with 360-degree hemispherical theaters.

Jenkins, the production coordinator for the film, worked for months with NASA engineers to provide thermal protection for the space camera carried aboard the *Challenger* flight in February, 1984. They also fabricated housing to insulate the exterior camera from vibrations and extremes of hot and cold and designed a power system for another camera in the crew compartment.

Using a Houston simulator, cinematographer Warren began training McNair and other astronauts in the techniques of filming in the 360-degree format under weightless conditions.

"Ron McNair really got into it," Warren said. "He was the one person most responsible for the film."

Shot aboard the 3-million-mile, 122-orbit flight, with some sequences made on a subsequent *Challenger.* flight in April of 1984, *The Space Shuttle: An American Odyssey* was filmed primarily by McNair, with considerable footage by astronaut McCandless.

In addition, the Jackson planetarium filmmakers shot several launches at the Kennedy Space Center. McNair made numerous trips from Houston to Jackson to work with Knapp, Warren and Jenkins on the planning, development and later the editing of the documentary.

During the 360-degree presentation of the film, the viewer has the sensation of experiencing a spaceflight. The *Challenger* blasts off, Earth slips away and the space shuttle streaks across the skies.

Then the viewer feels like a passenger inside the crew compartment as the astronauts go about their work.

There are lighthearted exchanges. McNair has a close-up of a gum-chewing astronaut and of a "Don't Panic" button tacked to a wall. The camera pans outside to Bruce McCandless, an untethered astronaut free-flying away from the shuttle in Buck Rogers fashion.

As a party to the awesome voyage 170 miles above the planet, the viewer sees the capture and repair of the Solar Max Satellite, with spectacular windows on the earth below—1,000 miles in all directions—and finally touchdown at Edwards Air Force Base.

Knapp recalled working with McNair: "We were all tremendously impressed with his intelligence, personal magnetism and energy. He put so much of himself into this project. He understood what we wanted. He knew the equipment, took the initiative to raise questions. He was always trying to satisfy us. He had good feelings about this community, and the community had good feelings about him."

"He was just a wonderful, warm human being," Jenkins said. "One of the touching things about this guy, he wasn't on an ego trip. No matter who you were, he was interested in you."

McNair was a special person in many ways to many people.

The son of an auto mechanic who never finished high school, McNair picked cotton as a youngster to help his family survive in a small back-country South Carolina town, Lake City.

He was valedictorian of his high school class, where he played saxophone in a jazz band and lettered in football, baseball and basketball. He attended North Carolina Agricultural and Technical State University on a scholarship and graduated magna cum laude.

McNair was a Presidential scholar and a Ford Foundation fellow at Massachusetts Institute of Technology, where he earned his doctorate in physics in 1976. An expert in lasers, he worked at Hughes Research Lab in Malibu, Calif., as a staff physicist for a year and a half until he was selected for the astronaut program in January, 1978.

"I gained qualities in that cotton field," he once said in an interview. "I got tough. I learned to endure. I refused to quit."

He had great concern for young people, challenging them to study, to work hard: "You can achieve your dreams," he said. "Look at me, a humble country boy. If I can do it, you can do it, too."

McNair died at age 35, leaving his widow, Cheryl, and two children, Reginald and Joy. The main street of his Lake City hometown is named in his honor and so is the junior high school he attended.

Science buildings at his alma maters, MIT and North Carolina A&T, carry his name. So does a park in Houston, a high school in Decatur, Ga., and a dozen other elementary and junior high schools across the nation.

The Ronald E. McNair Scholarship Foundation in Atlanta, its advisory board headed by Paul Gray, president of MIT, provides four-year university scholarships in science to students with academic merit, community involvement and financial need.

Among the photographs and exhibits about the astronaut in the Jackson space theater named in his honor is one showing him lifting a 360-degree camera aboard the *Challenger*. He inscribed it: "To my friends at Davis Planetarium. It's been great working with you—Ron McNair."

THIRTY-TWO

LOUISIANA

Sweet Life on the Bayou

FISHERMAN-TRAPPER INNERCE (NACIE) DARDA lives on Bayou L'Eau Bleu, five miles from the nearest town. Last year he went to town twice, both times reluctantly.

The town is Golden Meadow, La., population 2,200. Darda made his two 15-minute, five-mile trips by boat, both times to get a haircut.

"Every time I go to town I get nervous," he confided. "Too much noise. Too many people. Too much confusion. I can't wait to get out of there and return to the peace and quiet of my home."

His wife Ovelia shares his feelings about going to town.

No roads lead to the Cajun fisherman-trapper's camp where the couple live in the comfortable, weather-beaten, tarpaper house he built when he returned from World War II.

They live on a small patch of high ground in a vast swampland on the shores of Bayou L'Eau Bleu, which in English would be Blue Water Bayou.

The Dardas have no neighbors. They are self-sufficient, hunting wild ducks and geese, catching seafood and growing vegetables.

They catch shrimp, oysters, crabs and crawfish and trap wild mink, raccoon, muskrat, otter and nutria for a living.

Ovelia and Nacie raised seven daughters and a son in the lonely isolation of their bayou camp; all are grown, married with families of their own.

Darda never went to school. All his life he lived in the backwater bayous of southern Louisiana except for three years in the Army during World War II. He said he will never forget one day on the front lines fighting the Germans. He was a loader on a three-inch turret gun.

"When the gun jammed I smashed three fingers," he said, showing the permanently damaged fingers. "I didn't want to leave. We were shooting at the Germans across the Moselle River.

"My sergeant ordered me to go to a medic. As I was walking away a German bomb burst, killing all seven of my gun crew...." Tears welled in his eyes as he remembered.

Darda is one of the thousands of Cajuns who live in Louisiana's watery world of bayous, moss-draped cypress swamps, marshes, sloughs, lakes, lagoons, rivers and delta.

They live in America's largest wetland wilderness, a 20,000-square-mile area that takes up nearly half of Louisiana. More than a third of all the marshland in the United States is in this state.

Louisiana's wetland country produces more fish and game than any other natural water system in the nation.

Victoria Toupes, 62, lives in Bayou La Fourche. "Queen Victoria," as everyone calls her for miles around, has been a trapper since she was 8. She said her father taught her how to catch muskrats in the bayou.

"I growed up trappin'," the Cajun said as she hung her day's catch of muskrats to dry on a row of stretched wire.

"I don't want to brag, but I'm the toughest woman down in these places here on Bayou La Fourche. You have to be tough to be a trapper. It's dirty work. Full of mud all the time. Pullin' those animals out of traps, skinnin' 'em, puttin' 'em on the stretch."

Three times as many muskrats are trapped and skinned in southern Louisiana each year than are caught in all of Canada and the rest of America combined.

"I built this here shack I live in year-round," Toupes said with pride as she sat drinking a cup of syrupy Cajun coffee in her kitchen. "Nobody nailed one nail in it 'cept myself."

Forty percent of all the wild fur sold in America comes from animals trapped in the spongy marsh muck by thousands of independent trappers like Ovelia and Nacie Darda and Victoria Toupes. The watery world of southern Louisiana also supports half of America's migratory waterfowl. Swamplands here are dotted with rich oil and gas fields.

For the most part it's a good life. The people of the bayou's swamps and marshes live in homes on stilts above water. They feast daily on exotic Cajun and Creole cuisine—fried alligator tail steaks, turtle soup, shrimp *rémoulade,* stuffed catfish and crawfish heads, crawfish *étouffée,* red beans and rice, jambalaya, gumbo and other dishes that would make a gourmet green with envy.

Because the water table is so high, they bury their dead in concrete vaults above ground.

"Looseeann" is what blacks and Cajuns call their state. The word *Cajun* is a contraction of *Acadian.* Ancestors of the Cajuns came from French Acadia in Nova Scotia. Because of their sympathy for the French, they were banished from Canada by the British in the 1750s and 1760s. The first of the Cajuns began arriving in French Louisiana in 1762.

Today there are 300,000 Cajuns living in the 22 parishes of southern Louisiana, in the state's Great Atchafalaya Swamp and the Louisiana bayou country.

A celebration of Cajun life is broadcast each Saturday night from the 1920s-era Liberty Theater in Eunice, 150 miles west of New Orleans. The theater seats 800 and is always filled. It is part of Jean Lafitte National Historical Park.

The two-hour program heard over a number of radio stations is produced by the National Parks Service, the city of Eunice and the University of Lafayette. It features storytelling in Cajun French and zydeco and Cajun music.

Cajun band instruments always include a washboard and an accordion. Zydeco is a black version of Cajun music, played by blacks who grew up in the Cajun culture. The blacks call themselves Creoles.

There are black communities where entire populations speak a special Louisiana French patois, one being the town of Napville, population 1,500. "We all speak nothing but the Looseeann French here," said Mitch Williams, at work at Mary Jane's Grocery, his sister's country store. "Many of the older ones don't speak English at all."

Catholicism is the leading religion in Louisiana. The heritage of the church before the Louisiana Purchase in 1803 is reflected in the state's unique parish system.

All but two of the U.S. states are divided into political subdivisions called counties. The exceptions are Alaska, divided into 25 divisions, and Louisiana, which has 64 parishes. The parishes derive from the original ecclesiastical boundaries that existed under French rule.

A number of the parishes take their names from saints: St. Bernard, St. Charles, St. Helena, St. James, St. John the Baptist, St. Landry, St. Martin, St. Mary and St. Tammany.

There's a parish named in honor of Christ going to heaven—Ascension—and another in honor of the Virgin Mary going to heaven—Assumption. There are parishes recalling the Acadians' exodus to Louisiana—Evangeline and Acadia—and a parish named after the president of the Confederacy, Jefferson Davis.

Parishes have parish courthouses, parish seats and parish sheriff's departments. Each parish has a police jury comparable to a county board of supervisors. The elected parish legislators and administrators are called police jurors.

Several parishes along the Mississippi are sliced in two by the river. A network of ferryboats operated by the state carries pedestrians and vehicles back and forth across the Mississippi free of charge.

On the free ferry *Acadia*, skippered by veteran ferryboat Capt. Ferdinand August, three sheriff's cars were crossing from La Place on the east bank to Edgard, the parish seat of St. John the Baptist Parish, on the west bank.

"Riding the ferry is an everyday occurrence for most deputies while on duty," said St. John the Baptist Deputy Sheriff Rick Hylander. "There are no bridges crossing the Mississippi in our parish. The courthouse is on the west bank, the sheriff's headquarters and jail are on the east bank. We patrol both sides of the river, so we have to go back and forth on the ferry."

Alligators have always been a favorite food for the people of the bayou. Gator hides bring good prices. But for 18 years, from 1962 to 1980, hunting alligators was illegal in Louisiana because the animal population had dropped dramatically.

Sound management raised the number of alligators back to peak levels, more than 500,000. Since 1981, the state has permitted taking alligators each year during one month, September. In a typical September, 21,000 alligators will be harvested in Louisiana.

Hides are shipped to Japan and other Asian nations where the skin is converted into watchbands, belts, purses and luggage. The tail meat is frozen and served all year in Louisiana restaurants. Body meat is used to make gravies.

You see big commercial shrimp boats everywhere along the lower Mississippi, the lower regions of Bayou Lafourche and the Atchafalaya River. You see them unloading the latest catch, preparing to go out for another two weeks to a month in the Gulf of Mexico.

C.J. Pizani skippers the 86-foot shrimp boat *Mean Machine*. His father and grandfather are shrimpers. So are his three brothers. C.J. has been a shrimp-boat captain since he was 17. "It's in my blood," mused the 26-year-old shrimper. "What else can I do?"

Almost everyone encountered in the bayou country fishes or traps part or full time. In the town of Pierre Part, Marian Daigle was selling her catch of 462 pounds of catfish to seafood processor Claude Metrejean at 55 cents a pound. She wore green rain slicks and a bright orange and green crocheted hat. She crochets when she isn't fishing.

"Fishin' is my business," Daigle said. "It pays the bills. I set my nets in the bayous and come back a week later. You see what I make this week? $254.10."

At Leeville in Bayou Lafourche, Beatrice Duncan fishes from shore every other day using four long cane poles. "I'm the greatest fisherman up and down this bayou," she declared. At age 60, Duncan has been fishing 55 years. She catches blue crabs, crawfish, eel, catfish, redfish and trout using five pounds of shrimp for bait each outing.

"I eat the fish and crabs," she said, "give some to neighbors and sell some. Sometimes I fish with other ladies. I fish no matter what the weather, rain or shine." Her favorite seafood dish: catfish heads smothered in onion greens.

Lawrence Duet operates a moss gin in Labadieville, following in the footsteps of his "daddy, granddaddy and several more generations down the line." From their small boats, people in the bayou harvest Spanish moss from the tops of cypress trees using 14-foot-long poles with hooks on the end. They sell the moss to Duet.

He then hangs the moss out to dry in a curing process that takes several weeks and turns the moss from gray to jet black. The moss is used for stuffing furniture, mattresses and spawning mats in which fish lay eggs.

"It's a dying industry," Duet sighed. "In the old days moss gins were everywhere. Mine is one of the last that's left."

This, too, is the land of turtles, frogs, armadillos, cranes, herons, laughing gulls, marsh wrens and poisonous snakes.

"We have blue runner, cotton mouse and water moccasin in this swamp," said Carolyn Pepper. She lives on a two-story houseboat on Four Mile Bayou with her husband Jimmy and their nine children.

"Honey, if one of those blue runners gets ahold of you, you're dead. You might as well pick up an ax and chop off your hand or arm if a blue runner bites you there."

The Peppers live miles from their nearest neighbors and have a TV dish that brings in Philadelphia, New York and Chicago as clear as New Orleans.

"You might think it's funny us livin' out here on this swamp. But we paid off the houseboat in four years. It costs us $10,000. No way you can pay off a house in four years."

Philip Green has a small plot of land embraced by swampland in the hamlet of Darrow. He fishes, traps and farms. "I plant okra, bell peppers, tomatoes and snap beans," he said. "If the crops don't come up, that's God's business. I put them there and let the good Lord take care of it."

Throughout bayou country are antebellum homes and huge plantation houses, relics of pre-Civil War days. Like many of the castles in England, plantation homes cost so much to maintain that owners often conduct tours through them to help pay for the upkeep. Some operate as bed-and-breakfast inns.

Saturday night in the bayou is a time for *fais-dodos*, or Cajun dances. Music is provided by groups playing the squeeze box (tiny French accordion), fiddle, guitar, washboard and triangle.

One of the most all-time popular Cajun songs is "Las Pas Patate," or "Don't Drop the Potato," an old Cajun expression meaning hang in there. Such is life on the bayou.

THIRTY-THREE

TEXAS

Richest Little County and Texas Longhorns

L OVING COUNTY, TEX., is America's least populated and wealthiest county per capita.

As far as the eye can see, it is a flat, treeless sage land, broiling under a blazing sun and blistering wind through most of summer. It's alive with rattlesnakes, coyotes and cats.

Only 107 men, women and children lived in Loving County at the time of the last U.S. Census in 1990.

"There isn't another county in the country like this one," said Mary Belle Jones, the West Texas county's chief appraiser and historian. Her husband is county sheriff.

"You can't buy a loaf of bread or a pint of milk anywhere in Loving County," she said. "There is no store, no school, no doctor, no dentist, no ambulance, no fire truck, no lawyer, no bank, no cemetery, no saloon, no stoplight, no mail delivery or jail in this county."

The county has a cafe, a gas station and a post office—all in Mentone, population 15, the county seat. Up the road three miles is Creagerville, where 22 people live in six trailers and one house. The rest of the county's inhabitants are scattered on ranches all over the countryside.

Mattie Thorp, an 88-year-old widow, has been running the county's only gas station for more than 30 years. She serves as chairman of the Democratic Party's Precinct 1 in Loving County. But her gas station is plastered with pictures of Ronald Reagan and George Bush.

"I was elected," she explained when asked why a Democratic official kept photos of Republicans Bush and Reagan in her gas station. "I didn't ask for the job. I have voted for every Republican candidate for President as far back as I can remember."

"We all know one another," historian Mary Belle Jones said in her office in the two-story brick 1935 Loving County Courthouse. "Many of us are related. When anybody sneezes around here, everybody knows it. This place is so quiet you can hear rattlesnakes crossing the road...."

Most county officials are related. County Treasurer Fay Busby, for example, is the mother-in-law of Juanita Busby, the county clerk. County Judge Donald Creager is the brother of Royce Creager, one of the four county commissioners.

The U.S. Census Bureau reported that Loving County's per capita income of $34,173 for all residents older than 15 was the highest in the nation. "Three or four millionaire ranchers live in the county," Judge Creager explained. "That bumps up our average income considerably."

As longtime county judge, Creager not only takes care of judicial matters but presides over the Board of County Commissioners as well. He is the county's chief administrative officer. He proudly noted that no one in Loving County is on welfare. Ranching and oil fields are the county's two major revenue producers.

Elgin Jones, Loving County's sheriff for 22 years, never wears a uniform. He wears a big sweat-stained cowboy hat and drives an unmarked car. Asked about crime in Loving County, the lawman replied: "Well, it isn't as bad as it is in other places. Few people ever find their way here. We're at the end of the road. No main highway goes through the county. But we get our share of criminals now and then.

"I remember 1980. Now, that was a bad year, let me tell you. We had five burglaries by two men and a woman who came over here from San Antonio. That's crime. Imagine, five burglaries in one year in Loving County. By the way, we got all them burglars. They're still serving time."

What do people in Loving County do for excitement? Barbara Creager makes hat bands and belts out of rattlesnake skins. Her deep freeze is full of rattlesnakes.

"I hate rattlesnakes," she said as her son Devan brought one to her house. The snake continued to twitch after having its head cut off. "They're so deadly. A young man almost died the other day after he chopped the head off one. He was careless. That head without the body bit him on the hand. Luckily, his life was saved by surgery."

Creager has 14 cats. "Rattlesnakes feed on mice. We keep the cats to eat the mice and keep the rattlers away," she explained. "We keep so many cats because coyotes eat the cats, and we have to keep replenishing our cat supply."

She said the biggest pastime in Loving County is dominoes. "We get together at one another's house and play dominoes for hours in the evenings."

And twice a month the 11-member chapter of the only club in the county, the Texas Extension Homemakers, stages events. "We try to bring information and all sorts of timely subjects to people in the county, like AIDS," Creager said. She is president of the club. "We did a program on AIDS. No one has AIDS in the county so far as we know, but we thought people here ought to be made aware of that terrible disease."

Loving County had an elementary school until 1978 when the local school district merged with the district in Wink, 33 miles east of Mentone in Winkler County. The Mentone school had four pupils and two teachers when it closed. The handful of Loving County students are bused daily to Wink.

In 1887, Loving County was named after Oliver Loving, who also lent his name to the Charles Goodnight–Oliver Loving Trail. Loving was shot in 1867 by Comanches on the cow trail he made famous. He crawled five miles after the shooting, chewing on an old kid glove for food. His wounds were treated, but he died of gangrene. The county keeps his memory alive with a large plaque on the courthouse grounds.

Eighty-year-old J.D. (Jack) Phillips popped a red More cigarette in his mouth and ambled out into the pasture of his Battle Island Ranch, where his prized Texas longhorn steer grazed on lush green grass.

"Some longhorn steers are gentle; some are mean as hell," Phillips said, his eyes on 12-year-old Big Red, a 2,000-pound steer with huge sweeping horns. "Big Red looks mean, but we get along."

Phillips, 5-foot, 6-inches tall and weighing 140 pounds, knows as much about the breed as any man alive. His family has run Texas longhorn cattle since the 1820s, when Texas was first settled by non-Indians. One of the 1964 founders of the 3,000-member Texas Longhorn Breeders Assn., Phillips served as the organization's third president and never fails to attend the cattle group's annual convention.

The oldest breed of cattle on the North American continent, the Texas longhorn—like the Alamo—is symbolic of the Lone Star State.

"When you say longhorn, you're talkin' Texas," Phillips said. "That's what the breed is all about—hardy survivors, adaptable to everything an animal can stand, blazing heat, unbearable humidity, cold, freezing rain and winter blizzards."

T.D. Kelsey's *Texas Gold*, one of the largest bronze sculptures in the world, pays homage to the longhorn. Each of the seven animals depicted on the statue has a brand representing the seven families who owned purebred Texas longhorns in 1925, when the breed was on the verge of extinction.

Phillips' brand—J&P—is one of the seven brands on the statue. He and his father owned about 30 of the purebred longhorns in 1925.

That year, to make sure the legendary breed didn't vanish, the U.S. Forest Service gathered 30 of the animals and placed them on the Wichita Mountains National Wild Life Refuge in Oklahoma. Within a few years the federal herd increased to 300 and became the foundation stock for the 125,000 registered Texas longhorns scattered across the country today. Half are still in Texas.

Phillips may be long in years, but there's no slowing him down. He works six and sometimes seven days a week, riding 20 miles a day and more on his 13,000-acre ranch.

"I'd be riding with a bunch today, if I wasn't talkin' to you," he said with a laugh, the ever-present red cigarette drooping from his mouth.

Married 58 years, Phillips and his wife Carolyn have three children, six grandchildren and a great-granddaughter. The walls of their huge living room are covered with two dozen skulls and horns of longhorn bulls, cows and steers, a tribute to the animals they've loved. The front porch displays yet more heads of longhorns they've loved.

In the living room Phillips pointed to a mounted longhorn skull. "See that one in the middle? That's Texas Star, a steer that belonged to my wife. That old critter would stand outside the house all hours of the day lookin' in and watchin' Carolyn. He was fascinated by her. He never left his eyes off her. He was grand champion steer at the Denver Western in 1976."

Quilted pillows depicting longhorn cattle were on the couch. Several bronze statues of longhorns in the living room included one of Texas Ranger JP 3681, one of the all-time famous Texas longhorn bulls. Texas Ranger was in the Phillips' herd.

The old rancher pointed to another skull and horns, this one above the fireplace. "Some of my longhorns were in John Wayne's *Alamo* movie. That steer was in the movie. The head next to that one was from a cow that lived to be 32 years old."

It was Christopher Columbus who introduced longhorn cattle to the New World. He dropped them off on Santo Domingo Island on his second voyage to the West Indies in 1493. In 1521, the cattle were brought to Mexico from Santo Domingo, and in 1690 the first herd of 200 head of longhorns was driven north to present-day Texas.

After the Civil War, 10 million longhorns were herded north from Texas.

"When I was a child, this was all open range," Phillips said. "There was nothing but longhorns in this country. My father had 4,000 in the early days."

Phillips runs about 180 longhorn, 100 Brahma and 600 crossbred cattle on his Battle Island Ranch. He keeps about a dozen of the old longhorns with the huge horns.

"There is no breeding value for the ones with the big horns," he said, "just historical, colorful and nostalgic value. President Reagan was given one for his California ranch, and the University of Texas at Austin has one as a mascot.

"People like to have them around to show. They're a conversation piece. It was longhorns that put Texas on the map."

THIRTY-FOUR

OKLAHOMA

The Oklahoma Land Runs

I SUPPOSE YOU MIGHT SAY I'M IN A RUT," Fred Olds said with a laugh. Olds had just spent weeks painting a 30-by-15-foot 1889 Land Rush mural at the Oklahoma Territorial Museum in Guthrie, Okla. It was his 60th Oklahoma Run painting. A World War II B-26 bombardier who flew several missions over Europe, Olds is known throughout the state as the "Oklahoma Run artist."

His artworks depict dramatic episodes during the wild dashes for free land when the Oklahoma Territory was opened for settlement.

In five land runs staged between 1889 and 1895, more than 250,000 men and women raced across the open countryside on horseback, on foot, riding bicycles and oxen, in buggies, covered wagons, hanging from trains.

The artist described how the land-starved masses gathered behind a starting line. At high noon bugles blew, guns fired. The thundering herd of man and beast surged forward.

"It was like coming out of a starting gate," Olds said, explaining the exciting action depicted in his latest mural. "Some flew off their horses and were trampled."

Oklahoma had 50,000 eager would-be homesteaders at the 1889 run, 100,000 rushing madly out of the shoot at the Cherokee Strip Run in 1893, tens of thousands at the other runs.

There were many more people in the races than land to be had. They came from farms, small towns and cities all across the United States.

Today the runs are very much alive in the minds of the people of Oklahoma. Many still live on farms and town sites homesteaded by their grandparents, who came to run for several miles for a free piece of land.

Every year on run anniversaries, schoolchildren and townspeople reenact the historic event. Local fairs are held on run days. High schools, colleges, communities and little-theater groups stage plays about the land rush.

Helen Franks Miner, a popular African-American high school music teacher from Canadian County's El Reno, wrote and produced the community's annual land-rush play that reenacts the 1889 run.

"It was low-income people who came to Oklahoma, looking for a better life in the closing chapter of frontier America," Miner explained. "Blacks, Hispanics and Chinese made the runs as well as whites. And many descendants of the early settlers are still living on the old homesteads."

Nearly every city and town that sprang up overnight in an Oklahoma run has a land-rush museum or special exhibit commemorating the mad dash. The communities of Guthrie, Enid, Alva, Perry, Cherokee, Lawton, Shawnee, Stillwater and Woodward all have run museums.

Oklahoma City has the 1889ers Museum and the Museum of Unassigned Lands. It has land-rush exhibits in the Oklahoma Historical Society Building across from the Capitol.

A huge mural in the statehouse dome, depicting the 1889 run, depicts a giant banner exhorting: "Go Forth and Possess the Promised Land!"

As Minnie Rose Tellaro pumped away on her backyard well drawing water to do her dishes, the wail of a train crossing the bridge over the Cimarron River could be heard in the distance.

"In 1889 my grandfather, Andrew Tellaro, rode a train on those same tracks," Tellaro said. "He jumped off the train, ran across the prairie and claimed this land."

She was born and has lived her entire life on the quarter section, or 160 acres, her grandfather claimed on April 22, 1889, in the first of Oklahoma's great runs.

"I'm an old stuck-in-the-mud," said Tellaro, who never married. "It's because I like the old-fashioned ways of doing things, living the quiet life in the same old house, pumping my water, using the outdoor privy."

She had no electricity until 1979 and got her first TV on Christmas, 1985. But she still has no running water inside the house or indoor plumbing. "Except for the electricity and TV, I have pretty much left things like they always were," she said. "What you don't have, you don't miss."

Her grandfather never spoke English. Andrew Tellaro and his wife Rose were Italian immigrants. He was working in a coal mine in Missouri when he heard there was free land available in Oklahoma.

Many of the Oklahoma run homesteaders were immigrants—Germans, Italians, French, Danes, Poles, Scotch-Irish and others.

Out in the country, homesteaders erected a one-room school every three miles. Andrew Tellaro gave an acre of his land for a one-room schoolhouse, where children in the Abell Community of Logan County were educated from 1890 to 1947.

Minnie Rose's father graduated from the school. She and her brother James did too.

The original homestead cabin Andrew Tellaro built stood near Minnie Rose's house until one day in 1985. "It just wore out and collapsed," she said. "I went outside and there it was, crumbled, with the roof on the ground covering what was left."

Three generations of Tellaros raised hogs, cows and chickens for a living on their 160 acres. "If we were poor, we never knew it," said the homesteader's granddaughter.

Oh, the stories they tell, handed down generation to generation.

"My father was in the run," recalled Gabrielle Yenzer of Guthrie, "but he got a jail sentence instead of free land. Three homesteaders were on the same claim. The morning after the run, one was dead.

"Daddy and the third man wound up behind bars. I have a belt Daddy won in a wrestling match in jail. Finally the other man confessed. They let Daddy out."

Tiny Frazier, who operates an Oklahoma City limousine service, said that when he was a boy his grandfather showed him how he took a wooden stake and hammered it into the ground to claim 160 acres.

"People pulled up other people's stakes, but they never messed with my granddaddy's claim," Frazier said. "We'll never sell that land. It's the tradition of it, the prestige of it. It's been in the family all these years."

Women were entitled to make the runs if they were single, widows or legally separated from their husbands, over 21 and U.S. citizens.

Nanitta A.H. Daisey covered the runs for the *Dallas Morning News*. She, in turn, was covered by correspondents from newspapers all over the country who spilled a lot of ink about their colleague, some of it apocryphal.

On the first run, Daisey rode a train's cowcatcher with a six-shooter strapped to her waist. She jumped off the slow-moving train, ran across the open country, staked her claim, then with great joy fired her pistol into the air.

The New York Times published a story about her on a later run, reporting that correspondent Daisey and 20 other women filed claims to start an all-women's pioneering community called Bathsheba. Nothing more was heard from Bathsheba.

Edna Couch, 92, stood alongside Leonard McMurray's '89er statue in the heart of downtown Oklahoma City. The statue shows an '89er pounding his stake and taking his claim, his wife astride their horse beside him.

A message scrawled on the statue's plaque reads: "Strong men and women came upon a raw land with vision. They spanned rivers and prairies and mountains with determination. They created schools, churches, farms. They lifted great buildings to the skies...."

Couch serves as president of the 700-member 1889ers Society, founded by those who made the run and continued today by their descendants. Her grandfather, William L. Couch, was the leader of the Boomers and the first mayor of Oklahoma City.

"Our society perpetuates the pioneer spirit," she explained. "We have a big banquet every April 22 on the anniversary. We place a wreath at the foot of this statue that day."

Another group, the Sons and Daughters of the Cherokee Strip, makes its headquarters in Enid. It is made up of 1,000 direct descendants of those who made the Sept. 16, 1893 run.

Edna Couch's grandfather and David L. Payne were leaders of the Boomers. "Booming Oklahoma" was their slogan as they tried for 10 years to get the government to open up the unoccupied, unassigned lands of Oklahoma for settlement.

A year to the day after the run of 1889, Couch's grandfather was buried at the age of 39, dead from a bullet wound by another Boomer in a dispute over a 160-acre claim where the Oklahoma Municipal Auditorium stands today. It is one of the best quarter sections in the capital city.

Couch talked about the Sooners, those "that jumped the gun and got into the territory too soon."

Instead of joining in the race, the Sooners were already inside the unclaimed lands, hiding out, waiting to jump out and grab the choice land. Hundreds of Sooners were prosecuted in the courts when the dust settled.

"People got the Sooners and the Boomers mixed up," Couch said. "*Sooners* was a derogatory term for years. Now it has lost its negative connotation. The University of Oklahoma teams are called the Sooners. Oklahomans are called Sooners. People have forgotten that part of the history."

According to historian Bruce Joseph of the Oklahoma Historical Society, the 50,000 men and women in that first run claimed 2 million acres of virgin lands. They created 15 towns and settled farms in six present-day counties.

During the first few days after the run, troops stationed in Oklahoma City and the other towns tried to keep the peace, settling arguments among the Boomers and Sooners and others fighting over the same claims.

Joseph's grandfather, originally a Missouri schoolteacher, was an '89er. He built a school on his quarter section in Oklahoma and taught there the rest of his life.

"All that existed in Oklahoma City on April 21, 1889, were a half-dozen railroad buildings. That was it," Joseph said. "Overnight the raw prairie became a tent city of 10,000 homesteaders. The day after, trains came through carrying lumber to build houses, to build shops, to build a city."

THIRTY-FIVE

KANSAS

Mecca for Women Pilots

ATCHISON, KAN., a small Midwestern town, is a mecca for women pilots from throughout the world. Amelia Earhart was born here July24,1897.

When women fliers make pilgrimages to Atchison in their light airplanes, they land at Amelia Earhart Airport, the only airport in the United States named after the famed aviator.

In a nearby forest and in a downtown mall are two identical life-size bronze statues of the pilot depicted in her familiar short leather flight jacket, scarf and slacks, her hair tousled by the wind.

The local high school and college football stadium bears her name. The town's baseball diamond is called Amelia Earhart Field. The road from Atchison to Leavenworth is called the Amelia Earhart Highway.

"Way things are going around here, one of these days they might change the name of this place from Atchison to Amelia Earhart," observed Joe Carrigan, 78.

The former mayor remembered a visit by the pilot when he was in high school. "Every kid in town got to shake her hand," Carrigan said.

Atchison, population 12,000—birthplace of the Atchison, Topeka and Santa Fe Railroad—was named after David R. Atchison, a U.S. senator from Missouri—not Kansas—who visited his namesake town only once.

The large, two-story Victorian home where Amelia Earhart was born and spent her first 12 years sits on a bluff overlooking the Missouri River. The house, considered a shrine by women pilots, is owned by the Ninety-Nines.

Earhart was the first president of the Ninety-Nines, the international organization of women aviators she helped found in 1929. She suggested the name because there were 99 original members.

Every year Ninety-Nines from nearly every state—and from as far away as Australia, Japan, Mexico, Central and South America and Europe—fly to Amelia Earhart's hometown to visit the famed pilot's childhood home, to see the impressive collection of Amelia Earhart's possessions, memorabilia and artifacts housed in the Atchison County Museum.

They also fly in to visit the International Forest of Friendship.

It was Fay Gillis Wells' idea to establish the forest to further honor the memory of Amelia Earhart and pay tribute to other men and women who have made outstanding contributions to aviation.

In her younger years, Wells—87, of Alexandria, Va., one of 16 surviving charter members of the Ninety-Nines—was a noted aviator and newspaper foreign correspondent.

"The year 1997 will be the 60th anniversary of Amelia's disappearance," she noted, "and the 100th anniversary of her birth."

The Ninety-Nines, the city of Atchison and the forestry department of Kansas State University, Manhattan presented the International Forest of Friendship to the American people in America's Bicentennial year, 1976.

Wells, chairperson of the Ninety-Nines Bicentennial Committee, and Atchison's former mayor and civic leader Joe Carrigan, bicentennial chairman for the town, headed up the friendship forest project from its inception and have continued as its leaders.

Within the park overlooking Lake Warnock are trees from the 50 states; Washington, D.C.; the U.S. territories, and 33 foreign nations where Ninety-Nines chapters exist. At the foot of each tree, a granite marker lists its species and the state or country it represents.

There is a tulip tree from the White House, a cherry tree from Japan, a redwood from California. The English oak tree was a gift from British Ambassador Peter Ramsbotham, who flew out from the nation's capital to plant it.

There is a sycamore tree grown from a seed flown to the moon and back on a space shuttle flight. In a circle around the moon tree, granite markers honor the memory of astronauts who died in space-related accidents.

More than 550 aviation notables, both living and deceased, are honored with granite markers embedded in a mile-long walkway that winds through the forest.

The majority of those honored are women pilots, women like Amelia Earhart, Jacqueline Cochran, Alice Hammond, Neta Snook Southern, Shirley Chapfield, Louise Thaden, Lucille Wright, Tiny Broadwick, all of the original Ninety-Nines and Sally Ride, the first woman astronaut.

Among the 33 men and women honored in 1995 with granite markers is NASA pilot Lt. Col. Marie Collins, who became the first woman to pilot a shuttle when *Discovery* lifted off on Feb. 3, 1995.

Among the many famous male aviators honored are Charles Lindbergh, Wilbur and Orville Wright, Wylie Post, Jimmy Doolittle, Howard Hughes and Dwight Eisenhower, the first U.S. President with a private pilot's license.

In 1995 there were 6,375 members of the Ninety-Nines in all 50 states and 33 foreign countries, including Iceland and Russia.

The Ninety-Nines are headquartered in their own building at Will Rogers Airport in Oklahoma City. To be a member, a woman must be a certificated pilot. There is a monthly publication, *The Ninety-Nines News*.

To this day Amelia Earhart is remembered as the premier woman pilot in the world.

She was the first woman to solo across the Atlantic, May 20 to 21, 1932. She was the first woman to solo across the Pacific, from Honolulu to Oakland, Jan. 11, 1935. Among her many other distinctions, she was the first woman to fly solo round trip from the United States to Mexico City, the first woman to make a transcontinental nonstop flight and the first woman to receive the Distinguished Flying Cross.

Her last flight began from Miami with her navigator Fred Noonan as they attempted to fly around the world. They were last heard from when Earhart radioed, "Position uncertain." They were searching for tiny uninhabited Holland Island in the mid-Pacific.

Holland Island was one of the destinations on an around-the-world charter flight I took in 1973 with my wife Arliene and 154 other Southern Californians aboard a DC-8. The idea was to see as much of the world as possible from the air in two weeks.

The global odyssey was the brainchild of Stew Angle, chairman of Mount San Antonio College's aeronautics department, and Bill Arnot, a senior United Airlines pilot. The flight took us low over the North Pole, the South Pole, much of Europe, Africa (skimming 19,340-foot Mt. Kilimanjaro), India, 29,028-foot Mt. Everest in the Himalayas, Thailand, Australia and New Zealand.

The final adventure was retracing the route of Amelia Earhart and Fred Noonan in the mid-Pacific where they were lost in their twin-engine Lockheed 10 Electra on July 2, 1937.

Howland Island is one of the most remote places on the face of the earth. No one lives there, and virtually no one ever goes there. It lies on the Equator, is 1½ miles long and half a mile wide and rises only eight feet out of the water.

As we approached Howland Island, eight members of the Ninety-Nines stood beside the cockpit. The pilot banked the plane low, and a button pushed to lower the landing gear released a wreath and other mementos to the famed aviator.

Amelia Earhart was a multifaceted woman. She was a fashion designer for *Vogue, Harper's Bazaar, Vanity Fair* and *Woman's Home Companion* magazines. She was aviation editor for *Cosmopolitan.*

She authored three books. She took a course in photography at the University of Southern California and was a professional photographer. She was a poet and a painter.

She was a vocal pacifist and had a favorite saying: "Let there be peace on Earth and let it begin with me." She was a nurse in World War I, a social worker at Denison House in Boston and a premed student at Columbia. Her husband George Palmer Putnam, a publisher, died in 1950. They had no children.

Over the years numerous books, poems and songs have been written about Amelia Earhart. "Lady Lindy" and "Amelia, Queen of the Air" were popular songs in the 1930s. A fox-trot called the Earhart Hop was named after her. She loved to dance.

Schools carry her name. Postage stamps in the United States and several foreign nations have featured her. A street in Los Angeles and streets in other cities and towns are named after her. So is a mountain in Yosemite

National Park.

Speculation over her death has persisted and given rise to all sorts of stories. One rumor said that Earhart and Noonan did not perish at sea; they were captured by the Japanese, held prisoners and later executed. Another said that Amelia Earhart is alive and well and living today in America under another name.

"We've heard all the stories all these years and consider them ridiculous," insisted Muriel Morrissey, 95, Earhart's sister. "Amelia went down in the ocean near Holland Island."

Morrissey, retired and living in Medford, Mass., received her master's degree from Harvard and taught high school English in Massachusetts. Though never a pilot herself, she often flew with her sister. They were the only children of Ed Earhart, a railroad lawyer, and Amy Otis Earhart. Their grandfather, Alfred G. Otis, was an Atchison judge.

Morrissey wrote a biography of her sister, *Courage Is the Price*, published in 1963. For years she was a frequent lecturer about her sister before women's clubs. She has been guest of honor at numerous events pertaining to her sister over the years in Atchison.

From 1928 until her death, Amelia Earhart took great pride in her membership in Zonta International, a service club for executive women founded in 1919. Headquartered in Chicago, Zonta today has 36,000 members in 1,100 chapters in 68 countries. *Zonta,* a Sioux Indian word, means honest and trustworthy.

Each year since 1938, Zonta has granted $6,000 Amelia Earhart Graduate Fellowships in aviation (now aerospace), science and engineering to deserving women.

Since the inception of the program, 509 students from 48 nations have received $3.5 million in grants. Janice Voss Ford, an astronaut in the space shuttle mission of February, 1995, was a recipient of an Amelia Earhart Fellowship.

It was Zonta and the Jaycees of North Hollywood, Calif., that placed the Ernest Shelton statue of Amelia Earhart at the front of the North Hollywood Library.

On July 2, 1987, the 50th anniversary of Amelia Earhart's disappearance, Ninety-Nines throughout the world took to the air in hundreds of small airplanes. Each pilot broadcast an identical message on the same line of frequency during the hour they remained aloft:

"The search for Amelia's dream for excellence in aviation continues. Amelia Earhart is the legend of aviation. Her name still rings bells. The magic is still there."

THIRTY-SIX

NEBRASKA
Homesteading and Sodbusters

WHEN YOU'RE TALKING about the early days in Nebraska, you're talking about homesteading and sod houses. A greater percentage of land in Nebraska was given free to homesteaders by the federal government than in any other state. A total of 22,253,314 acres of land was granted to 104,260 Nebraskans by the Homestead Act.

"I am in favor of cutting the wild lands into parcels," Abraham Lincoln said as he signed the Homestead Act into law May 20, 1862, "so that every poor man may have a home."

The act became effective Jan. 1, 1863.

It provided that any citizen—or anyone who declared his intentions of becoming a citizen—could file claim to 160 acres of unappropriated government land and, after cultivating it for five years, receive title to it.

The Homestead Act had a profound impact on the Great Plains. It played a key role in the winning of the West. Nothing of its magnitude ever occurred before or since in any country on earth.

Five miles west of Beatrice, Neb., the Homestead National Monument of America occupies the first 160 acres granted by the act. The monument was established by Congress and President Franklin D. Roosevelt in 1936 to honor the memory of all American homesteaders.

Daniel Freeman, an itinerant doctor who administered medical aid from a medicine wagon, was the first homesteader under the act. In his writings he explained how he became the first of nearly 1.7 million persons to homestead 270 million acres of land during the century the act was in existence.

"I was at Brownville, Neb., as a Union soldier sent there to do some secret service work," Freeman wrote. "The town was the seat of the government land office in Nebraska. Fate seemed against me. I was ordered to St. Louis and had to leave early Jan. 1, 1863, the day the Homestead Act went into effect."

New Year's Day, of course, was a holiday. Land offices would not open until the next day.

But Freeman sought out the registrar of the Brownville Land Office. He found him at a dance and prevailed upon the man to let him file his claim immediately after midnight. Freeman then left promptly for St. Louis by horseback.

His claim encompassed 160 acres on Cub Creek west of Beatrice, present-day location of Homestead National Monument.

Galusha Grow, author of the Homestead Act and speaker of the U.S. House of Representatives, years later noted two interesting instances connected with the final passage of the bill: "First, it took effect on the day of Lincoln's Emancipation Proclamation. Second, the first settler under the homestead bill, which provided free land for free men, was named Freeman."

Thousands of Civil War veterans headed to the Great Plains and the Far West to take advantage of free land. Thousands of immigrants came from Europe. Thousands fled the sweatshops and factories in Eastern cities to settle and work their own 160 acres. Thousands of blacks started new lives as homesteaders.

Virtually no land was homesteaded east of the Mississippi.

Homestead National Monument is one of the least known and least visited of the parks and monuments administered by the National Park Service.

"That's mainly because Homestead is not on or near a transcontinental highway," explained Vince Halvorson, grandson of a North Dakota homesteader and superintendent of the national monument for most of the 1970s, "and because most Americans nowadays know little or nothing about the Homestead Act."

In exhibits at the monument's visitors center, the history of the Homestead Act and its importance in the development of America and the winning of the West is explained in great detail.

The one-room school Freeman attended and a homesteader's 1867 log cabin are located on the monument grounds. Some 100 acres of the original homestead grant are planted in tall prairie grass to show what the land looked like when Freeman first acquired it.

The national monument celebrates Homestead Days the third weekend of June each year with demonstrations of 19th-Century skills such as blacksmithing, spinning and weaving.

"Each year about 30,000 people visit the monument," noted monument superintendent Constantine Dillon. "Many are descendants of homesteaders; a few are descendants of Daniel Freeman.

"As far as I know, this is the only park commemorating a law. People often ask if it's still possible to homestead land in America. I tell them that homesteading hasn't been possible since the 1960s in the Lower 48, but that the federal government gave up 10% of federal land to homesteaders when the act was in effect."

Dillon's goal is to have the monument become the national repository for all government records on homesteading. The records are currently stored in the national archives, which lack easy access.

The graves of Daniel Freeman and his wife Agnes rest on a hill overlooking the national monument.

Born in Preble County, Ohio, April 25, 1826, the strong-willed, bearded Freeman was a graduate of the Cincinnati School of Electric Medicine. He served as a Pinkerton detective for six years before joining the Army.

He divorced his first wife after she deserted him and disappeared with their four children.

Two years after filing his claim for the 160 acres, at the age of 39, he took a new wife, Agnes Suiter, 22, daughter of a Mississippi riverboat pilot. They moved to the Nebraska homestead where their eight children were born.

He farmed the 160 acres and augmented his income with money made from operating his medicine wagon.

He served as justice of the peace at Beatrice and later as sheriff of Nebraska's Gage County.

Freeman continued to live on his homestead until his death at the age of 82 in 1908. His widow lived in a primitive cabin on the land until her death at the age of 88 in 1931.

A few weeks after Freeman's death, a bill was introduced in Congress to set aside the original homestead as a national park. But no action was taken until 1936 when legislation was again introduced and this time passed, with President Franklin D. Roosevelt signing the bill that created Homestead National Monument.

Thousands of Nebraska homesteaders lived in sod houses, worshipped in sod churches, attended sod schools and worked in sod structures.

The Sod House Society began in 1956 with 300 members. To be a member one had to have lived in a sod house, worshipped in a sod church, taught or attended a sod school or worked in a sod building.

In 1995, only a handful of the original members—men and women in their 80s and 90s—met the original requirements for membership. Most of the society members were descendants of those who lived in sod houses. The rules for membership had changed.

Sod buildings were constructed of three- to four-inch thick slices of raw prairie held together with grass roots. Nebraska had thousands of sod houses built by the homesteaders in the 1800s and early 1900s.

There are still sod houses scattered throughout Nebraska, some intact, some in ruins, some framed or stuccoed over.

"We're the surviving generation of sodbusters," said Faye Stevens, 80, president of the Sod House Society since 1976. "Nebraska was a rockless, treeless prairie settled by homesteaders following the Civil War. The only material available to construct homes was the soil and grass."

Stevens, who lives in Holdrege, explained that the Sod House Society meets twice a year, in June and October. "We sit around and talk about what life was like living in the soddies, sharing cramped quarters with bugs, occasional snakes and a lot of dirt."

In Gothenburg in central Nebraska, Linda and Merle Block have operated the Sod House Museum since 1988. It features a typical 12-foot by 20-foot sod house filled with period furniture including a rope bed, corn-husk mattress, crude table, benches and an old stove.

Merle, 58, and Linda, 57, are fifth-generation Nebraskans, descendants of immigrants from Sweden and Germany. Their great-grandparents, grandparents and parents lived in sod houses.

The Blocks also operate a Pony Express and barn museum. "We added the sod house in honor of our parents, grandparents and all the Nebraska homesteaders," Linda said.

In 1973, Vesper Einspahr, 63, and her brother Gustave, 72, were living in an 1881 sod house on a 160-acre homestead in the tiny German community of Holstein.

"There are wonderful memories in these old sod walls," Miss Einspahr said. "Seven of us kids were born here. The soddy is cool in the summer, warm in the winter. We heat it in winter with a blazing fire of corncobs in our pot-gut stove."

To keep the soddy's clay floor clean they sprinkled it with water, then swept it.

Miss Einspahr's lifestyle wasn't much different from that of her mother or grandmother before her.

She still baked all her own bread, "10 loaves at a shot." She made her own soap and milked her cows by hand. She and her brother had a barnyard full of chickens. They kept their perishables in a "cave"—a hole in the ground.

The late Dr. Glen Auble, who was born in a sod house and served as president of the Sod House Society, contributed to the organization's four-volume journals called *Sod House Memories—Treasuries of Soddy Stories*.

"Those hardy pioneers hand dug their own wells," he wrote. "Their only source of food was wild fruits, wildlife, chickens, cows and gardens. The only remedies for the sick were hot water, salt, turpentine, mustard, goose grease and skunk oil."

The journals are filled with turn-of-the-century photographs, true stories of soddy living by Sod House Society members, sod house songs and poems such as one from Della Harrison of Norfolk, Neb. It begins:

> *Humble little old sod shanty,*
> *Yet it was like a shrine to me,*
> *Better than the great mansions,*
> *For it was home, you see.*

THIRTY-SEVEN

SOUTH DAKOTA

Shrine to Music

IN 1984, THE UNIVERSITY OF SOUTH DAKOTA's Shrine to Music Museum & Center for Study of the History of Musical Instruments paid $3 million for 75 violins, cellos, lutes and guitars. It was the largest sum ever paid for a collection of antique musical instruments.

It came as no surprise to anyone interested in the history of musical instruments. It was something to be expected from America's smallest state university.

For years the world's leading instrument makers and music scholars have been beating a path to Vermillion, S.D., a tiny Midwestern town on the Great Plains. They come to visit the Shrine to Music, solely dedicated to the documentation of music history and musical instruments.

When the historic purchase was announced, *The Strad*, the prestigious London-based music journal founded in 1890, reported:

"The Shrine to Music has acquired the world's finest assemblage of Baroque violins in original condition, as well as some of the earliest and best-preserved historically important musical instruments."

An anonymous Southern California alumnus of the University of South Dakota put up the money. The $3-million group of early Italian stringed instruments, known as the Witten–Rawlins Collection, includes 5 of 16 instruments constructed by Andrea Amati, the 16th-Century master whose violin patterns became the world standard.

And so here in this windswept settlement, a town of 10,000 (half of them students), is what is reputedly the world's greatest collection of antique musical instruments. It's housed in a square neoclassic building at the University of South Dakota.

It is the only museum in the United States, and one of the few in the world, dedicated to the history of musical instruments.

The University of South Dakota boasts the only music department in the country offering a master's degree in the history of musical instruments. Though the department is too small for a doctoral program, Ph.D. candidates come here from other schools do their research.

Joseph Johnson of Titusville, Pa., was at the university preparing his thesis on mandolin orchestras of the 1880s through 1920.

"There were hundreds of mandolin orchestras all over America," he said. "It was a vogue, like rock 'n' roll. But by the end of World War I, most of the mandolin orchestras were disbanding. They could no longer compete with jazz."

In addition to musical instruments, the Shrine to Music has an excellent music library.

"Here you do more than just read about the history of musical instruments," Johnson said. "You see the original old instruments. You touch them. The instruments here, more than 6,000 from all over the world, go back to the 1500s."

To demonstrate his point, Johnson went to a display case and picked up one of two surviving guitars made by Antonio Stradivari. The other is in the Ashmolean Museum at Oxford University.

The guitar was made by Stradivari in Cremona, Italy, in 1680. It appears almost new. It has the five double strings typical of the 17th Century rather than the six single strings found on modern guitars. The museum paid $165,000 for the instrument. Many scholars claim it is the finest guitar ever constructed.

Also part of the collection is one of the few Stradivari violins in existence with an original neck. The instrument was made in 1693 and cost the Shrine to Music $550,000.

The museum acquires its musical treasures through gifts, bequests and purchases.

How did tiny University of South Dakota become the repository for such an outstanding musical treasure chest?

It happened because of a small-town high school teacher's obsession with musical instruments.

"My father was a pack rat," said the teacher's son, Andre Larson, professor of music and director of the museum. "I grew up in a house that had little room because musical instruments were cluttered floor to ceiling. Dad's collection really took off in 1920 when Congress passed a bill establishing A440 as this country's official pitch."

Until that time, all musical instruments in America had a pitch of A466, higher than the pitch in other nations.

Andre Larson's father, Arne B. Larson, was 81 in 1986 and music professor emeritus at the University of South Dakota. During a visit to the Shrine of Music that year, he reminisced about his early days of collecting.

"When American military bands went overseas in World War I, they were unable to play with British and French bands," he said. "It was the difference in pitch in their instruments. It was a horrible racket when they played together.

"But then the pitch was changed. All the American musical instrument factories had to gear up. Times were booming for the instruments factories—for me, too."

People either gave Arne Larson their instruments or sold them to him for a pittance. He especially searched out instruments that had been in families for several generations.

At the end of World War I, Larson recalled, many Britons suffering hard economic times sold family heirlooms, including musical instruments, for very little money.

He collected instruments from Europe, Asia, Africa, South America and the islands of the Pacific. In 1966 he came to the University of South Dakota as a music professor, bringing his collection of more than 2,500 musical instruments with him.

What instrument was first in the collection? He reached into a display case and brought out an ocarina that his Norwegian grandfather played as a soldier in the Civil War. Larson played "Ich Hat Ein Hut," or "I Have a

Hat," an old German folk song, on the blue terra-cotta wind instrument with finger holes and an elongated ovoid shape.

Arne Larson grew up on a Minnesota farm, in a family with its own orchestra. "I played everything. I still do." He lifted a long African kudu horn to his mouth and played a tune.

"People down through the centuries have been most ingenious when it comes to making music," he said with a twinkle in his eye.

In 1972, Andre Larson joined his father on the faculty of the University of South Dakota, also as a music professor.

"We wanted to do something special with dad's collection and decided to use it as a nucleus for the establishment of a major museum," the son explained. Arne Larson donated his instruments; and on July 1, 1973, the Shrine to Music became a reality with Andre Larson as the founder-director.

In 1979, Arne Larson sold his Minnesota farmhouse and the 160 acres his grandfather had purchased a century earlier. He donated the money from the sale to the museum for future acquisitions.

"My grandfather bought the farm in 1870 for $3 an acre," he said. "It took him 40 years to pay it off, and we sold it for $364,000."

Arne Larson died at the age of 83 in 1988.

In the late 1980s nearly a million dollars was spent renovating the museum. New galleries and exhibit areas were constructed.

Then in May of 1995, two additional galleries opened, making eight in all. One of the new galleries chronicles the American music industry as it grew from humble 19th-Century beginnings to the large musical instrument factories of the mid-20th Century. The other new exhibit highlights musical innovations of the Industrial Revolution.

Acquisitions in 1995 included four of Adolphe Sax's personal saxophones. Sax, who lived from 1814 to 1894, was a French maker of musical instruments and the inventor of the saxophone. He also made wind and brass instruments as well as pianos, harps and guitars.

"South Dakota is a rural state with about 700,000 people," noted Andre Larson. "We do not have the corporate base or proliferation of foundations larger states have. So for support we depend upon the 700 members of the Shrine to Music Foundation, from interested parties throughout the world and from our alumni."

The museum is filled with gifts. Fireman George V. Hendricks of Etna, a tiny hamlet in northern California, donated his collection of a dozen select bass instruments, including a fine double-bell euphonium and a four-valve sousaphone in B-flat.

A family in Tipp City, Ohio, sent a 1799 tenoroon (tenor bassoon) made by William Milhouse in London. Their great-grandfather, William Wardell, a tailor who lived from 1815 to 1874, brought the tenoroon with him from England to New York in 1855.

Concerts are performed throughout the year at the museum, with artists from the United States and many parts of the world playing the rare instruments.

In 1995, for example, two of the world's great young harpsichordists, Ursula Duetschler and Menno van Delft of the Netherlands, gave a concert on a 1785 French harpsichord built by Jacques Germain of Paris and a copy of that rare instrument.

The collections include Native American instruments of North and South America; instruments played by Civil War bands; instruments used by folk musicians of northern Europe, central and eastern Europe and the Mediterranean countries; Austrian, Bohemian, Dutch, English, Flemish, French, German, Polish and Swiss instruments from the 16th, 17th and 18th centuries, and exotic instruments from the great civilizations of Asia, Africa and the Pacific Islands.

"Many people phone or write us about old instruments they find in attics and old trunks, hoping to learn that they are of value," Andre Larson said. "Hardly a week goes by that we don't get letters or phone calls about a Stradivari from people believing they have found a fortune.

"At the turn of the century, thousands of reproductions were made. Sears Roebuck sold them through the catalogs. The violin the caller or letter writer believes might be worth $500,000 or more is probably worth about $5. They are so excited about the find. I hate to knock the wind out of their dreams of a new-found fortune."

THIRTY-EIGHT

NORTH DAKOTA

Cruel, Cold, Blustery Winters

A COUPLE DOZEN FARMERS took shelter in the small cafe in downtown Starkweather, N.D. They played cards as the wind howled outside, blowing snow like a blizzard. The temperature was 15 below zero; with the wind chill, minus 45.

"Warm day," allowed the operator of the local grain elevator, Hank Schaack. "Last week it was 38 below; with the wind chill, 74. Sometimes it gets so cold in Starkweather it turns your eyeballs."

Half the farmers were playing a card game called Smear, the other half played Buck Euchre, as was their custom nearly every winter afternoon at Kathleen Besse's K-B Cafe. Besse, 83, had owned and operated the eatery since 1931.

"One good thing about a day like this—the mosquitoes aren't biting," farmer Dave Anders said with a laugh as the cafe owner made her rounds refilling the card players' cups with hot coffee.

It was March, and the end of winter in North Dakota was nowhere in sight. March is traditionally North Dakota's worst time of the year for blizzards. North Dakota has blizzards in April, sometimes in May and June.

Cruel, cold, blustery winters are a way of life in North Dakota, the heart of the great central prairie where there are no mountains to break the fast-moving Arctic storms coming out of Canada. The storms blow in so fast, locals call them Alberta Clippers.

Residents of the sparsely populated state brave some of the coldest day-in, day-out temperatures recorded in America, as well as some of the fiercest storms.

No wonder North Dakota had fewer people in 1990—638,800—than it did in 1920—646,872.

It is so cold in North Dakota that undertakers place the dead in unheated concrete holding buildings at local cemeteries to await the spring thaw for burial. The ground in winter freezes four to six feet deep.

High school athletic teams in Starkweather, population 210, are called Storm Kings and Storm Queens.

In Jack Case's "Etc." column on the front page of the *Bismark Tribune*, his parting words were:

"What's black and blue and bloody and crawls on its hands and knees in the gutter?

"The next S.O.B. who asks if it's cold enough for me."

In Bismark, the state's capital, upwards of 500 hikers show up every day as early as 6 a.m. to get their exercise in the warmth of the Kirkwood Mall. Shops open at 10 a.m., but the front door of the mall opens four hours earlier to accommodate the "wall walkers."

"They call us wall walkers because we walk through the corridors along the shop walls where distances are marked from one point to another," explained Wendelin Doll, 66, who walks eight miles a day inside the warm building.

"Walking outside in this cold weather is unthinkable. People of all ages and descriptions get their exercise in the mall every day no matter how bad the weather outside."

At Grafton, one of the coldest spots in the state, four mailmen are "out in it" every weekday, no matter how unthinkable the weather. They each walk about 12 miles a day. The postmen are Dennis Lykken and Jim Byzewski, both with 18 years on the job; Bob Mlcoch, with 21 years, and Gene Pribula, with 27 years.

They claim to have the coldest foot-mail route in the nation.

"It's not an easy life, let me tell you," Lykken said with a sigh. "People say they get used to North Dakota cold. The four of us have been out in it for years, and we will never get used to it.

"We freeze our faces several times each year. It happens on a day when maybe the temperature is zero or as high as 10 above and there's no wind and we forget our protective face masks and a sudden Arctic storm blows in. Freezing your face is like getting a bad sunburn. The skin blisters and peels off."

Each Grafton mailman wears long johns, three pairs of trousers, a heavy shirt, two sweaters, a parka with a hood, boots and gloves. The snow and ice never melt all winter in most places in North Dakota.

"The post office shows us films every year," Lykken said, "about how to fall on ice, what to do when you're going down. Trouble is, we don't have the time to think about the right way to fall when we slip on the ice."

At Pembina, population 700, the coldest weather station in the state, weatherman George Motl, who also runs the local water plant, noted that the lowest temperature in town was below zero every day from Dec. 16 to Feb. 20 that particular winter, and the highest temperature was below freezing during the same period.

Daily lows in Pembina from the 1st to the 18th of February were all below zero: -30, -30, -31, -32, -30, -32, -28, -19, -28, -30, -38, -15, -14, -18, -8, -15, -9 and -5. The coldest temperature during the period, accounting for wind chill, was minus 90.

On Feb. 21, the town had its first break in nearly two months when it warmed up to a low of 10 above and a high of 33. A couple of days later, however, the temperature again plummeted to below zero as the state was raked by blizzards.

North Dakota is wide-open spaces, mile after mile of grain farms and a sprinkling of tiny towns, each with a grain elevator. The wind seldom lets up.

Snow blows from one end of the state to the other almost incessantly. The countryside is desolate, empty and cold in winter with lonely farmhouses, barns and granaries dotting the prairie.

Emil Langowski, an employee of the Walsh County Road Department, spends his winters shoveling ice off railroad tracks crossing county roads. "If a train derails," the Minto resident said, "and the railroad can show that it was the county's fault for not clearing the ice where a track crosses a road, they can have us for damages."

At Nash Elementary School in Nash, population 40, the 23 first through eighth graders may go outside for recess if it isn't any colder than 10 below and the wind is quiet. The school's four kindergartners do not have outside recess in winter.

Kindergarten teacher Linda Johnston recalled leaving Nash one day to drive 10 miles to Grafton with her 2-year-old and 5-year-old. All of a sudden a storm blew in.

"I could not see the front of my car," she said. "I could not see to turn the car around and go back. I backed up my car the two miles to the Nash school. It took me nearly an hour. I was terrified.

"What especially terrified me is that we are told to get out of the car and check the tailpipe to be sure it isn't plugged up, as that could cause carbon monoxide poisoning. No way could I get out of the car in that storm. I was lucky I didn't back into anybody."

"It's life-threatening stuff," said attorney Gary Thune of Grand Forks. "If your automobile stalls, ice forms on the whole inside of the car. It's like a freezer. If you're out in the country and you leave your car to find a farm, with the wind blowing the snow around—blinding your way—you may well freeze to death."

People freeze to death every year while stranded in storms on lonely North Dakota roads.

At Hector Field, the Fargo airport, there's a huge billboard with giant letters: CALIFORNIA, ARIZONA, FLORIDA. The sign shows the front end of a Northwest Airlines jet and people in swimsuits under sunny skies at the beach. There are no other words on the sign. They're not necessary.

Hundreds of grain farms across the state are locked up and abandoned for the winter while the farmers escape to warmer weather until spring thaw. Not all farmers are so lucky. Many tough out the winters, especially those with livestock like Sharon Blumhagen and her husband Jerome at Harvey, population 2,527.

In summer, Jerome grows grain on his 1,700 acres. In winter, he struggles to keep his animals fed, milked and in good health. Sharon milks the family's 30 cows at sunup and at sundown. She feeds the cows each evening with the help of her 12-year-old daughter Traci and spreads hay in the cows' stalls to bed the animals down.

Jerome cleans the animals and the barn. He takes the cows out in the cold to give them exercise. "But I can't leave them out too long," he said.

His 85 head of beef cattle remain outdoors, but he must watch them closely and feed them daily. He brings newborn calves into the barn to prevent them from freezing. Every winter he loses a couple of animals from the weather.

Why does he do it?

"I enjoy farming," he explained. "I enjoy the land, the open spaces. I love this country up here and our way of life. People are honest in North Dakota. We don't have to lock our doors. We feel safe. It is the only life I know.

"In winter, sure, it's a struggle. A struggle to save the cattle, to keep them going so I'll have something to sell later in the year to pay the bills."

Then there are the people like Clara Krahler, 95, in Fessenden, population 761, who never misses a local high school basketball game in winter, although it means walking three blocks through the snow.

And the people like the ice-fishing folks at Devils Lake, who drill holes with ice augers through four feet of frozen water, bait their hooks, drop their lines and wait at times for hours in the cold before they get a bite.

In Harvey, scraping the ice off the windows of her car as she does every day all winter, Mavis Kanwischer, a grocery store clerk, mused, "Everybody in North Dakota spends all winter dreaming of spring...."

Newspapers run daily listings of activities going on in North Dakota's small cities and tiny towns. Mert Armstrong, executive director of the Mental Health Assn. of North Dakota, explained how important it is that people avoid cabin fever and get out of their houses.

"Those who never leave the house get a lot of depression," she said. "We encourage people to join clubs, to be active."

She mentioned "pity parties," where residents of rural areas get together and air their complaints at social gatherings. "People sit around feeling sorry for themselves no matter what during the long winter," she said. "But this is people feeling sorry for themselves and getting together and hearing out one another's complaints, having a lot of good laughs and feeling much better for it the next day."

Life is difficult, indeed, for those like North Dakota's firefighters, who brave the outdoors as a daily diet. House fires are common in severe winter weather.

"Many people have switched from fuel to wood-burning stoves because of the high energy cost," noted Grand Forks Battalion Chief Clarence Coss, who counts 39 years with the department. "Their chimneys fill up with creosote, which now and then suddenly goes off like a blowtorch.

"Fighting fires is no picnic in -20-, -30- and -40-degree-temperatures on a day when the wind chill is -60, -70 or -80. Hose lines freeze up. When water hits the fire it condenses into steam.

"As soon as water hits the ground it freezes. We slip and slide all over the place. Hoses freeze to the ground. We have a hell of a time finding fire hydrants covered with snow."

Yet Coss said he wouldn't move to a warmer climate on a bet. "I've been to 36 states. I wouldn't trade one of them for North Dakota. That includes California and Florida. Sure, we have tough winters. But we know how to dress for them. We know how to cope with it.

"You live through a North Dakota winter, and spring is like being in heaven. I like the four seasons. Spring, summer and fall in this country can't be beat. And, you know, it feels so good in winter to be inside out of the terrible cold."

THIRTY-NINE

MONTANA

Charlie Russell, America's Cowboy Artist

*There ain't but one spot on Earth that I want to see, and that's
my Montana home. I want to stay here as long as I live....*
—CHARLIE RUSSELL

NO STATE IS IDENTIFIED with an artist as much as Montana is with
Charlie Russell.

Known as America's premier cowboy artist, Russell lived from
1864 to 1926, capturing on canvas the colorful life of the Big Sky State's
early days. He chronicled the buffalo in the wild, the Indians, cowboys,
early settlers, the open range and the spirit of the West.

Charlie Russell Country, the official designation given the north-central
sixth of Montana—the nation's fourth largest state in area—includes the
artist's hometown of Great Falls and Helena, the capital.

Also bearing his name is the Charles M. Russell National Wildlife Refuge,

120 square miles of scenic wilderness that embraces the Missouri River and Fort Peck Lake in northeastern Montana. High schools and elementary schools are named after him. So is a mountain.

An annual statewide contest for Montana schoolchildren invites them to write an essay, "Why I Like Charlie Russell." The winning composition is read in Great Falls at the widely acclaimed C.M. Russell Art Auction each March, Charlie Russell Month in Montana.

Every schoolchild in Montana knows all about Charlie Russell, along with everyone else who calls Montana home.

Each state honors two of its most famous citizens in Statuary Hall in the nation's Capitol. Montana's statues are tributes to Russell, the only artist so honored, and Jeannette Rankin, the first woman elected to Congress.

A square block of Great Falls, population 60,000, honors the memory of the cowpuncher turned artist, sculptor, poet, author and storyteller. The block includes his home, built in 1900, his 1903 log studio next door and the C.M. Russell Museum, one of the nation's leading centers of Western art.

Charlie Russell's wife Nancy, who died in 1940, donated the studio and sold the house to the city. Josephine Trigg, a Great Falls city librarian who was a neighbor of the Russells, willed her property and collection of 175 Charlie Russell originals to perpetuate his memory and art.

In 1953 the people of Great Falls raised $79,000 to establish a gallery of Russell's works with the Trigg collection as its nucleus. A $500,000, 15,000-square-foot wing was added in 1969. The museum gained an additional 26,000 square feet in 1985 at a cost of $3 million.

Today the museum contains the best overall collection in existence of Charlie Russell paintings, sculptures, illustrated letters, postcards and memorabilia.

Russell, who was born in St. Louis, left home for Montana at the age of 15. He lived in a trapper's log shack the first year, cowpunching in the Judith Basin east of Great Falls. He was a night herdsman who lived and rode with the Indians.

And he sketched.

He sketched almost everything in sight. In the beginning he got $5 for his drawings or paintings and figured he was lucky.

"I am an illustrator," he wrote later. "There are lots better ones, but some worse. Any man that makes a living doing what he likes is lucky and I am that. Anytime I cash in now, I win."

Russell died a wealthy man and counted many famous individuals in his circle of friends. President Theodore Roosevelt bought one of Russell's bronze sculptures. Humorist Will Rogers was a buddy, as were actors William S. Hart and Douglas Fairbanks, Sr., and oil magnate E.L. Doheny.

During Russell's lifetime, his paintings, watercolors and bronze pieces were featured in exhibits in Los Angeles, Chicago, New York and London. He wrote and illustrated books under his own name and the name of Rawhide Rawlins. He illustrated books by other well-known Western writers and stories for the *Saturday Evening Post*.

In 1911, the state commissioned him to paint the 12-by-25-foot mural that hangs above the speaker's platform in Montana's House of Representatives.

The mural, *Lewis and Clark Meeting the Flathead Indians at Ross' Hole*, is considered Russell's masterpiece.

"We often speculate about the value of that mural, Charlie Russell's largest painting," said Ed Smith, chief clerk at the House of Representatives. "Charlie was paid $4,600. It took him six months. It's got to be worth at least $5 million to $10 million now."

Indians on horseback dominate the painting. Lewis and Clark are insignificant figures. It was Russell's way of reminding the viewer that Lewis and Clark were intruders on land that belonged to the Indians.

When the Land Belonged to God, showing wild buffalo on a bluff overlooking the Missouri River, was painted for the 110-year-old Montana Club in Helena and completed in 1914. Russell received $3,000 for the painting. The club sold it to the state in 1977 for $450,000. The painting hangs in the Russell Gallery of the Montana Historical Society across from the Capitol.

Today, 70 years after Russell's death, his oils sell for $100,000 to $1.5 million; his watercolors, $45,000 to $500,000; letters to friends, $7,000 to $60,000; one-of-a-kind illustrated postcards, $5,000 to $10,000, and bronze pieces, $3,500 to over $100,000.

The Montana Historical Society in Helena has major Charlie Russell works in its collection, as does the Amon Carter Museum and the Sid Richardson Collection in Fort Worth, Tex.; the Cowboy Hall of Fame in Oklahoma City and the Thomas Gilcrease Institute in Tulsa, Okla.; the Buffalo Bill Historical Society in Cody, Wyo.; the Rockwell Museum in Corning, N.Y., and the Norton Foundation in Shreveport, La.

Altogether, about 4,500 Russell originals are on exhibit and in private collections, although there is no complete record of everything he did.

In 1995 the C.M. Russell Museum began work on a catalog listing every known piece of art Charlie Russell ever did and the history behind each work.

"We expect it will take at least 10 years to complete and will not be published for another 12 years," explained Elizabeth Dear, curator of the museum. "We have an enormous amount of work ahead of us. We have to do a lot of research on every single piece he ever did."

The curator and Lorne Render, director of the museum, are on a committee for the project that includes advisors and scholars from outside the museum.

"We know there is Russell art out there we are unaware of," Dear continued. "There are other pieces we know of but have no idea where they are. We hope to hear from everyone who can enlighten us. We know there are letters we don't know about. Early on he painted on everything he could find—shirt collars, shirt boxes, ends of tobacco kegs, satin robes—and he gave them all away. We want a record of everything."

Jerry Goroski, former assistant director of the museum, said he was never surprised when something new of Charlie Russell's came to the museum's attention. "Charlie did his artwork on tablecloths, tent canvas, wood, metal, tin and glass. The buffalo skull was his emblem. It went along with his signature on everything he did."

Charlie Russell's log studio looks the same as the day the 62-year-old artist died of a heart attack, Oct. 24, 1926. In 1994, over $250,000 was spent on a major restoration.

"Nearly all the artworks and memorabilia in the 24-by-36-foot studio were conserved and put back where they originally were according to old photographs," Dear said, "including the props he used for his paintings: guns, saddles, boots, Indian feather capes, a cradle board and a travois."

Prior to the restoration, his easel held an unfinished painting. "But it had started to warp," Dear said. "It looked pretty bad and needed conservation work, so we put a copy of one of Russell's works on the easel. A grizzly-bear skin hanging from a wall was removed because it was in shreds, but the elk's head is still there."

For years guides in the studio, Russell's home and the museum were often people who knew the artist when they were children. They would reminisce about their relationship.

Art Jacques, a Great Falls ham radio operator and Charlie Russell's neighbor, was one of the guides. He was 10 years old when the artist died. "A bunch of us kids would walk down his alley to and from school," Jacques recalled.

"We would stop and look at his saddle horse, Neenah, tied to a tree behind his studio. We'd peek in the studio and watch him paint. We never bothered him; he never bothered us.

"My dad was a streetcar motorman in town. Charlie would ride the streetcar downtown almost every day to visit his cronies. He would sit up in Dad's motorman seat, his arms dangling out the window, waving and shouting to people he knew. He liked to do that."

John Kegler of Palos Verdes Estates, Calif., remembered Charlie Russell from six summers spent at Lake McDonald in Glacier National Park. Kegler's father ran a string of saddle horses at the lake.

"Charlie loved horses," Kegler said. "He would stop by to visit with Dad. He painted in Bull Head Lodge, his summer cabin on the lake. I would watch him paint in his studio. He was a wonderful guy as far as this little boy was concerned."

For years Joan Stauffer of Tulsa traveled throughout America presenting a performance called *Behind Every Man: The Story of Nancy Russell*. Director emeritus of the board of the Thomas Gilcrease Museum Assn., Stauffer thoroughly researched Charlie Russell's wife, who she said "guided her gregarious, unambitious husband along the road to artistic and commercial success."

Raphael Cristy crisscrosses the United States doing dramatic interpretations of the artist's life. Cristy, a Stanford graduate who at one time operated a bookstore in Palo Alto, Calif., relocated his family to Montana in order to be close to source material about Russell. Cristy later worked on his Ph.D. at the University of New Mexico. His dissertation subject: Charlie Russell, of course.

In Paradise Valley, Ariz., Fred Renner and his wife Ginger, leading authorities and authors of books about the artist, dedicated their lives to the pursuit of information about Russell. Renner knew America's premier cowboy artist as a young man.

When Charlie Russell died, every store in Great Falls closed for his funeral. He hated automobiles. As a concession to his wish that his body not be carried off in a gas-engine hearse, a horse-drawn hearse bore his coffin from his home to the church and cemetery. The hearse was acquired by the museum in 1994 and is now on permanent exhibit.

Elizabeth Dear, the C.M. Russell Museum curator, believes that as time goes on Charlie Russell is becoming more and more popular. "Young people in their 20s and 30s have taken to him in recent years," she said. "People interested in cowboy culture and anyone who knows anything about Western art knows Charlie Russell. Western artists idolize him.

"We have a very strong collection of Russell's Indian paintings. He depicted

Indians with so much dignity and respect. Indians from all over the country come to see his work, his home, his studio. Many have a great affection for Charlie Russell."

In August, 1944, a group of Great Plains Indians held a three-day encampment on the grounds of the C.M. Russell Museum, erecting and staying in a teepee village to show their appreciation for the artist. They repeated the encampment in August, 1995, and said they planned to make it an annual event.

Charlie Russell is revered not only by Americans but internationally as well. Every year hundreds of people who admire this man, his paintings, his sculptures and his writing travel to Montana from Germany, France, England, Spain, Scandinavia, Australia and Japan.

They come to Great Falls to visit Charlie Russell's hometown and to see his studio and the great museum that honors him.

FORTY

WYOMING

America's Lonesome Cowboy State

PERSPIRATION POURED from the young cowboy as he kept the 450- to 500-pound yearling heifers separated in the long chute. The chute led to the squeeze, where the animals were being spayed.

He wore a black dirt-splattered hat, chaps, spurs. His face was burnt bright red from the scorching sun. His lips and teeth were smeared with chewing tobacco. He was one of the cowpunchers on the Nevada Palace Ranch in Wyoming.

"It's spring, time of no sleep," the 21-year-old cowboy muttered. "We're underpaid, overworked. Haven't been to town in two months. I can't wait to get to Casper to chase the girls...."

He allowed as how a person has to have one heck of a sense of humor to be a cowboy, then quickly added, "I wouldn't trade this life for any other on a bet."

All of Wyoming is range land. From Cheyenne to Cody. From Sundance to Rock Springs. It's one of the last vestiges of the Old West, wide-open country where antelope roam freely—best grassland on God's green earth, as the cowboys say.

Wyoming is cattle, 1.4 million head. Wyoming is sheep, more than 850,000 of the woolly critters. It's the smallest of the 50 states in population. Only 453,588 people lived in the state when the 1990 census was taken.

Jim Geringer, a Republican, was governor in the mid-1990s. He's a rancher. More than half the governors in the state's history have been cowboys.

Wyoming *is* the cowboy state.

Its license plate since the 1930s has been a cowboy on a bucking horse.

Cowboy ballads are about all you hear on Wyoming radio stations—stations like KTWO, KSHY, KSIT AND KWYO—songs like "City Girl and Country Boy," "I'm a Lonesome Cowboy," "I Don't Need a Four Leaf Clover" and "Black Days and Blue Nights."

It's a state where everybody wears boots. Where beef and lamb are the main dishes. Where people turn up their noses at the mention of chicken and fish. No poultry farms here.

The Nevada Palace Ranch was one of seven ranches spilling over 200,000 acres owned and operated by Webb Stoddard and his sons Bob, Paul and J.R. They ran 5,000 head of cattle and 600 sheep.

Like ranchers throughout the nation, the Stoddards were having a rough time making ends meet because of agricultural economics. Beef consumption had declined and Wyoming land prices plummeted.

Webb Stoddard had recently lost a finger when a horse threw him into a barbed wire fence. "Man takes his life in his own hands out here," the rancher said with a laugh.

Stoddard was standing by the squeeze where a heifer was being spayed by "Doc" Rich Johnson. When Stoddard released the squeeze, the heifer did not budge. "Get 'em, Rooster," Stoddard shouted to his Australian cattle dog. The dog darted over and nipped the yearling on a leg. The heifer bolted from the squeeze.

Rooster ran around the squeeze and guided the heifer toward the others huddled in the corral. The dog ran on three legs. One leg was crippled from a steer falling on it.

"People don't know what a rough life ranching is," Stoddard said. "They think it's all peaches and cream and glamour. They think all ranchers are wealthy. I can assure you that isn't true. We're barely surviving in today's tight economic crunch.

"It's up before dawn and working into the late hours of the night, skimping here and there to keep this outfit going."

Webb Stoddard wouldn't have done it any other way. A lifelong cowboy, Stoddard loved ranching. He loved Wyoming. He died in 1993 at age 82.

Wyoming is America's lonesome state.

Mile after mile of open spaces. Highways and byways with hardly a car. Ranches 30, 40, 50 miles from the nearest town—and the nearest towns aren't much: a handful of people, a few stores, a couple of bars. They're towns with names like Bill, Buffalo, Chugwater, Horse Creek, Jay Em, Kaycee, Lightning Flat, Lost Cabin, Medicine Bow, Moose, Pitchfork, Spotted Horse and Ten Sleep.

Lost Springs claims to be the smallest incorporated town in the nation—population 4. Incorporated in 1911, it has never gone out of business.

Leda Price, who owns the local bar, has been mayor 20 years. Her bar doesn't keep regular hours. In fact it's seldom open.

Lost Springs' other three residents all serve on the town council: Clara Stringham, the postmaster who also runs the Lost Springs General Store; Clara's husband Bob, a retired cowboy, and Edith Dorset, the mayor's mother.

Council meetings are held once a month in the Lost Springs Town Hall.

"Lost Springs is like any other town," Stringham said. "The council has to meet and take care of town business. We keep on top of everything that needs to be done around here."

What's crime like in Lost Springs?

"We have never had crime in Lost Springs," Stringham said. "Crime is something that doesn't happen in our little town. I guess you could call us lucky."

A large sign in the Lost Springs General Store proclaims: "Just Because Everything Is Different Doesn't Mean Anything Has Changed."

The general store has a few shelves of groceries, fan belts and other auto parts, cough medicine and aspirins, a refrigerator with soft drinks, some candy. It has a vacuum cleaner in a corner for sale.

"I bought eight vacuum cleaners 12 years ago," Stringham said. "I thought some of the ranchers around here might need them." Two years went by before she finally sold her first vacuum cleaner. Now, after 12 years, it looks like it shouldn't be too long before she finally gets rid of her last vacuum cleaner.

Such is life in America's smallest incorporated town.

To give another example of how lonesome it is in Wyoming: A few years ago Bob Cardwell and his wife wrote the Carbon County School District in Rawlins from their ranch in the Shirley Mountains requesting that the board consider establishing a school for their daughter Brenda.

"They lived in an extremely isolated area reached by a rutted, rough road 60 miles from the nearest school," explained Robert Randall, superintendent of the school district. "It's a ranch completely cut off from the outside world each winter. No way could that child get out to go to school, so we brought the school to the child."

Cardwell Elementary School was a one-student, one-teacher school in Wyoming's outback. It was the smallest school in Wyoming, maybe in America.

The Cardwells provided the school district with a three-bedroom home for the teacher, Anita Kaessenger. One of the bedrooms was converted into the schoolhouse with a desk for the teacher, a desk for Brenda and a chalkboard. Brenda was 6 years old and a first grader at the time.

Buck Holmes' 8,000-acre registered purebred bull ranch is on Little Bear Creek down the road from the town of Chugwater. Holmes, a rugged 6-foot, 200-pound cowboy, lost a leg when his horse threw him against a gatepost when he was 17.

"It kept me out of Vietnam," he mused over a bull steak dinner with his wife Eva Jeanne and daughters Britt and Heather. "Maybe if I'd been in Vietnam, I'd have had my head blown off."

Three Holmes families operate Holmes Herefords, the families of Keith Holmes, his son Buck and son-in-law Dick Drake. They run 200 head of highly sought after breeder bulls. Buck has a degree in animal science from the University of Wyoming.

"Sure, we miss out on some things being so far out in the country," Buck Holmes admitted, "but it's a good life."

His wife Eva Jeanne, who teaches a business course at "L Triple C" (that's what everybody calls Laramie County Community College), said they could not imagine living anywhere else. "It is so peaceful and quiet out here. The fresh air. The deer and the antelope. So good for the girls to grow up in the country."

Ranchers from as far away as Iowa, Nebraska, Colorado and Utah come to the Holmes Ranch each summer for the family's bull auction. They come to buy bulls that will upgrade their herds. The Holmes women spend two weeks preparing lunch for those attending the auction and dinner for those who buy the bulls.

Ranch women are kept busy as homemakers, getting the children ready for school and often transporting them several miles over four-wheel-drive roads every morning and night, to and from a school bus. They cook for cowboys during calving and branding time, vaccinate animals, care for newborn, young and sick livestock and join their husbands on horseback during long cattle drives.

Nearly all Wyoming ranch women are members of the American National CattleWomen, an organization of 11,000 women in 38 states. The CattleWomen up until recently were known as the Cowbelles, but the organization changed its name. With headquarters in Denver, the group promotes beef consumption, publishes cookbooks with favorite beef recipes and lobbies for legislation benefiting ranchers on both state and national levels.

When it's springtime in the Rockies, Wyoming is alive with newborn lambs and calves. As far as you can see, from one end of the state to the other, from the endless grasslands to the high mountain pastures, there are bands of ewes with lambs, herds of cows with calves.

Creeks bubble over with runoff from melting snow. Wild flowers are everywhere. The music in the air is a delightful dissonance of baas and moos.

Novels about the Old West relate countless stories about wars between sheepmen and cattlemen, especially during the late 1800s. There are many recorded instances of animosity and bloodshed between the two groups.

On Green River in the 1880s, masked cowboys tied up sheepherders and clubbed 8,000 sheep to death. Cattlemen at the time mapped out a 55-mile-long, 28-mile-wide stretch—a million acres of public land—and ordered sheepmen to stay out.

Now the majority of Wyoming ranchers run both sheep and cattle. John Etchepare, his brother Paul, Jr., and their father run 5,000 cattle and 25,000 sheep on 200,000 acres north of Cheyenne.

"In the old days it was cattlemen against cattlemen," John Etchepare said, "sheepmen against sheepmen and cattlemen fighting sheepmen, all scrambling for range land. It just happened that sheepmen versus cowboys got played up more than the others.

"We Wyoming ranchers do so much better utilizing our forage with a diversified operation—sheep and cattle. One market may be up; the other may be down."

Etchepare's grandfather, a Basque, came from France in the late 1800s as a sheepherder. He was paid in sheep instead of money. When his numbers of sheep were big enough, he started an outfit of his own. Land was free; first come, first serve.

Grayce Miller's 25,000-acre ranch is headquartered at Crazy Woman Creek. "Incidentally, the creek was not named after me, although many swear it was," the lifelong rancher said with a smile.

In the blizzard of April, 1984, Miller lost 2,500 ewes and lambs, animals that froze to death or were smothered with snow. Wyoming lost over 250,000 sheep in that blizzard. Miller also lost 300 head of cattle in the storm.

"My father always told me to run horses for pleasure, cattle for prestige and sheep to pay the bills," she said. "I go right along with that theory."

In 1993, the Nature Conservancy acquired the 120-year-old, 35,000-acre Red Canyon Ranch south of Lander. Fifth-generation Wyoming rancher Robert W. (Bob) Budd was hired to manage the ranch, to show that economic use of resources and the enhancement of biological diversity are compatible.

"It's my job to demonstrate that it's possible to retain rare plants and wildlife while ranching," he said, "and that ranches are more user friendly to the ecology than subdivisions."

Budd, whose family began ranching in Big Piney, Wyo., in 1878, was executive director of the Wyoming Stock Growers Assn. for 10 years before heading up the Nature Conservancy's ranch with 1,000 head of crossbred Angus.

At the Nevada Palace Ranch, when one of Bob Stoddard's daughters married a cowboy, Stoddard remarked: "I'm glad she wants to stay on the ranch. It's a better way of life. Our family has been ranching Wyoming four generations. We've got to keep these longtime family operations going. If we don't, big corporations will take over and phase out the Wyoming way of life, and Wyoming will never be the same again."

FORTY-ONE

COLORADO

The Loftiest State

WITH MORE THAN 1,000 MOUNTAINS over 10,000 feet in elevation, Colorado is America's highest state.

Waitresses at the Summit House atop 14,110-foot Pikes Peak, the nation's highest restaurant, are ever alert for "pale faces," as they call those about to faint.

"Almost every day we get one or more customers who pass out as we take their orders or deliver their food," Jill Knudson said. "They can't take the high altitude."

What do you do when that happens?

"You remain calm," she replied. "Only thing you can do. We have oxygen and smelling salts ready. Hopefully, you catch them before they hit the floor."

Colorado, the state with America's greatest concentration of towering peaks, is one of only four states with mountains soaring above 14,000 feet.

No wonder Colorado's license plate shows a series of snow-crowned Rocky Mountain peaks.

Colorado has 54 peaks higher than 14,000 feet. Alaska has 19. California has 12—including Mt. Whitney, at 14,494 feet, the highest in the contiguous 48. Washington has 3.

Seventeen of Alaska's highest peaks are higher than Mt. Whitney. Alaska's Mt. McKinley, at 20,320 feet, is the highest in North America.

Pikes Peak, Colorado's 31st highest mountain, is the highest place in the United States where people live and work on a continuous basis several months of the year.

In summer, 30 men and women, two dozen of them college students, work at the restaurant and gift shop atop Pikes Peak.

"Everybody who works here gets sick the first night they spend on top of the mountain," said Bill Carle, owner of the Summit House. "Dizziness, headaches, nausea. They toss and turn, unable to sleep. It's like being on a ship on a rough sea the first night out. It takes three or four days to get adjusted to this altitude."

He ought to know. When we met him he had spent six to seven months on top of Pikes Peak for 36 years. Before Carle took over, his wife's parents had owned and operated the restaurant and gift shop since 1916.

People who meet the Pikes-Peak-or-bust challenge generally spend, at most, an hour or two in the thin air. To reach the top they drive 20 miles on a narrow, winding road—half paved, half dirt—or ride the 8.9-mile Pikes Peak Cog Railway.

They take in the incredible view, maybe have a bite to eat or at least a cup of coffee, perhaps buy a "We Made It! Pikes Peak" bumper sticker or other souvenir, experience shortness of breath—the weird, woozy lightheaded feeling—and then leave.

Even Carle has problems with thin air. "I'm beginning to puff a little now that I'm getting older," he said. Instead of sleeping on top of Pikes Peak, to be more comfortable he drives down to the Glen Cove Inn, run by his wife at 11,425 feet.

Yet Carle's mother-in-law, Grace Wilson, was active running the place and living on top of Pikes Peak until she was 87.

Valerie Voyles, manager of the mountaintop establishment, has been coming up in the middle of April and staying until mid-November for 18 years.

"I feel better up here," she said. "I think living at this altitude improves your health and life expectancy. You've heard about people living to be 120,

130 and 140 in the Himalayas and high mountains in South America?

"It's the pure air up here on top of Pikes Peak. You have to breathe slow and deep. I walk a lot. I love it. It's like being on top of the world. In the mornings when it's socked in, it looks like you could walk to Kansas on the clouds below. And Kansas is 150 miles from here."

She told of the magnificent night sky, with a moon you can almost reach out and touch, the dazzling lights of Denver below and looking down the backbone of the Continental Divide from Wyoming to New Mexico.

Voyles said that when she vacations, she likes to travel to high mountain country in Scandinavia and Europe. She avoids lower elevations.

No carbonated soft drinks are sold on Pikes Peak. Carbonated beverage cans explode at the high elevation. No alcoholic beverages are sold either. Flatlanders can't handle alcohol at that elevation.

"Everything about cooking is different up here too," said Leona Reinert, a Pikes Peak cook during summer. Reinert works in a ravioli factory the rest of the year in her hometown of LaPorte, Ind. "It takes two hours to boil water up here. Oh, it boils before that, but doesn't get hot enough. It takes twice as long to bake a cake. It takes half an hour to get a soft-boiled egg."

Bryan Staddon, engineer on the Pikes Peak Cog Railway, talked about the lightning storms.

"Lots of lightning on top," he said, "especially summer afternoons. Static electricity is everywhere in the air. You can smell it. You can feel it. Your hair stands on end. Static is all around you. It stings your ears."

Staddon's train has carried passengers to the top of the mountain since 1890.

Temperatures are generally in the 40s and 50s on summer days. It freezes nearly every night. A snowstorm may happen any day of the year.

Wellesley College English professor Katharine Lee Bates visited Pikes Peak in 1893. She was so inspired by what she saw, she sat down and wrote the words to this nation's national hymn, "America the Beautiful."

The highest road in America isn't the one up Pikes Peak; it's the 27-mile, narrow paved road from Idaho Springs to the top of Mt. Evans, with an elevation of 14,264 feet.

The road winds its way around the shoulders of Colorado's 14th highest peak without a protection rail. It hangs precariously over steep cliffs that drop off several hundred feet.

A small University of Denver high altitude research lab on the peak is used by scientists from time to time during the summer.

Denver scoutmaster Al Vitil and three Boy Scouts, Scott Unruh, 11, Doug Rothenburger, 14, and Mark Thompson, 12, were hiking up Mt. Evans. They hiked six miles up and six miles down to earn the Boy Scout Fourteener Patch, given to Colorado scouts for climbing any one of the state's 54 peaks over 14,000 feet high.

One of the most spectacular scenic drives in America is the 48 miles through Rocky Mountain National Park on Trail Ridge Drive. The drive skirts 62 snow-shrouded peaks, all higher than 12,000 feet. A third of the park is above the tree line.

Eight miles of the road lie above 11,000 feet, three miles above 12,000 feet. The highest point, Iceberg Lake, is 12,183 feet above sea level. Trail Ridge Drive is said to be the highest continuous road in the United States.

In the park near the ghost town Lulu City, a pip-squeak of a stream forms the headwaters of the mighty Colorado River. Headwaters of the Rio Grande and Arkansas rivers are also in the Rocky Mountains of Colorado.

Leadville, with an elevation of 10,188, claims to be the highest incorporated town in America.

Because of the town's high elevation, Leadville High School's athletic teams have ranked among the top school teams in the state and nation for years.

Coach Frank Mencin's boys' track team won 13 of 18 state championships. His girls' team won five championships in a row to tie a national championship.

"Anywhere we run is lower by thousands and thousands of feet than Leadville," Mencin explained. "Our kids produce more red blood cells, carry more oxygen. They train running trails up to 13,000 feet, six days a week."

Leadville High football coaches plant "Welcome to Leadville, Elevation 10,138 Feet" signs on the edge of the football field to psyche out visiting teams. The visitors take oxygen during the games to keep them going.

At Leadville's St. Vincent's Hospital, nurses and doctors call summer "the heart-attack season," as each year several visitors unaccustomed to the high altitude have heart attacks.

Mine tailings are piled high above Leadville, one of the richest silver camps in the nation a century ago. Many famous characters of the Old West called Leadville home—Unsinkable Molly Brown, Leadville Johnny, Broken Nose Scotty and Soapy Smith.

It was here that Horace Tabor made a fortune and lost it. On his deathbed he told his wife, Baby Doe, to hang on to the Matchless Mine as it would make millions. She hung on for 36 years in poverty. She was found frozen to death in an old miner's shack in 1935.

This is the town that constructed the gigantic Leadville Ice Palace, a 450-foot-long, 320-foot-wide, 60-foot-high castle made of 5-foot-thick blocks of ice.

Inside were a huge ice rink, a hall of ice statuary, exhibit booths and special rooms. The Ice Palace, said to be the largest ice structure ever constructed, was open to the public from Jan. 1 to March 28, 1896.

It began to melt March 15, and on March 28 it was closed for safety reasons.

Colorado has many towns 8,000 feet and higher. These include Breckenridge, with an elevation of 9,534 feet; Buena Vista, 8,094; Central City, 8,516; Creede, 8,854; Crested Butte, 8,867; Cripple Creek, 9,591; Georgetown, 8,489; Silverton, 9,032, and Telluride, 8,744.

Among the peaks more than 14,000 feet high are many with intriguing names, like 14,150-foot Mt. Sneffels, its name taken from Jules Verne's *Journey to the Center of the Earth.*

People make pilgrimages to 14,005-foot Mount of the Holy Cross, where a giant cross forms in the snow each year. In 1951, a U.S. postage stamp honoring Colorado's 75th anniversary as a state featured the cross on the mountain.

There are the Collegiate peaks: Mt. Harvard, at an elevation of 14,420 feet; Mt. Oxford, 14,153; Mt. Columbia, 14,073; Mt. Yale, 14,196, and Mt. Princeton, 14,197.

Mt. Bierstadt, 14,060 feet, is named after the famed landscape artist Albert Bierstadt. Peaks are named after botanists Asa Gray, 14,170 feet, and John Torrey, 14,267. Quandary Peak, 14,265 feet, was so named because miners were in a quandary about a mineral found on it.

There's Mt. Lincoln, 14,286 feet, named in honor of the President. There's Mt. Sherman, 14,036 feet, named after Gen. William Tecumseh Sherman. There's Mt. Democrat, 14,148 feet. There is no Mt. Republican.

Named after Indian chiefs are Mt. Antero, 14,269 feet, and Mt. Shavano, 14,229. A 14,165-foot peak is named after Kit Carson. El Diente, 14,159 feet, is Spanish for "The Tooth." Culebra Peak, 14,047, takes its name from the Spanish word for snake.

Scientists have discovered that plants and animals in Colorado's higher elevations live longer than their counterparts in lower areas. At the 9,896-foot-high town of Fairplay, a monument pays tribute to Prunes, a burro who packed supplies to miners for more than 60 years.

The University of Colorado's High Mountain Research Station, 25 miles west of the Boulder campus and 5 miles north of the hamlet of Nederland, is the oldest and largest year-round high altitude research center in America. The station, at 9,500 feet, was founded in 1914.

Alpine textbooks have been written entirely from studies conducted at the station. Scientists call the surrounding mountains the best-known piece of alpine real estate in the world for research.

"Scientists use the station as their base," explained Pat Webber, UC Boulder professor of environmental biology. "The log cabins you see clustered around the lab buildings are used for housing. They were constructed by the professors themselves in the early days."

From here the researchers go out into the field to the tundra country above the tree line in four-wheel vehicles and snowmobiles. They conduct studies in environmental sciences, biology, geography, geology and all the various disciplines pertaining to alpine research.

Botanist Oren Pollak was the first person to study the longevity of the American bistort, a plant producing dazzling white puffball flowers. Working out of the UC High Mountain Research Station, he discovered that the plant's caudex, or underground woody stem, bears a scar for each leaf of its existence. Bistorts grow an average of four leaves a year. This provides a dating record similar to tree rings.

The American bistorts Pollak found growing on 11,300-foot Niwot Ridge live twice as long as the plants do in the meadows of the 9,500-foot research station.

"I could not believe what I was seeing," he said. He lay flat on his stomach, his nose up to a plant on the slopes of the windswept ridge. "Something was wrong, I thought. None of these plants were dying as the other plants were."

Pollak dated one of the bistorts on Niwot Ridge at 74 years old.

To survive through the fierce winters, American bistorts in the high elevations of the Colorado Rockies produce special salts and proteins–their own form of antifreeze—to prevent them from freezing.

Another scientist, Rick Brown from the University of California at Davis, was working on Niwot Ridge as well. He was weighing a round-eared cousin of the rabbit, a pika. The four-to-five-inch-long mammal is one of the very few animals found at this elevation in Colorado.

Pikas dwell in large rock piles above the tree line on the steep slopes of Niwot Ridge, five miles east of the Continental Divide. One always knows when pikas are close by from the serenade of their delightful squeaks.

Like the American bistorts, Niwot Ridge's pikas are long-lived. They live about 12 years, twice the average life span of their cousins at lower elevations.

Pikas are active year-round and do not hibernate like other small mammals. They spend the summer harvesting flowers, grasses and other plants and stashing them in hay piles in rocks for winter food supplies.

"It's like working on top of the world," Brown said, looking out over miles of towering snow-covered mountains. "Incredible view, isn't it?

"We get lightning strikes almost every afternoon up here. Lightning bounces all over the place. Scares the hell out of me. Scares everybody with any sense."

Niwot Ridge is one of the windiest places on the planet, with wind velocity recorded in excess of 150 m.p.h. The wind velocity is outdone only by that on Fujiyama in Japan and Mt. Washington in New Hampshire.

To get to Niwot Ridge, scientists drive two miles from the mountain research station to where snow fields stop their progress. Then it's a mile-and-a-half walk the rest of the way. The thin, high country air has only 70% of the oxygen found at sea level.

"It's amazing anything survives in this high alpine tundra," said Mark Noble, year-round resident field director of the research station. "This environment is truly as tough and resilient as any other system on the planet."

Grand Lake, elevation 8,153 feet, has been boasting since 1902 that it is the location of the world's highest yacht club.

Ted James, defensive end on the University of Nebraska's 1952-53 football team and commodore of Grand Lake's yacht club in 1980-81, insisted that Grand Lake's was the world's highest yacht club, as did all 300 members. James, who lost his sight late in life, believed he was the only blind person ever to be commodore of a yacht club.

But at Dillon, another town in the high country with a lake at an altitude of 9,017 feet, another yacht club claims to be the highest on earth. Members wear jackets embossed "World's Highest Yacht Club."

"They're a good bunch of people at Grand Lake," said attorney Vern Corporon, commodore of the Dillon Yacht Club.

"They were the highest yacht club for so many years. When we formed in 1968, they just didn't have the heart to admit someone else finally topped them. They still won't admit it."

FORTY-TWO

NEW MEXICO

Land of the Pueblos

OCHITI PUEBLO'S LANGUAGE TEACHER Ray Trujillo pointed to the drawings of animals and insects on his classroom walls. The adobe schoolhouse is perched on the crest of a spectacular mesa 42 miles north of Albuquerque, N.M.

As he came to each object, the sixth graders chanted the proper Ko-'chits word: dog, *tiya;* butterfly, *puraka;* pig, *pirs-kuchi;* roadrunner, *shash-ku.*

Trujillo tested the youngsters with words spelled out phonetically on flash cards. The students repeated the words and gave English translations. They went through the colors: *ku-chini* means yellow, and so forth. Then they went through the words for family members. Girls and women in the pueblo have different ways of expressing kinship than boys and men.

Sa-mii-mii, for example, is "brother" when spoken by a female; *sa-ti-um-sha* is "brother" when spoken by a male. *Sa-ta-uu* is a female's word for grandmother; *so-muu-muu* is a male's word for grandmother.

Ko-'chits is the Cochiti dialect of the Keresan language of the Pueblo Indians. Each of New Mexico's 19 Pueblo tribes speaks a different language—Keresan, Tiwi, Tewa, Towa and Zuni—or a unique dialect of one of the languages. The languages and dialects are not written. They have been passed down orally, generation to generation, for untold centuries.

In Cochiti Pueblo, population 920, there has been a tendency among children and parents of the present generations to speak only English and to ignore the ancient language of their ancestors. The same is true in several other pueblos.

"If the language goes, our rich culture goes," Trujillo told his sixth graders. "Everything will be lost if we lose our language. You have a big responsibility.

"Nobody else on this earth speaks our language. We are the only ones who know it, and there are only a handful of us. That is why it is very important you learn it; otherwise it will die."

Trujillo, a Cochiti Pueblo Indian himself, was teaching all 107 kindergarten through sixth-grade students their native tongue each day in seven hour-long classroom sessions. He received his degree in elementary education from the University of New Mexico.

The program was in its third year at Cochiti Elementary School, a Bureau of Indian Affairs schoolhouse on the lonely mesa. The program operated at the request of the pueblo's governor, village elders and religious leaders.

Throughout the language lesson, the students paid close attention to their teacher. Each responded quickly and correctly during the exercise.

"Now I am beginning to understand my grandparents when they are talking Indian," 11-year-old David Garcia said. "I have heard these words all my life. But I never knew what many of them meant before learning from Mr. Trujillo."

Trisha Moquino, 10, added: "It is easy to learn because the language is deep down inside me."

These are exciting and significant times for northern New Mexico's 50,000 Pueblo Indians. They live on 19 small reservations to the north, south and west of Santa Fe and Albuquerque. The largest group is the Zuni, with 8,300 people; the smallest is the Zia, with 690 resident tribal members.

Each tribe, no matter how small, has its own government headed by a religious leader, called a *cacique*, and a governor. Each tribe has its own unique history, traditions, ceremonies and arts and crafts.

The *cacique* is protector of the pueblo's sacred and secret rites and artifacts and is held in great esteem by the tribe. He is responsible for the well-being and perpetuation of his people. He is trained for years as an understudy to previous *caciques* and holds the position as long as he lives.

Abraham Lincoln has been dead for more than 130 years, yet his name is still law for the 50,000 New Mexico Pueblo Indians.

When the pueblos' governors sign important papers for the tribe, they declare: "By the authority of President Abraham Lincoln, I do hereby affix my name to this document...."

Lincoln's name is invoked daily as the authority for rulings governing the 19 New Mexican Indian tribes.

The symbol of every Indian governor's authority is an ebony cane with a silver head inscribed "A. Lincoln, President [the name of the tribe appears], 1863."

Lincoln presented the canes to the governors of each of the Pueblo tribes in a ceremony at the White House.

A visitor to a pueblo seeking the village leader is often instructed to "go to the house of the Lincoln cane," where the governor lives.

Four of the pueblos elect their governor through a popular vote by members of the tribe. In the 15 other pueblos, the governor is appointed by the *cacique*.

The governors wear many hats—chief administrator, judge, chief of police. The governor heads the tribal council.

"It is hard work being governor," said Raymond Herrera, the longtime governor of Cochiti Pueblo. "I have to settle disputes, do all the tribal business. Sometimes there is a fight in the middle of the night and I am awakened to calm the fighters down."

He receives no monetary compensation for his position, "just the honor and respect," he said.

The Lincoln cane is used in secret ceremonials and carried by the governors on special occasions and during fiesta parades.

Some years back, a Lincoln cane was misplaced in one of the pueblos, rendering the governor powerless.

There was a great deal of uneasiness in the village. A massive search was launched. In the interim, the federal government gave the pueblo a substitute cane, but the people would not recognize it. Nor would they recognize the governor.

Fortunately, the cane was found several weeks later and tranquillity was restored.

"In recent years there has been a very positive, renewed attitude, a rekindling of the spirit as to who we are and where we are going," said Frank Tenorio, governor of San Felipe Pueblo. His pueblo, population 2,400, lies on the west bank of the fast-flowing Rio Grande in the shadows of towering Black Mesa.

The Indians of San Felipe live in adobe homes built in the 17th, 18th and 19th centuries. The homes line narrow, winding, dusty, dirt streets. Many families have a horse or two in a backyard corral. They grow crops for their own use on family plots outside the village.

Men of the pueblo work as skilled tradesmen in Albuquerque and Santa Fe—as carpenters, cement finishers, roofers, plumbers, boilermakers. Some San Felipe men and women hold college degrees and work as engineers, nurses and teachers.

Men, women and children often augment the family income by making turquoise and *heishi,* or shell-bead, jewelry. The women of San Felipe are known for their embroidery and weaving.

Pueblo Indians on all 19 reservations live in traditional adobe homes in the old villages or in modern, albeit modest, homes on village perimeters. New housing is not permitted in the village proper, although in some pueblos—like Acoma—in recent years several badly deteriorating ancient mud houses have been razed and replaced with replicas.

Each of the pueblos is renowned for a particular type of art or craft, such as the three-dimensional corn-dance figures of Santa Clara Pueblo—especially those by Michael Naranjo, an artist blinded in the Vietnam War.

Individual styles of pottery among the pueblos include the famous black-on-black pots created by the late Maria Martinez at San Ildefonso Pueblo, a tradition carried on by her family. Distinct styles of jewelry include the widely heralded inlaid work of the Zunis. The artisans of Cochiti Pueblo are particularly known for their clay storyteller figurines and drums.

"Our people are feeling better about themselves than at any time that I can remember in the past," Tenorio mused. "We have a purpose in life. We have a renewed interest and pride in our heritage, and we are doing everything necessary to preserve and perpetuate that heritage. This wasn't true a few years ago. We are a blend of the old and the new."

He said that as governor of San Felipe Pueblo he is determined to make certain young people are bilingual, fluent in English and in the language of the tribe.

"With more of our young people sticking it out in school, he said, "our future looks a lot brighter. I am optimistic for my people."

New arts and crafts centers have been constructed in the pueblos as outlets for talented village artists and craftsmen. Many pueblos have erected stores, gas stations and other businesses along highways on the outer edges of reservation land for their own use and the use of non-Indians.

Merle L. Garcia, governor of Acoma, stressed the importance of Acoma Indians fending for themselves, becoming self-reliant. "We are trying to find ways to survive instead of being dependent on the government," he said.

Acoma, population 4,350, consists of three villages at an elevation of 7,000 feet. The villages rest at the base of a towering sandstone mesa that rises 367 feet from the mountain it crowns. On top of the mesa rests 70-acre Sky City.

Dating back to at least AD 900, Sky City is said to be the oldest continuously inhabited village in America. By tradition, homes in Sky City have no electricity or running water.

Taos, the northern pueblo with a population of 2,200, is another highly traditional village and perhaps the best known of the 19 pueblos. Taos Indians, living in centuries-old, four- and five-story adobe structures at the base of the Sangre de Cristo ("Blood of Christ") Mountains, also choose to forego electricity and running water.

When the Spaniards arrived in New Mexico in the 16th Century, they were amazed at the development and sophistication of the Indians. The Spaniards' word *pueblos,* or "villages," referred to the Indian's permanent settlements with well-organized religious systems and local governments. The lifestyle was highly distinct from other Southwest Indians, who were mostly nomadic.

The Pueblo Indians clustered around the Rio Grande and other ample water sources. They were farmers with excellent irrigation systems.

When the Spanish sought to impose their culture, the Pueblo tribes staged the most successful revolt in North American history. They drove the Spaniards out of the area in 1680.

But the Spaniards returned a dozen years later, and the Indians eventually adopted aspects of the Spanish way—governors and lieutenant governors to administer the civil activities of the pueblos and the Catholic faith. At the same time they maintained their traditional religious leaders and practices. They kept the *kiva* (the building where religious ceremonies are held), the *cacique* and their war chiefs.

The traditions of the past are just as alive today in the villages as they were centuries ago. There are age-old dances for planting crops, for rain, for snow in winter, for thanksgiving.

Pueblo Indians have always been great runners. Foot races are as popular in every village as they were in prehistoric times, when runners provided the communication between the 19 tribes who joined together in common defense against marauding Apaches and other Indians.

In the backyard of nearly every pueblo home there is a beehive adobe oven for baking bread. The bread is baked by burning branches and heating lava rock foundations, then raking out the coals and putting in the dough. Women and young girls are up at daybreak in all the pueblos, baking bread in the ovens.

It is early morning in Isleta Pueblo, population 3,000. Muffled voices echo through the dusty dirt streets. The crisp, daybreak air is alive with the delightful aroma of baking bread.

The centuries-old ritual is taking place in Isleta, which is known in the Isleta Indians' native Tiwa tongue as the village of *kleo-ron-tieba-who-pan*, the "women who bake bread."

Nowhere else is Pueblo Indian bread produced and sold on the scale it is in Isleta, where bread is the mainstay of the economy.

Every day at least 50 backyard ovens, or *hornos*—and as many as 200 on weekends and holidays—fire up. The women sell their fresh bread door to door in Belen, Bosque, Los Lunas and Albuquerque. They sell it by the road, from the kitchens of their adobe houses and from stands in the village plaza in the shadows of Mission San Agustin de Isleta, erected in 1630.

Each woman bakes one or two batches of 25 loaves. The bread sells for $1.25 to $2 a loaf.

The bread makers start a fire of cottonwood branches about 6 a.m. on the oven's lava-rock floor. The fire burns for about an hour, then the coals are swept out.

Next the tins containing the loaves of bread are placed inside the oven with a long paddle. In less than an hour the bread is done. The steamy, hot bread is retrieved with the paddle and placed in a wicker basket.

Each loaf of bread has a different design. "We learn the secrets of making bread as little girls from our mothers, grandmothers and aunts," explained Lou Abeita, 60, on a warm summer day in 1995.

"It is an honor," she said, "to be a bread maker. Each person has a different way, a slightly different touch. One good thing is that the young women today are continuing this time-honored tradition."

New Mexico's state flag shows four rays bursting in each direction from the sun. It is the ancient, sacred sun symbol of the Zia Pueblo Indians. Each of the four bars represents the four seasons, the four directions, the four periods of each day, the four divisions in life and the four sacred obligations: strong body, clear mind, pure spirit and devotion to the well-being of mankind.

The Zias call themselves the "Come-Back" Indians. Scientists in the late 1800s predicted the tribe would soon vanish from the face of the earth.

In the 17th Century there were 6,000 Zias. By 1890 there were only 89 Zias left, survivors of the "white men's" diseases that decimated their numbers. By 1995 there were 690 Zias.

They live on 117,000 acres of land 40 miles northwest of Albuquerque. They farm and run cattle. They make pottery. Zias have long been known as potters.

The main village of Zia Pueblo crowns a scenic mesa dotted with adobe homes, narrow dirt streets, a 17th-Century adobe Catholic church and two round *kivas* where ancient Indian ceremonies are performed. They are a proud, modern people steeped in time-honored traditions that date back centuries.

"We have obligations each step of life, as Zias have had for generations." said Peter Pino, a tribal administrator with a master's degree in business administration from the University of New Mexico. "There are all kinds of procedures we follow from birth to death. For example, when a boy reaches the age of 18, he becomes 'a man among men,' a voting member of the Zia Tribal Council."

The Zias live in Sandoval County in the state of New Mexico in the United States. They are governed by the laws of the nation, the state, the county and the laws and traditions of their pueblo.

It is a complex society.

The person held in greatest esteem by the Zias is the *cacique*, the religious leader and protector of the sacred rites and artifacts. He is responsible for the well-being of the people, and the people are responsible for his well-being.

Next in rank among the Zias is the war captain.

"In the old days, he was the commanding officer of our forces, the man responsible for the defense of the tribe," Pino explained.

"Today, he makes sure the inner workings of the tribe are carried out, the traditions, the ceremonies, the dances as prescribed by the *cacique*.

"The war captain has a number of other duties. He is in charge of the reservation lands. He determines how the land is to be used."

The governor of Zia Pueblo represents the tribe in dealings with the outside world and presides over tribal council meetings by the authority of the Abraham Lincoln cane.

"Few non-Indians have the slightest inkling what it takes to make an Indian," Pino said. "Even in a tribe as small as ours there are many clans and societies. We abide strictly by our customs and traditions. We are caught in the middle of two cultures. It is not easy at all times."

At Isleta, Joseph Juancho, head of the pueblo's arts and crafts center, said people ask why Indians, especially those like him who are well educated, live in these old villages in this day and age when everybody else is trying to get ahead, to live in the most modern, up-to-date homes.

"There is something that draws you back or keeps you here," he explained. "We never have had a big exodus from the pueblos, even among young people. We have many Indians with good paying jobs who could live in better homes, but they chose to live here. People on the outside don't understand the depth of our culture.

"The Pueblo villages have a special meaning you don't find in the outside world, a meaning you cannot fully understand unless you are Indian. Being here gives our people peace of mind. The Indian way of life is something money cannot buy."

FORTY-THREE

ARIZONA

Saguaro, Lord of the Desert

S AGUARO NATIONAL MONUMENT in Arizona is an 83,000-acre federal reserve set aside to preserve and protect an enormously appealing species of giant cactus.

Among the largest and tallest plants on earth, the saguaro grows only in southwestern Arizona; northern Sonora, Mexico, and the southeast edge of California. Saguaro National Monument boasts the heaviest concentration of the strange desert giants anywhere in the world.

These fluted, thick green cacti grow as tall as five-story buildings, up to 40 or 50 feet high. Many live to be 200 years old and weigh as much as 10 tons.

When cartoonists do humorous sketches of the desert, saguaros almost always appear. Charles Schulz, from time to time, will show one of Snoopy's relatives in sandy surroundings hanging a hat on a saguaro.

Reg Manning, Arizona's "Cactus Cartoonist," was a Pulitzer Prize-winning political cartoonist for the *Phoenix Arizona Republic* from 1926 through the 1980s. His signature at the bottom of his cartoons was automatically followed by a smiling, stubby cactus.

Manning did more to introduce the public to the saguaro than any other writer or artist. His book *What Kinda Cactus Izzat?*, first published in 1941, is into its 35th printing with nearly 400,000 copies sold.

Sprinkled with humorous illustrations of cacti and other desert flora, *What Kinda Cactus Izzat?* is a who's who of strange plants in the Southwestern American desert. Manning's favorite cartoon subject was the saguaro. He showed it doing everything from waving to passing motorists to hitchhiking and dancing.

"Because of Manning, Schulz and other cartoonists, many believe wherever you have a desert, saguaros are sure to be found," said Richard Hayes, a ranger-naturalist at Saguaro National Monument. "But that isn't true. Saguaros only grow in the Sonora Desert.

"Not everybody knows or can pronounce the name [sa-waur-o]. But nearly everyone can relate to the shape, thanks to the cartoonists."

Arms start growing only when the plant reaches a height of 20 feet, about the time it is 75 years old. Botanists believe the arms provide balance for keeping the saguaro upright.

Some arms curve and stick straight up. Others point outward, hang down or have grotesque and twisted shapes. Some saguaros have arms that appear to be waving.

Some saguaros stand side-by-side and embrace one another with arms that may be as long as 15 feet.

Granddaddy Saguaro in Saguaro National Monument has 51 arms. It stands more than 40 feet tall and is estimated to be between 150 and 200 years old. Few visitors see this monster; it takes a hardy soul to hike the 10 miles of desert terrain to reach Granddaddy.

The Tohono O'Odham Indians call the saguaro "lord of the desert." For centuries the Tohono O'Odhams, whose reservation spills over into three Arizona counties and occupies part of Mexico, have had a sacred relationship with the saguaro.

Until 1986, the Tohono O'Odhams were known as the Papago Indians. But *papago* means pinto bean, a name given the Indians because the beans are a favorite food of the tribe. The tribe decided "Bean" Indians was demeaning, so they changed their name to Tohono O'Odham—which means the Desert

People in their language. In 1995 there were 8,697 Tohono O'Odhams.

Saguaro National Monument consists of two segments 35 miles apart, one to the west of Tucson, the other to the east. The Tohono O'Odham reservation abuts the western portion of the monument.

Tohono O'Odhams are the only people permitted to gather the fruit of the saguaro. In late June, July and early August—when the red, chicken egg-sized fruit ripens—Tohono O'Odham families bring firewood and kettles into the national monument.

Following an age-old tradition, they tie together long poles made from dead saguaro stalks and place a hook on top to harvest the fruit, which grows only on the saguaro's crown and arm ends. The giant desert cactus bears fruit for the first time in its 50th year.

The hook frees the fruit and it falls to the ground. The Indians then gather and boil the fruit in kettles, making a preserve. They also crush the more than 2,000 seeds per fruit to make a flour paste.

Saguaro is one of the staples of life for the Tohono O'Odham people. Birds, coyotes, deer, fox and many other animals of the Sonora Desert also look to the seeds and fruit of the giant cactus for nourishment.

The saguaro provides a home for many birds. Gila and gilded flicker woodpeckers drill holes deep into the cactus and nest inside. The woodpeckers clean out a large L-shaped hollow, called an Arizona boot because of its shape.

Nature protects the giant cactus during this house-building process. Sap from the exposed plant tissue dries and forms a hard, thick lining that prevents the plant's moisture from leaking out.

When woodpeckers abandon a saguaro, the residence is taken up by other birds such as elf owls, purple martins, screech owls, sparrows and cactus wrens. It is an air-conditioned home. In the scorching heat of the summer, it is 10 to 15 degrees cooler inside a saguaro.

Saguaros are shallow-rooted, but the root system fans out in all directions as far as 100 feet. The plant slurps up nearly every raindrop before the precipitation has a chance to percolate into the soil.

When there is plenty of moisture, saguaros are fat and full of water. They are the camels of the plant world. They can store enough water to last four years, bloom and bear fruit without another drink. In dry years, saguaros become skinny, shrinking to perhaps half their girth.

The white saguaro blossom, Arizona's state flower, blooms only 10 hours. During this time, it is up to the white-winged dove, the long-nosed bat, bees and butterflies to pollinate the flower.

The worst enemy of the saguaro is freezing temperatures. The youngest and oldest plants perish after 19 hours of temperatures below 25 degrees. Wipe-outs of vast stands of saguaro forest have occurred in particularly cold years.

In summer, when temperatures sizzle on the desert, coyotes, rattlesnakes, Gila monsters, javelinas, geckos, fox, frogs, tortoises, lizards, skinks (a variety of lizard), whiptails and other desert animals stretch out in the shade of the saguaro.

Poaching is a problem in the two segments of Saguaro National Monument, and the park locks its entrance gates at night as a deterrent. In 5 to 10 minutes, a poacher can dig out a 5- or 6-foot-tall saguaro worth as much as $500 to $1,000.

"Poachers pay heavy fines when caught," Ranger Hayes said. "But it is difficult catching them, especially since budget cuts reduced park service patrols."

Saguaro lovers can buy specimens of their own, however, thanks to commercial growers who cultivate small plants for sale. The law requires these greenhouse-grown plants to be labeled accordingly.

FORTY-FOUR

UTAH

The Great Stone Gallery

TO REACH THE GREAT GALLERY, you drive 70 miles over nearly impassable dirt roads. You take a precarious hike down a steep cliff, followed by a five-mile walk along a creek bottom in a narrow canyon flanked by towering walls.

You're in Utah's Canyonlands National Park, one of the most remote and inaccessible regions in the continental United States.

The haunting, elongated, bigger-than-life human figures are etched high on the pink sandstone cliff. They form the mysterious mural known as the Great Gallery, a magical art exhibit left over from the distant past.

Who were the artists? How many centuries have the bug-eyed drawings been starring into space? What message does the giant sandstone billboard convey?

Archeologists theorize that the prehistoric mural may be the work of ancient Indians dating back 1,500, 2,000 or 3,000 years.

"You can read whatever you want into it," observed Gary Cox, a volunteer National Park Service ranger in Horseshoe Canyon, a seldom-visited slice of Canyonlands National Park in southeastern Utah.

Cox was resting after the strenuous hike through the hot summer sun. He sat on a rock at the foot of an eight-foot-high, bug-eyed pictograph he called the Holy Ghost. The figure has a huge head and triangular-shaped body surrounded by seven creatures resembling mummies.

The Great Gallery, a giant mural composed of hundreds of eerie human and animal forms, is a long-to-be-remembered highlight of a visit to Horseshoe Canyon, the Maze, the Island in the Sky, the Needles and the Doll House of Canyonlands National Park.

Located here are what are considered the finest examples of prehistoric rock art in America.

The surrealistic figures on the sandstone cliffs of Horseshoe Canyon are enigmatic and strangely compelling.

There are human figures without arms or legs. Some hold snakes. Some wear what appear to be shields. Others hold spears. There are numerous bighorn sheep, deer, bison, birds.

One huge panel shows figures holding implements like sickles. They're bent over as though harvesting grain.

In one section, 275 six-inch-tall human forms line up side by side. They're in two rows, in marching formation.

Film director Godfrey Reggio was so taken by the mural on the sandstone wall of Horseshoe Canyon, he introduced and ended his 1983 film *Koyaanisqatsi* (a Hopi word for "life out of balance"), with footage of the Great Gallery.

(*Koyaanisqatsi* has no actors, no plot, just 87 minutes of sound and imagery—clouds racing by mountains, Lake Powell, Black Mesa, skyscraper canyons of New York City and people pouring out of subway shafts there, Los Angeles freeway traffic, offices and factories, atomic bomb blasts. The frenzied pace is accompanied by a score by Philip Glass, interspersed throughout with Hopi chants.)

Horseshoe Canyon is a world of mysterious rock art, of kangaroo rats, bats, deer, whiptail lizards and rock wrens that warble a weird song of descending notes.

Gary Cox, the 6-foot-2, red-bearded, red-haired bachelor ranger, gave up Chicago's urban civilization and set out backpacking through the West.

He hiked the High Sierra, the Cascades of Oregon and Washington and several peaks over 14,000 feet in Colorado, then wandered down into

Utah's Canyonlands.

"I liked it so well here, I decided to stay," he said.

"I tried to hire on with the National Park Service, but there were no openings. So, thanks to district Ranger Ed Forner, I'm a $3-a-day volunteer ranger. I'd rather be making $3 a day out here than $30,000 a year in the city."

Cox is provided housing in a trailer at remote Maze Ranger Station. He lives on whole-grain rice, corn, beans, squash and trail mix.

He patrols Horseshoe Canyon in the Maze, a jumble of canyons described as a 30-square-mile puzzle in sandstone. He works 10 days on, 4 days off. His days off are just like his days on. He hikes through the wild country as much as 30 miles a day.

"I'm a walking fool," he admitted. "I provide directions and advice to the few people who find their way to this faraway place. Sometimes I go days without seeing anybody."

He is forever on the lookout for new artwork on the sandstone walls and in hidden caves. He watches for remnants of ancient Indian dwelling sites, for baskets, pottery, arrowheads and other artifacts.

He discovered three never-before-reported series of pictographs. One life-sized drawing looks like two humans shaking hands.

Horseshoe Canyon has both pictographs and petroglyphs. Pictographs are prehistoric paintings of mineral or vegetable pigment on stone. Petrogylphs are images cut, pecked or scratched into the rocks.

"It is generally believed that two prehistoric cultures were responsible for the petroglyphs and pictographs in Canyonlands," Cox explained, "the Anasazi and the Fremont Indians. Both groups mysteriously vanished from this area 800 to 900 years ago. That is the latest dating on the artifacts found here."

The age of the prehistoric art is generally correlated with artifacts found in the immediate area.

Cox said he envisions Indians gathered in Horseshoe Canyon at ceremonial sites and hunting camps. "As I hike alone I feel the presence of the spirits of these departed people. In my mind I see shaman artists painting the figures on the sandstone cliffs...."

"Rock art is the orphan of archeology, ethnology and anthropology," Alex Patterson said. Patterson and his wife Mary, who both belong to the 500-member American Rock Art Research Assn., were visiting the Great Gallery from their home in Greenwich, Conn. At his home studio, Alex was classifying and identifying more than 3,000 photographs of prehistoric drawings for the Museum of American Indians.

"Scientists pretty much ignore rock art," he said. "There is no accurate way of dating the drawings with present technology that we're aware of. Efforts are being made to find a way to date the paint. Lichen and desert varnish [a chemical buildup in the rocks] could also offer clues."

The Pattersons and Cox discussed rock art in general and offered their ideas on the interpretation of the paintings at the Great Gallery. They exchanged views about the weird and mysterious drawings left behind in many parts of the West by ancient Indians.

"Have you seen or heard about the petroglyph in Natural Bridges National Monument that's a dead ringer for a dinosaur?" the ranger asked.

"Now, how do you explain that one?"

FORTY-FIVE

IDAHO
Tending the Flock

"G ABON ON BAT ETA URTE BARI ASI!" everyone shouted in the packed auditorium in Boise, Ida., as Jim Jausoro's band struck up the first tune at the annual Sheepherders Ball.

Five hundred Basques were greeting one another with heartfelt "Merry Christmas and happy New Year" in the ancient language of their forefathers. The language has no linguistic relatives. It's so old and so different from all others that its origins have been lost in antiquity.

Idaho's 20,000 Basques represent the largest concentration of Basques in America as well as the largest in the world outside Spain and France. For Idaho's Basques, the Sheepherders Ball is the biggest social event of the year. It's held each year during Christmas week by Euzkaldun-Etxea, America's largest Basque club.

Band leader Jausoro's first song was a favorite Christmas carol, "Ator Ator

Mutil Etxera." The song is about a mother and father calling their sheepherder son home from America to the Basque country of Spain and France for the Christmas holidays.

Colorful banners from the four Spanish Basque provinces and the three French Basque provinces hung from the ceiling of Boise's big Basque Center, in the shadow of Idaho's capitol. A giant Basque flag, red field with green X and white cross, hung from a wall. A huge map showing the seven Basque provinces—Araba, Benabarra, Bizkatia, Caburdi, Gipuzkoa, Nafarroa and Zuberoa—adorned another wall.

Basques come to the Sheepherders Ball from throughout Idaho, Nevada, Oregon and Utah. A few come from as far away as California and Hawaii.

"Five of us drove over in a van from the Salt Lake area," explained Jim Sangroniz, an engineer from Midvale, Utah, and the son of a sheepherder. "We came for the good time, for the dancing, to see old friends we haven't seen since the last Sheepherders Ball, to get together with other Basque 'cousins' we haven't seen in years. There is nothing like this in Salt Lake City."

Sangroniz and his friends drove 350 miles just to go the ball. They arrived a few hours before the dance. They would leave the next morning to return to Utah.

It was the liveliest, noisiest, happiest, most free-spirited ball imaginable. First the widely acclaimed Boise Basque Oinkari dancers got everybody in the mood. The Oinkari dancers (oinkari refers to people who do something with their feet) have performed throughout America and in the Basque country of France and Spain as well.

For a solid nonstop hour the 90-member, colorfully costumed troop did a series of centuries-old Basque numbers accompanied by rousing cheers, claps, yells, whistles and shouts from the crowd.

"Ori, ori," shouted the dancers and the spectators. Ori, ori means "That's the way to go!"

Dancers spun, kicked, clicked castanets as they leaped high off the ground. The haunting sound of the txistu, the ancient Basque flute, brought somber moments.

Next came the traditional auctioning of a lamb. The same animal was auctioned several times, fetching $3,400 for the Basque club's charities in coming months.

"Proud people, aren't they?" mused auctioneer Dick Davis of Emmett, Ida., one of the few non-Basques at the ball.

After that the sheepherders, ex-sheepherders and descendants of sheepherders danced with as much enthusiasm and exuberance as the Oinkari dancers, leaping, kicking, clapping, throwing their arms into the air to the spirited music.

It was the late Jon Ashabal, who had one of the biggest sheep outfits in the West, who came up with the idea of having a Christmas dance for Basque sheepherders. The year was 1928. The ball has been held every year since.

"When I was 8 years old I went to the first Sheepherders Ball, and I haven't missed but one or two since," said Ramon Ysura, 75. He wore a red *txapella*, or Basque beret.

Ysura, who still works for the county clerk–recorder's office in Boise, was manning a steaming pot at the Sheepherders Ball, selling Basque chorizo sausages wrapped in hot dog rolls for the Basque Center benefit. Chorizo is a traditional snack at the annual dance.

In 1928, Ysura said, "99% of the Basque people in Boise worked with the sheep. The men grazed the animals out on the mountain and foothill ranges. Many of the women ran boardinghouses for the sheepherders when they came to town on occasional visits for a good Basque meal, for a day or two of rest."

Pete Cenarrusa, 77, had been Idaho's secretary of state for 28 years in 1995. The dean of America's secretaries of state was a three-term speaker and 17-year member of the Idaho House of Representatives before that.

In 1907, Cenarrusa's father came to Idaho from Spain's Basque country to be a sheepherder. The secretary of state and his brother still owned and operated a flock of 10,000 sheep in 1995, the 88th continuous year the Cenarrusa family had a sheep outfit in Idaho.

During the early years of the Sheepherders Ball, most of the sheepherders were rounded up and driven into town for the big event, though there were always a few less-fortunates left tending the flocks. The daughters of Basques who came to Idaho beginning in the 1890s would be dance partners for the sheepherders.

"The sheepherders would shower and shave for the dance," Cenarrusa said. "At the ball they would get all the news from the old country and meet other sheepherders working that lonely, isolated existence."

Basques who migrated from Europe in recent years and continue to tend flocks were at the most recent Sheepherders Ball as they always have been in the past.

Felix Otazua, a sheepherder who cares for 2,000 sheep, was the focus of a lot of attention throughout the evening. In a blizzard the previous January he became separated from his sheep and was lost three days without food or water.

"I was hungry, you betcha," Otazua recalled with a big grin. "But I got back to the sheep and my camp."

The common thread of all 20,000 Basques in Idaho and Basque centers throughout the West—in Nevada, California, Oregon and Utah—is sheep and the sheepherder.

Many former sheepherders or descendants of sheepherders at the dance were doctors, lawyers, accountants, teachers, policemen, firemen, businessmen and from various other walks of life.

"All of us Basques in America trace our roots to a sheepherder like my father," said Gloria Totorica, a postgraduate student in political science at Boise State University.

She talked proudly about the giant statue of a sheepherder dedicated in 1989 at Reno, Nev., in San Rafael Park. Basque sculptor Nestor Basterretxea came from Spain to create the 28-foot-high statue of a sheepherder holding a lamb.

Totorica explained that the statue was erected by the Basque community in America as a tribute to the sheepherders and a thank you to America from the Basques who came here to tend the flocks. Totorica's father, Ted Totorica, immigrated to the United States from Spain in 1952.

In July, 1995, Boise, home of the Basque Museum and Cultural Center, hosted the international Basque festival called Jaialdi. Held every five years, it is a gathering of Basques from throughout the world to celebrate the ethnic group's rich heritage.

A special Basque Mass was held in Boise's St. John's Cathedral during the Jaialdi. Parishioners carried a statue of St. Ignatius of Loyola. The saint, who was born in a Basque province of Spain, founded the Jesuit order and is patron saint of the Basques.

At midnight, two hours before the Sheepherders Ball ended, Esperanza Goitiandia, whose husband was a sheepherder, started preparing *berakatz sopa*—a strong garlic soup that is the traditional nightcap for the party.

A final playing of the popular "Dringilin Dron"—it means "We're getting together and having a good time"—then the celebrants said their goodbyes, wished one another *"Gabon on bat eta urte Bari Asi"* and headed for their cars and pickup trucks parked along the icy, snow-blanketed Boise streets in the crisp 15-degree air.

Two days after the Sheepherders Ball, shrill whistles and repeated shouts by two sheepherders pierced the still, cold air of Gem County, Ida.

In response, three black-and-white dogs bounded up a hill, circled the band of 4,200 sheep and turned the woolly animals toward a better crop of alfalfa stubble.

Rolling pasture land and towering, snow-shrouded mountains were visible in all directions. But there were no signs of other human beings—no houses, barns or roads.

There was nothing but open country.

Sheepherding in the foothills and mountains of southwestern Idaho's remote outback is one of the loneliest jobs imaginable.

"I don't mind taking care of the sheep," said Vicente Valle, a short, leathery-skinned Peruvian. "The hard part is the solitude and being separated from my wife and 9-year-old daughter month after month for three years."

Valle, 31, had left his home in Juancayo, Peru, a year previously. He is one of a few hundred men who have left their native lands of Mexico, Peru and the Basque country of the French and Spanish Pyrenees mountains to tend sheep in the United States.

They all come for the same reason. The dollar.

"In Peru I was lucky to make $60 a month as a laborer," Valle said. "In America I make 10 times as much: $600 a month watching the sheep. It means my wife and I have more money than we ever dreamed possible."

Like nearly all foreign sheepherders in this country, Valle knew nothing about sheep before he came.

"Everybody thinks that we Basques were all sheepherders in the old country before coming to America. Not so," said Eusebio Jayo, 61. He and Valle were taking time out for lunch in their covered wagon home parked on a hilltop half a mile from the grazing sheep. "I never ran sheep in Spain.

"It just happened that when Basques first started migrating to America in the late 1800s, they hired on as sheepherders. It was an available job. Ever since, the cousins, nephews, sons, grandsons and great-grandsons of those original Basque sheepherders have been working the sheep in America."

For Jayo, the years since he left his home in Guernica, Spain, 18 years ago have become a blur.

He is with the sheep week in, week out, winter, spring, summer, fall. In all this time he has never returned to Spain, not even for the funerals of his mother and father. He has never left the sheep except for an occasional night in a small Idaho hamlet if his flock was grazing nearby, or on even rarer occasions to spend a day or two in Boise.

"I give it another year, then I go home to the Basque country in Spain where I retire," Jayo said. He stood on the ladder of his covered wagon. A recently butchered sheep from his flock—frozen in the midday 24-degree temperature—hung from the back of the wagon.

"When I came here 18 years ago," Jayo continued, "I earned $225 a month. Owners of the sheep provide us with food. Now I get $700 a month. I saved almost every penny I made in America, enough money to live out the rest of my life in comfort without ever working again when I go back to Spain."

Jayo is a lifelong bachelor. "I'm hiding out from the women over here," he joked. Will he marry when he returns to his beloved Basque country in the Pyrenees?

He replied with a grin: "God only knows the answer to that."

Many Basques who come to this country under contract to care for sheep wind up becoming American citizens. Many others take their accumulated savings home and retire in style after years of the lonely, lonely life.

Valle and Jayo are alone with their sheep for days, sometimes weeks without seeing another person.

Jose Arrieta, a Basque sheepherder for 28 years, in recent years has been a camp supplier for a dozen sheep outfits. He brings food and supplies in a four-wheel-drive truck every couple of weeks to each pair of sheepherders.

Arrieta and his son Jon, 9, had brought Jayo and Valle fresh fruit and vegetables, canned food for their three sheep dogs, canned goods for the two shepherds, coffee, cereal, milk, eggs, mail, books and magazines.

"For Vicente this life is a killer," Jayo said, "being alone like we are. He's homesick for his wife Irma and his daughter Danitza. For me it is not a lonely existence. I relish this life alone.

"At night we read by the light of a lantern. Vicente and I talk about our countries. He tells me about Peru. I tell him about the Basque country. We talk about our hometowns, about our family and friends, about good times and bad times we remember."

The two men live in the covered wagon during December, January and February. Inside are two bunk beds, tiny stools, boxes of food, a wood stove for cooking and heat. Temperatures outside often drop below zero. But the sheepherders are comfortable.

They listen to shortwave radio, getting news from Peru and Spain.

Jayo is the cook. He also breaks camp almost every day, moving the wagon from one pasture to another while Valle watches the sheep. The wagon is pulled by two mules. They are constantly on the go as the sheep munch their way from one pasture to another.

During the nine months the sheep spend in the high mountains, the men sleep in tents and move from meadow to meadow on pack horses. They brave blizzards, sub-zero temperatures, hailstorms, lightning and heavy rain as their sheep eat 100 miles into the mountains and 100 miles back to the foothills in the yearlong cycle.

For nine months they never leave the sheep. There are no towns within walking distance.

During the three winter months in the foothills, now and then one of the men will go to town, take a day off, while the other remains with the sheep.

In January their band of sheep was at its lowest number, 4,200 ewes. "Hopefully all pregnant," said Jayo. From August through mid-December, 80 to 100 rams lived with the ewes. Lambing begins in January and continues into March. The 4,200 ewes would give birth to over 6,000 lambs, many born twins.

In August the lambs would be removed from the band and taken to market. Once a year the sheep are sheared.

Jayo gave a wry laugh after describing the cycle. "I keep telling Vicente, 'How can you be lonely with all this endless work we have to do?'"

FORTY-SIX

WASHINGTON

Life in the Rain Forest

I T WAS RAINING BUCKETS. Really coming down.

But nothing to get excited about. Washington's Olympic Peninsula is the wettest spot in the 48 contiguous states.

Only a handful of people, 150 at the most, live year-round in the Hoh, Queets and Quinault rain forests—the three temperate-zone rain forests in northwestern Washington.

Few others could take it.

Average rainfall is 12 to 17 *feet* a year.

It's eerie. Moss-draped branches of towering trees canopy the dense forest, carpeted with a thick jungle of lush green plants, herbs, huge ferns, giant edible orange and yellow chicken-of-the-woods mushrooms and other exotic fungi.

The forest is alive with wildlife. Big ravens, crows and flying squirrels inhabit the trees. Now and again, the bugling call of a male Roosevelt elk may interrupt the sound of steady rain.

Cougars live in the woods, too, along with black bears, deer, bobcats, minks, otters, skunks, shrews, mice and a raft of other animals. It is one of the most primeval chunks of virgin wilderness in America.

One would almost expect to see elves and leprechauns sliding down the drooping, moss-laden limbs or taking cover from the downpour under the wings of the gigantic mushrooms.

Those who live in the woods may not be leprechauns, but most are certainly of a different cut from the folks in drier climes. To live where it rains all the time and not go bananas takes a special kind of person.

"It's hard to keep your nose above water, that's for sure," said Gene Owens, unofficial mayor of the Hoh and the owner-operator of an A-frame general store on the slopes of 2,486-foot Mt. Olympus at the edge of Olympic National Park.

Seven families, 35 people in all, live in the tiny community in the Hoh Rain Forest. A sign along the road approaching their seven scattered homes and the general store proclaims: "Congested Area."

Owens was playing solitaire. He finished out the game, then looked up. Business is always slow. Solitaire is his favorite pastime. Most who stop at the store stop not to buy but to ask how far is it to the Hoh Rain Forest Visitors Center.

Behind the storekeeper hung a faded sign his son printed several years ago. It reads: "13 Miles to Olympic National Park Visitors Center."

"Yes," Owens admitted, "it does get a little depressing when it rains day in and day out for three weeks or more without letting up. But it's the floods that get downright discouraging. The road was out one year for 122 days. But somehow we manage."

Nevertheless, Owens said he likes the rain forest so much he only leaves twice a year, in April and in November, and then only for a few hours to go shopping for supplies in Forks, population 3,000, the nearest town some 25 miles from his house.

It's the hunting and fishing that have kept Owens and his wife Mary in the rain forest. He dug into a counter drawer and came up with an *Outdoor Life* that attested to his skill. A story in the magazine was about four master fishermen. He was one of them.

"I catch 40-pound king salmon out of the Hoh River behind my house," he said, "catch giant steelhead in the river. I have raised my family in the rain forest and never bought fish or meat. Buying fish and meat is against my religion. I get an elk every year, and if we need more meat I get a deer or two."

How many umbrellas does he go through in a year?

"Who uses umbrellas? It's too troublesome. People who live in the rain forest wear wool. Even when it's drenching wet, wool keeps you warm."

The bearded mayor of the Hoh always wears a cap. It's said he has no hair, just moss.

"Do you know how to tell an Olympic National Park ranger from rangers in other national parks?" asked ranger Harry Terry. He quickly answered his own question: "Olympic National Park rangers all have athletes foot. Fungi grow best in moist, warm places like between the toes...."

"Is it wise for a person to live in a rain forest?" Bright-eyed Minnie Peterson repeated the question on the porch of her homesteader's cabin in the Hoh. She lives on a 160-acre ranch down the road from Owens.

"Well, I'll tell ya," she said. "I'd say it's wonderful after living in the rain as long as I have. I was born and raised in the rain forest. Lived here all my life. Never left. I'm 87 and still going strong. The rain hasn't hurt me none."

Peterson's parents came to America from Sweden. "I'm grateful to my folks for settling here. They came clear across the country from one coast to another looking for a place to settle down. They would still be going yet if the Pacific Ocean hadn't stopped them. This was as far as they could go. And here they stayed."

Peterson and her late husband Oscar, a blacksmith also of Swedish parentage, married in the rain forest in 1915. For their honeymoon, they rode horseback to San Francisco and back, 1,600 miles round trip, just to take in the Panama Exposition.

For 50 years, from 1927 through 1977, Minnie Peterson was a packer-guide. She led groups on horseback to spectacular Blue Glacier, one of 60 glaciers in Olympic National Park. Now she was living by herself, caring for 10 holstein cows and three horses, Pinky, Mandy and Freddie.

"I bummed up my knee and haven't ridden a horse in two years," she said, "but the knee's gettin' better. I plan to saddle up Freddie any day now and ride down to my blueberry patch where a big band of elk ran through my fence. I got to see how much damage they did and repair that fence.

"I would hop on Freddie today except one of my cows backed up and stepped on my big toe. I have to wait until that heals."

Would Peterson ever move out of the rain forest?

"I should say not," she snorted.

A state campground in the rain forest is named in her honor.

Three generations of women run a 160-acre black Angus ranch up the road from Gene Owens' store—Marie Huelsdonk Lewis, 83; her daughter Marilyn Lewis, 43, and Marilyn's daughter Emmi Brown, 20.

Marie is a widow. Marilyn has been divorced twice. Emmi is single.

"This is hard country," Marilyn said. "You have to have a deep appreciation for what it is.

"I have had two husbands. Both told me to sell the ranch and get the heck out of this godforsaken rain forest. Both were from drier places. They could not take the rain. They left."

She told of leaving the rain forest once herself—for four days when she flew to Oklahoma. "I thought the sky was going to fall on me. I am not accustomed to seeing a blue sky. I don't like the heat. I don't like open spaces. I was glad to get back."

"You can't be depressed by the rain," her daughter said. "You are awed by it. I love to hear the rain on the roof of our house: bang, bang, bang, bang. Hardly ever pitter-patter. It rains so hard on our roof you can't hear yourself talking.

"I love the isolation. I guess I'm a hermit at heart."

Marilyn and her daughter work as summer rangers at Olympic National Park. They know the rain forest better than any of the other rangers who come here from other parts of the country.

"It's tough on rangers," Marilyn said. "Tough on their families. They're not used to anything like the rain we get. The weather makes some of them sick and they have to be transferred out.

"They're expected to spend at least a year at a duty post like this. As soon as the year is about up, out go the resumes to the other parks."

The three women run a pack outfit, guiding visitors to many of the 60 glaciers in Olympic National Park.

"Never a dull moment, I'll tell you," Marilyn said. "We don't have time to let the rain get us down. You have to think positive, not think depressed." Once she walked in on a mama bear with cubs. Another time she turned around and facing her 10 feet away was a cougar. She let out a whoop, and the cougar took off.

"We don't take anything for granted," she said. "You have to respect the elements. We go to town once a month for provisions and always take a chain saw and a shovel with us. No telling when a tree will be blown across the road in a storm."

Marilyn's mother, Marie, is one of the four daughters of legendary John Huelsdonk, "the Iron Man of the Hoh," known as one of the last of America's great frontiersmen. He was the first settler of the rain forest in 1891. A man of tremendous strength and endurance, he is credited with Herculean feats.

He opened the rain forest by building roads and trails into it. They say he wrestled a wild bear and escaped. While he was still alive (he died in 1946), the exploits of this seemingly superhuman being were featured in such magazines as *Time, National Geographic, Saturday Evening Post* and *Adventure.*

The Iron Man's daughter, granddaughter and great-granddaughter are chips off the old block.

A narrow 13-mile winding road leads to the ranger station in Queets Rain Forest, home of a 6-foot-5, 210-pound ranger by the name of Woody Rambo.

Rambo was the only person living full time in Queets Rain Forest, a favorite but little-known place for fishermen. Paul Moneymaker, a cabinet-maker from Kirkland, Wash., and his wife Doris were vacationing in the Queets as they had every year for 30 years.

They fished and enjoyed sitting in the rain under a plastic cover stretched out from their camper, "a grandstand seat for a marvelous display of all kinds of wild animals wandering by," as Moneymaker described it.

Earlier, a five-point elk had strolled by, bugling at the top of his lungs for a female elk.

A couple of years previously, the Moneymakers spent three weeks in the rain forest. It rained 19 days straight.

The Moneymakers' philosophy: Let it rain. "It guarantees our privacy," Doris Moneymaker explained.

Another rain-forest community lies along the north shore of Quinault Lake, just outside the national park. It was claimed by homesteaders in 1889 when a few lots on a narrow corridor fronting the lake were opened for settlement.

The father and grandfather of Orlo R. Higley, 81, were homesteaders on Quinault Lake. The retired schoolteacher has lived in the Quinault Rain Forest all his life, as has his wife Iva. A mountain peak overlooking the lake and a local creek are named after the Higleys.

Higley admitted to a great affinity for this wild, wet country but called himself a johnny-come-lately. "There were Indians all over this country for centuries," he said, "and there still are."

He explained that the Quinault Indians still own Lake Quinault. The tribe has always lived around the edges of the rain forests. The Quinaults might go in to gather wild berries, mushrooms and other edible plants, to hunt deer and elk; but as far as is known, they never lived within the areas of the great downpours.

The Indians say they were too smart for that.

Berdelle Christinsen, a widow who owns and operates an eight-unit motel on the lake, called living in the rain forest a tradeoff. "We do get the rain," she said, "but then we have all this beauty—and the cleanest air in America."

FORTY-SEVEN

OREGON
Portland, City of Parks

O F ALL THE CITIES IN AMERICA, Portland, Ore., has one of the highest percentages of land dedicated to parks—9,422 acres, 12% of its total area.

Portland's 180 parks are special in so many ways, from tiny Mill Ends Park, 24 inches in diameter and listed in the Guinness Book of World Records as the world's smallest park, to huge Forest Park, an 8-mile-long, 1¹/₂-mile-wide urban forest filled with hiking trails.

A 140-mile trail encircles the city.

There are parks everywhere throughout the city and always have been, ever since Portland was incorporated in 1851 and several blocks were set aside as parkland.

In many cities, wide swaths of downtown have been removed to make way for freeways. In Portland, two miles of four-lane expressway fronting the Willamette River in the civic center were removed to make way for—you guessed it—yet another park, Waterfront Park.

It is against the law in Portland's city parks to stand on a toilet seat and whistle or to dance, sing or roller-skate in public rest rooms. Really. The ordinance is still on the books.

A square block was set aside in the late 1800s as a park for women and children exclusively. Men entering the downtown Portland park unaccompanied by a woman were subject to arrest. Benches were marked "Women and Children Only."

"Womens' Park is a throwback to more graceful and genteel times," said Ross Walker, director of communications for the Portland Bureau of Parks and Recreation. "With women's liberation and changing times, it became an anachronism."

Men are no longer arrested for using the park.

Mill Ends, the world's smallest park, is part of a median strip of Front Avenue in the heart of the city. The circular, 452.16-square-inch park was declared a city park in 1976. This oversized flowerpot planted in marigolds is embraced by concrete, marked with a plaque and bordered on one side with two posts linked with chain.

Mill Ends was the brainchild of the late newspaper columnist Dick Fagen of the old *Oregon Journal*, who looked down from his editorial office window on a hole in a median strip meant for, but never filled with, a lamp post.

Fagen fancied it as a park for leprechauns presided over by the chief leprechaun, Patrick O'Toole. It was the subject of many of his columns.

Several weddings have taken place at Mill Ends Park—in the middle of busy Front Avenue. There is a big celebration there every St. Patrick's Day. Don't ask how many can squeeze into the park at one time.

Cathedral Park lies under the eastern approach of St. John's Bridge that spans the Willamette River and is named after the bridge's magnificent Gothic archways. Concerts take place in the natural amphitheater under the arches.

The city's 11 acres of park department-maintained cobblestone street medians, pedestrian plazas and downtown malls are dotted with large attractive kiosks, trees, flowers and fanciful bronze statues.

Downtown Portland is filled with statues.

Favorites include the sea otters and baby bears clinging to the sides of one fountain. A bronze adult bear standing inside the fountain clutches a salmon in its mouth.

A lifelike statue of a man holding an umbrella seems especially appropriate in Portland, where rain is frequent. (A T-shirt slogan proclaims: "Oregonians don't tan, they rust.")

Portland's popular bearded mayor, Bud Clark, was well known as a saloonkeeper before he became "his honor." A poster shows him from the back, standing before a Portland statue of a nude woman. In the photo Clark wears a flop hat, boots and long overcoat that he has pulled open in front of the statue. The caption reads: "Expose yourself to art."

Portland's towering Portlandia statue, whose image appears on the city seal, kneels and holds a trident. Dedicated in 1985, the copper lady is reputedly the largest hammered copper sculpture since the Statue of Liberty.

Then there is the 1905 statue of Sacajawea, the only woman in the Lewis and Clark expedition. Wrought by sculptor Alice Cooper, the statue was paid for by contributions from women in every state and unveiled by Susan B. Anthony.

Pioneer Courthouse Square, Portland's brick-terrace park in the center of the city, is affectionately called "Bang Heads Park."

More than 60,000 Portlanders paid $15 each to have their name inscribed on a brick in the park. Unfortunately, the bricks are not alphabetically arranged. So every day scores of people spend hours, heads down and sometimes banging heads, looking for their brick.

The 320 drinking fountains in downtown Portland are cared for by the parks department. The drinking fountains were gifts of lumberman Simon Benson in the early 1900s. Why he gave them to the city isn't clear.

One story has it that Benson wanted people to drink water instead of beer, wine or hard liquor. Another is that he was irritated because he could never find a place to get a drink of water in downtown Portland.

The city has many spectacular fountains. The most famous, Ira's Fountain, covers an entire block. It was named after the late Ira C. Keller, chairman of the Portland Development Commission.

A walk in the park is a popular Portland pastime during lunch breaks, in early morning, early evening and on weekends.

Portland has 650 men's and women's softball teams, over 10,000 adults who regularly play baseball in city parks until 11 p.m.

Getting to the parks is a simple matter in Portland. Tri-Met, Portland's public transit system, has gained national recognition for its excellent service.

In "Fareless Square," a 340-block downtown section of the system, passengers can ride anywhere within the area free, any time, any day.

Portland author Beverly Cleary wrote 20 children's books centered around Grant Park, where her main character, Henry Huggins, dug for worms.

Mt. Tabor is a city park with an extinct volcano used as a natural amphitheater for concerts.

Elk Rock Island is a 15-acre park in the middle of the Willamette reached only by boat. In summer the park department takes boatloads of children to Elk Rock Island for treasure hunts.

Mt. Hood, four other Cascade peaks and the Portland skyline are seen from a splendid vista point in the internationally acclaimed Washington Park Rose Gardens, the oldest public rose garden in America.

While walking through the rose gardens, visitors can see Portland's official bird, the great blue heron, with six-foot wingspan and S-shaped curved neck, soaring past downtown skyscrapers.

At Hoyt Arboretum, trails wind through 214 acres of dense forest. The 600 species of trees include the largest collection of conifers anywhere.

Kelly Park's picnickers watch a daily parade of ships from around the world beside the confluence of the Columbia and Willamette rivers.

Throughout the parks are huge boulders called "talking rocks," with plaques honoring Portland citizens who have made their mark and historic events. One of the talking rocks, for example, thanks Canada for helping free the Iranian hostages.

"Our parks represent the value system of Portland," said Park Superintendent Cleve Williams. "Residents here take great pride in their parks. This is one of the cleanest and most livable cities in America. Unlike other cities, there is virtually no litter or graffiti.

"Our parks are safe and receive tremendous loving care from our citizens."

Four times a year the park department publishes a 40-page paper filled with more than a thousand activities and special events in the parks.

FORTY-EIGHT

NEVADA

Gypsy Librarian

THE 30-FOOT VAN pulled by diesel cab rolled through northeast Nevada, along the seemingly endless dirt road of desolate Ruby Valley.

It was Elko County Library's silver and blue Nevada Rural Bookmobile on its 4,000-mile monthly odyssey over one of the most remote slices of America.

Bookmobile driver-librarian Lorry Moiola was on the longest bookmobile route in America.

The bookmobile delivers an average of 5,000 books each month. It brings knowledge, romance, science and adventure to 2,000 men, women and children scattered throughout the state's towering mountains, rugged terrain and bone-dry desert.

The library-on-wheels crisscrosses four counties. It covers more than a third of Nevada, an area larger than 13 states.

Isolated ranches, tiny towns no more than wide spots in the road, one-room schools, mining camps, Indian reservations, power-line and highway maintenance crews, prison camps and numerous other out-of-the-way places and faraway people lie on Moiola's route.

As the first red bands of a new day flashed over distant snow-shrouded mountains in the clear, crisp dawn, Moiola gassed up the big bookmobile at the County Yard in Elko, his home base. He would be on the road delivering his cargo of precious printed words until sundown, when he would check into a motel in Ely.

His first stop was Currie, population 15, located 115 miles southeast of Elko. The bookmobile pulled up in front of Louise Garcia's six-student, one-room trailer school.

Moiola had several volumes ready for the grade-school boys and girls, books they had ordered during his last visit two weeks before.

"Here are Milena's books on Australia and Jennifer's *Animal Doctors*," the librarian said as the students piled into the bookmobile. Milena Parker, a 12-year-old seventh grader, hoped to be an exchange student in Australia. Jennifer Chandler, an 11-year-old fifth grader, wanted to be a veterinarian. The children at Currie school live on ranches in the area.

Deanna McCall, 27, mother of fourth-grade twins Katie and Terri McCall, 9, noted that Currie had been without a school for six years before the school reopened the previous fall.

"To have a school in Nevada," she explained, "you need a minimum of seven students in the beginning and four to keep it going. We didn't have enough kids until this year to get the school reopened."

McCall, her husband David and their twin daughters live without electricity on a 75,000-acre ranch 15 miles by dirt road from Currie. McCall taught the twins their first three grades at home.

"It's good for them to have a regular teacher like Louise Garcia, important for them to have contact with other children," McCall said. She was selecting 10 books for herself—biographies, histories and best-sellers—and 10 Westerns for her husband.

Once a month, the couple take the twins 75 miles from Currie to Ely, the nearest town, "just to expose them to the outside world."

Many of the books brought along by the librarian were special orders from mothers living on isolated ranches miles from their next nearest neighbors. These mothers teach their children at home; the nearest school may be 75 to 150 miles away by dirt road.

At Currie, as on other stops along Moiola's journey, the children's favorite authors included Judy Blume, Beverly Cleary, Marguerite Henry of *Misty of Chincoteague* fame and Walter Farley, who wrote the *Black Stallion* series.

At Donna and Tom Korby's Currie store—the Best & Worst Place in Town—ranch wife Kathy Lear, a voracious reader like so many others who live in this lonely part of America, said the arrival of the bookmobile was "the biggest social event we have." Lear said she reads "everything so long as it's clean. Unfortunately, so many of the best-sellers aren't clean."

Currie's Best & Worst Place in Town is a grocery store, gas station, cafe and bar with an old wooden wagon on the roof and jack-rabbit milk for sale by the can. The school and the store are Currie. That's it. There are no telephones in Currie.

Moiola has been a resident of Nevada's outback all his life except for two years as a gunner's mate on the destroyer *Mansfield* during the Korean War. He knows just about every cowboy, Indian, miner, schoolteacher, bartender, store owner, correction camp prisoner and hermit in the northeast part of the state.

"Sometimes it's sad," the librarian mused. He was thinking of Elmer Hall, 79, of the old mining town Mountain City, where all 75 residents expect a gold rush momentarily. Hall and his wife Margaret, 74, were regulars on the bookmobile stop for years.

"Elmer would draw 10 Westerns every visit," Moiola recalled. "Then two months ago he failed to show up. He died. Margaret is back getting books for herself, but it's not the same."

White Pine County's Preston is on the map, but there is nothing there but 20 mailboxes side by side along the road. When the bookmobile shows up at the assigned time every other week, ranchers are waiting by the mailboxes on horseback, in pickups, on motorcycles and three-wheelers.

At Boise Ranch, the bookmobile pulled up in front of the cookhouse at lunchtime and the cowhands poured out. In Baker, Moiola greeted bartender Al Genz, the library's best customer. Genz checks out 20 romance books every other week for his wife and a like number of Westerns for himself.

Moiola made another bookmobile stop on the west side of Pequop Summit, at a prison facility called Wells Conservation Center. "Without Lorry we'd be sitting around in the evenings twiddling our thumbs," volunteered an old con.

The inmate said he fought in Germany during World War II as a staff sergeant with the First Division 26th Infantry. He reads everything about

World War II he can.

A 35-year-old convicted robber likes books about old-time criminals. "This man is the greatest," the inmate insisted, putting his arms around the librarian's shoulders. "You want a book? He gets it for you."

Another prisoner ordered every book available on the Cosa Nostra.

The bookmobile remains in Elko every other Thursday. That's the day Moiola washes it, greases it, changes the oil "and crawls under the son-of-a-gun to see what ails it and what's falling off."

The bookmobile is the only library for residents of tiny towns throughout sparsely populated Lander, Elko, Eureka and White Pine counties—places with names like Lages, Lund, Lamoille, Jiggs, Jackpot, McGill, Ruby Valley, Huckeley, Tuscarora, Dumphy, Contact, Carlin and Wildhorse.

"The bookmobile is our library," said Geraldine Jones, secretary at the Duck Valley Indian Reservation Owyhee School. "It is extremely important not only to the 315 children in kindergarten through 12th grade, but to all the Indian families here as well."

The reservation straddles the border of Idaho and Nevada. Both states have bookmobile card holders at Duck Valley.

Moiola is also librarian for Utah residents. He stops every other Tuesday at Wendover, a town divided by the state line of Utah and Nevada. Children from both sides of the border draw books from the bookmobile. They attend elementary school in Nevada and high school in Utah.

The nomadic bookmobile is also the library for Great Basin National Park, Nevada's only national park and one of the newest to be created by Congress. After Great Basin, the bookmobile visited power-line crews at Mariah's Junction and the families of an isolated highway maintenance crew.

At the one-room, 11-student school in Oasis, teacher Beverly Roesch noted that the bookmobile "is our only readily available source of reading material. The bookmobile is an invaluable aid for our school and for the community. We're all insatiable readers here."

Until the mid-1980s, Oasis was the Nowhere Saloon. Now it's the World Brotherhood Colony, home to 90 men, women and children. Most of the adults are graduates of the University of California at Santa Barbara.

Disciples of Paramahansa Yogananda, they bought the tiny town of Oasis and the ranch that surrounds it and live in trailers behind the town's school, store, cafe and auto garage. They run 2,000 head of cattle and maintain studios where they throw pottery, knit, quilt and make leather goods. The land is held in common by members of the group.

"We came here because of the isolation, the clean air," Roesch said. "We are linked together spiritually. We're not drug users, don't smoke or drink.

"And we love the bookmobile. It's one of our most important links with the outside world."

Other stops that day included Jean Stevens, an amateur archaeologist who lives alone at an archeological dig.

"My life revolves around the bookmobile," Stevens said. "When I need documentation for my work, Lorry provides me with scientific texts, journals or papers."

Lorry Moiola—Nevada's gypsy librarian—said he's delighted to bring the library service to this lonely territory. "For me this is a free and easy job. I enjoy meeting people. Nevada is the last frontier. It has all the free life that's left."

FORTY-NINE

CALIFORNIA

*Ralph Moore's Roses,
From California to the World*

WHEN RALPH MOORE WENT to his bank in Visalia, Calif., he took along a miniature rose plant with pink and yellow blossoms.

He stopped by the desk of Mary Hill, the assistant vice president and his longtime banker.

"What a gorgeous rose," Hill said. "It's my favorite color, pink."

"It's my newest flower," Moore explained. "I want to name it after a friend, but I need her permission first."

"What a lucky person," the banker replied. "She'll just love it."

"Will you give me your permission?" Moore asked.

Hill broke into a smile as she recalled the moment. "I was flabbergasted," she said. "Imagine having a rose named after you. It immortalizes you.

"Especially miniature roses created by Ralph Moore. They go all over the world."

The names of ordinary people from Visalia, population 65,000, are known throughout the world thanks to Ralph Moore. Few rose fanciers know that many of their favorite miniatures are named after the banker, the baker, the cop on the beat, the beautician, the kid down the block and scores of others in the central California town.

Moore, 88 in 1995 still as busy as ever, is one of the world's best-known rose breeders.

Over the last 74 years he has developed and named more than 350 varieties of plants, 90% of them miniature roses. He's been naming the flowers he creates after people, places and events since 1921, when he was a 14-year-old sophomore at Visalia High School.

His miniature roses grow in every state, in Canada, all over Europe, the Middle East, Africa, the Far East, Mexico, South America, Australia and New Zealand—and practically everywhere else in the world.

Many are named for Visalia residents like Mary Hill.

"I named the first rose I originated after one of my best friends in high school, Shelby Wallace," Moore recalled. "He died when we were both sophomores."

Moore named Anita Charles, a coral-red on yellow miniature rose, after a good friend who sings in his church's choir.

Rose Gilardi, a slender, mossy red and pink-striped rose, is named after a woman he knows who runs a beauty shop.

He named Little Mike for a grandson who was a baby at the time and is now a sixth-grade teacher.

He named the popular Ann Moore, a bright orange rose, after his wife.

Bit O' Sunshine got its name years ago from a little girl in a Sunday-school class Moore taught. "I brought in this new flower and she piped up, 'Mr. Moore, that looks just like a bit of sunshine.'"

A couple of years ago Moore named a warm, lush yellow rose after one of his favorite schools, California Polytechnic State University, San Luis Obispo.

"I called it Cal Poly, the school's nickname," Moore said. "Now the school has beds of the miniature yellow roses all over the campus."

Some plants name themselves. As Moore walked through one of the many greenhouses at his six-acre Sequoia Nursery, he pointed out a bed of roses called Ring of Fire. Their glowing yellow blooms etched with red look just like a ring of fire. The red-edged white blooms of another variety, Magic Carousel, resemble tiny merry-go-rounds.

He named Over the Rainbow because its colors made him think of the song from *The Wizard of Oz*.

He came up with Earthquake, a striped red and yellow miniature rose, around the time of an earthquake in Coalinga, Calif.

When the Armenian community in Yettem, a small town near Visalia, celebrated its 75th anniversary, Moore named a miniature purple rose St. Mary in honor of its church.

"*Yettem* means Garden of Eden in Armenian," Moore said. "The community put on a big banquet for their 75th anniversary, and my wife and I were special guests."

Another time, he was watching Dorothy Hamill skate on television when he decided to name a rose after her.

"I wrote her agent for permission," Moore recalled, "and he wrote back saying he wasn't interested.

"Dorothy Hamill probably never saw the letter. It's too bad. That rose, now called Rise 'n Shine, is considered the best yellow miniature in the world today."

More than 200 of Moore's flowers are patented. He receives 8% of the retail price for 17 years and derives a large part of his income from these royalties. He has 10 employees at his nursery. He spends all of his time developing new varieties.

Years ago when his daughter, Eleanore Bergthold, now a teacher in Roseville, Calif., attended Westmont College in Santa Barbara, Moore named a new shrub the Westmont Arborvitae. He donates all royalties from the plant—$35,000 to date—to the school's student loan fund.

One of his latest flowers to achieve international acclaim is a lilac, Blue Skies.

Moore lives next to his nursery and, when not on the road, can be found seven days a week breeding and developing new miniature roses and other flowers in his greenhouse.

Pretty good for an old-timer.

"Oh, I'll keep at it as long as I keep breathing," he said. "Each day I wake up and can't wait to get out into the greenhouse."

He attends rose shows and conventions and delivers papers and programs about miniature roses throughout this country and overseas.

He holds numerous awards. He's one of only three Americans to receive the prestigious Dean Hole Medal from the Royal National Rose Society of England. He has authored three books about miniature roses and is working on a fourth.

Moore has never named a miniature rose after himself. But another breeder did name a test variety developed by Moore's nursery after the famed horticulturist. He called it Ralph's Creeper and the name stuck. Its blooms are bright red with large yellow eyes.

Moore sees his creations whenever he travels. While attending a World Rose meeting in Israel, for example, he visited the nation's biggest kibbutz.

"My wife and I had a big thrill there," he said. "At the entrance to the kibbutz there was a large bed full of miniature roses. They were Mona Ruths, a rose I developed and named after our daughter, Mona Ruth Sorenson."

FIFTY

HAWAII

Curses, Spirits, Luck and Blessings

WHEN THE POLICEMEN OF KAUAI go on duty, they carry pistols in their holsters. And in their pockets, most of them carry a little salt wrapped in ti leaves.

In both cases, the objective is to protect from evil; in the case of the ti leaves and salt, it's evil spirits.

At police headquarters in Lihue, the county seat of Kauai, Officer Frank Medeiros explained that the plant, which also puts the rustle in the hula skirt, is widely known to ward off evil spirits.

Spirits and ghosts are plentiful throughout Hawaii, but especially on the island of Kauai.

Antone K. Vidinha, Jr., three-time mayor of Lihue (which means goose pimples in Hawaiian), blamed his defeat for a fourth term on a ghost that haunted his political headquarters.

During the heat of his last campaign, Vidinha moved out of his headquarters when heavy footsteps were heard clumping back and forth in the attic.

Intrigued by the wealth of stories about ghosts and spirits on the island, the author sought answers from Kauai's Big Kahuna—some say the most important kahuna of the Hawaiian archipelago. The search led to 70-year-old Margaret Kupihea, better known as Kahana, or "Breath of Life."

A kahuna, according to Hawaiian tradition, may be a priest, sorcerer, witch doctor or medicine man. Kupihea has the reputation of being a mixture of all four and much more.

It was difficult to track her down. No one wanted to give her name or address. When her whereabouts were finally learned, the source wanted sworn assurance that the Big Kahuna would not be told where the information came from.

Kupihea proved to be a warm, friendly and engaging individual, a descendant of Hawaiian royalty and a mother of 27 children, 52 grandchildren and 46 great-grandchildren.

Seated on the porch of her home at Kapaa, which overlooks a cemetery in one direction and her herb garden in the other, Kupihea readily admitted to being a *kahuna hola*.

"That's a healer," she explained. "I have had powers of healing all sorts of sicknesses since I was 7 years old.

"It's a God-given power passed to me through my great-grandfather, who died at the age of 115. The power has been in my family for centuries.

"Before my great-grandfather passed on, he told me: 'My love, I will be going back to almighty God shortly. You will carry on my work.'"

Islanders are in awe of Kupihea. Civic leaders, doctors, police and others attribute scores of cures to the woman, who admittedly had no formal education and who speaks Hawaiian most of the time.

"I heal by touch and with prayer," the Big Kahuna said, "and with herbs from my garden."

The prayers are ancient Hawaiian chants.

To mainlanders visiting Hawaii, stories about ghosts, magic and witchcraft in the Honolulu and outer island newspapers may seem strange. But to islanders, the stories are commonplace.

The front page of the *Honolulu Advertiser,* for example, reported that Paul Yamanaka, curator of the Kapiolani Rose Garden, hoped he had found a way to stop vandalism at the botanical showplace. Yamanaka arranged for sacred kahuna stones to be moved to the gardens as guardians, hoping their presence would discourage those who had been stealing rose bushes.

Kupihea said she once owned a similar stone.

"It was a strange and beautiful three-cornered rock that glowed in brilliant rainbow colors," she said.

"I found it on the beach near my home. I asked the rock: 'Does this rock have a name?'"

"The rock replied: 'Kamealii—King of the Fish.'"

She said that from that day on, she became the best fisherman in the islands. The islanders confirm that she never went down to the sea without returning with a huge basket of fish.

"I dive with goggles," Kupihea said. "I catch the fish with my bare hands under rocks."

She believes the sacred rock not only brought her good luck with the fish but was responsible for her success as a kahuna.

"I kept it under glass in a box beside my bed," she said.

"One day a nephew of mine died. He was only a child. Some in the family blamed the death on my sacred rock.

"My husband asked the rock: 'Rock, did you do this?'"

"The rock jumped up and down in the box, bumping its head on the glass top. It cried like a pigeon cooing.

"Soon a man came to our house and said he was a kahuna from the island of Oahu and had instructions to take the sacred rock with him."

Kupihea reluctantly gave the rock to the man, but with a warning: "The rock will kill you if you are lying."

Kupihea had intended no curse.

"But I admit the truth," she confided. "It was a curse. The man sold the rock to the Bishop Museum in Honolulu. He took the money, got drunk and was found dead. So help me God, that is what happened."

"It's spooky, I tell you, the things that occur on this island," said Pat Naea, public information officer for the city of Lihue.

"People are constantly leaving offerings, usually food, to the spirits on the grounds of civic center buildings. No one touches the offerings. No way."

Naea told of the time when many owls were found dead on the island.

"Boy, that was something. Owls are supposed to be the spirits of those who died. We were all running around picking up the dead owls, making little coffins for them and giving them proper burials."

Malcolm Kight works at the county jail on Kauai, a two-story structure with nine cells on the ground floor and six on the top. None of the prisoners want to stay in second-floor cells, he said. They believe the second floor is haunted.

"We never put anyone upstairs if we can help it," the jailer said. "Prisoners held in the upper-floor cells can't sleep. They complain of ghosts walking back and forth and talking loudly to one another all night."

Kight admitted to hearing the noises.

"To me they sounded like loud mumblings. One time I heard the mumblings when I knew there was no one being held upstairs.

"I went up, turned on all the lights, checked all the cells. There was no noise when I was up there. But just as soon as I came downstairs, the mumblings started again."

Here's another example of an island belief:

Two neighbors on Kauai had a falling out.

One woman placed a stick in the ground, a stick topped with the carving of three fingers pointed in her neighbor's direction—an omen of bad luck.

On seeing the evil sign, the other woman placed a mirror in the ground to reflect the evil sign back to where it came from.

Now the lawn separating the two homes is filled with two rows of mirrors bouncing the evil sign back and forth.

These are not isolated instances.

Hawaiians are among the most superstitious people on earth. Only they don't think so.

"It isn't superstition," Naea insisted. "It's for real.

"It's something the Hawaiians live with every day of their lives."

When Hawaii became a state in 1959, the Rev. Abraham Kahikina Akaka gave the blessing.

Akaka, 78 in 1995, has been Hawaii's official blesser for nearly 50 years.

Hardly a day goes by without the pastor emeritus of Honolulu's oldest church giving one or several of his special blessings.

He carries an ancient Hawaiian calabash filled with water to the colorful ceremonies. He pronounces the blessings in Hawaiian as he flicks water from the calabash with a ti leaf.

Polynesians have been living and burying their dead on the islands since the time of Christ. Because many burial sites are unknown, ti leaves are tied to bulldozers for good luck in case a blade should strike a bone. No sense taking any chances with the spirits of those suddenly unearthed. All work comes to a halt when bones are struck. Construction workers refuse to return to the job until the blesser appears to bless the site and rebury the human remains in a cemetery.

Akaka, it seems, blesses everything.

A new fleet of buses in Honolulu was not driven until Akaka performed a blessing of the buses.

When huge resort hotels are completed, Akaka sprinkles water from his calabash in the lobbies with a ti leaf and says his prayers at the dedications.

He once flew to Seattle to bless three 190-passenger boats under construction at Boeing. When the hydrofoils arrived for inter-island service, he blessed them again.

"The blessings are in the tradition of old Hawaiians and also in the Christian spirit," Akaka explained. The minister is three-fourths Hawaiian and one-fourth Chinese.

"Everything was religiously oriented with the early Hawaiians. If they went fishing, prayers were said by the kahunas acknowledging the sovereignty of higher powers over the sea.

"There is always a beginning and continuation of enterprise with purpose. The blessing and prayers are a recognition of human dependence on God."

Sometimes, when Akaka feels "the vibrations are not quite right," he refuses to give his blessing.

He recalled the groundbreaking for the Halawa Stadium and his disapproval over the manner in which the property had been acquired from long-time Hawaiian residents.

Construction on the stadium was fraught with problems. At one point a workman fell to his death on the job and 200 of his co-workers laid down their tools and refused to continue the project.

The workers insisted there was a curse on the place and said they would not return to their jobs unless Akaka gave his blessing.

After he felt proper restitution had been made to the people who once lived on the site, the minister gathered the construction workers together.

"We prayed as a group on the stadium site," he said. "I blessed the project. They went back to work."

Owners of one hotel figured they could get along without the blessing. The hotel burned down three weeks after it opened.

Akaka has blessed everything from a neighborhood poodle grooming parlor to airline terminals, the start of new television series, state office buildings, new parks.

As one of Hawaii's best known public figures in the last half of the 20th

Century, Akaka is spokesman for the Hawaiian community. He was pastor of Honolulu's Kawaiahao Church for years and is now pastor emeritus. He served as regent of the University of Hawaii and chaplain for the territorial and state senates. He preached at the White House and was photographed by Ottawa's famed Youssuf Karsh.

He was the eighth pastor of the majestic coral block "mother church" of Hawaii's Congregational churches. Called the Westminster Abbey of Hawaii, Kawaiahao Church was the church of the kings and queens of the Polynesian islands.

It had its origin in Boston in October, 1819, when 14 Americans and 3 Hawaiians took Communion together and construction of the church began shortly after.

Akaka delivers two sermons every Sunday in the mother church, one in Hawaiian and one in English.

And he's called upon to bless the opening of just about every roadway, building, shop and store in the islands.

"It is of great importance to the people that I do the blessings," he said. "They have great faith in this relationship to God."

FIFTY-ONE

ALASKA

World's Largest Gathering of Eagles

I T WAS THE LARGEST GATHERING of bald eagles on Earth. Hundreds upon hundreds of American bald eagles converged at the Chilkat Eagle Preserve in southeast Alaska as they do every year from mid-October to mid-January.

As many as 3,988 bald eagles have been counted in the preserve at one time. Forty may occupy a single cottonwood tree. The dark brown birds sport seven-foot wingspans, white heads, white tail feathers, yellow talons and huge yellow beaks.

What draws the eagles is a late run of salmon in the Chilkat River, along a three-mile stretch that's warmed by underground springs. All the other Alaskan rivers used by salmon are normally frozen when the bald eagles converge at the preserve.

For three miles along the shallows of the free-flowing river, scores of bald eagles were ripping away at spawned-out salmon carcasses.

It was a noisy feast.

As the birds devoured the fish, other bald eagles flew back and forth a few feet overhead. They were eager to land and share the spoils.

But the diners were gluttons, refusing to share their bounty. Between gulps, they glared and shrieked raucously at the hovering birds. The air was alive with the sound of screeching eagles.

When the airborne eagles attempted to displace the diners, shoving matches ensued. The piercing cries of eagles berating one another echoed throughout the snowy wilderness.

Alaska State Park Ranger Bill Zack viewed the scene on the shores of the Chilkat River. "See? Sometimes their talons lock," he said, "but they never seem to inflict serious harm to one another. There are no bloody battles. And they become a lot less aggressive as their stomachs get full."

Between snacks, hundreds of eagles bided their time on the limbs of snow-covered cottonwood trees lining the river. Magpies and seagulls stood in the river shallows waiting for leftovers.

Other wildlife was close at hand. The woods and snowy meadows along the river were crisscrossed with fresh bear, deer and moose tracks.

Zack—a tall, husky, black-bearded, ruddy-complexioned man—is Alaska's eagle ranger. He's been the only ranger assigned to the 48,000-acre preserve since it was set aside by the state in 1982.

Michael Jacobson, U.S. Fish and Wildlife eagle management specialist stationed in Juneau, reports that the highest count of eagles in the Chilkat Eagle Preserve was 3,988 in 1984 with the average peak count of 2,500 eagles a year.

"In 1994 an unusually large number of bald eagles, 3,769, were counted in a census along the Cheakamus River near Brackendale, B.C., Canada, but the previous high there was 2,500 with the count much lower in other years. Year-in and year-out the heaviest concentration of bald eagles on Earth happens along the Chilkat River in Alaska," noted Jacobson.

Zack administers first aid to sick eagles and to eagles that have been shot or hit by vehicles on the two-lane Haines Highway next to the Chilkat River.

He explained that sometimes an eagle flying with a fish in its talons may drop the meal onto the road, swoop down and continue to eat it there. If a fast-moving vehicle approaches, the bird may take off too slowly and be struck and killed or injured.

Zack also provides information about bald eagles for the preserve's human visitors and makes sure they do not disturb the birds.

Every year there are fender benders and more serious accidents along Haines Highway in the area where the eagles are feeding.

Pete Lapham of the Alaska Department of Highways said the turnouts on the highway in the eagle preserve are kept free of snow so people can easily park their cars for viewing.

"Even so," he said, "people often get so excited when they spot the first eagles, they slam on their brakes, stop their cars in the middle of the road, run out and start shooting pictures."

Photographers come from all over the United States and from many parts of the world to capture the great congregation of bald eagles on film.

Manabut Tozuka, a Tokyo noodle maker, said he saved up for three years to fly to Alaska just to photograph the eagles at Chilkat Eagle Preserve.

"Seeing those wonderful birds all over the trees and feeding on salmon up and down the river is the most exciting adventure of my life," Tozuka said. "I'm going to start saving as soon as I get home for my next trip here."

"This is my sixth year," said Frank Oberle of St. Louis, Mo. "Each time I've spent a month photographing the eagles, from mid-November to mid-December. To me, this is the ninth wonder of the world."

The tiny town of Haines bills itself the "American Bald Eagle Capital of the World." It lies 120 miles north of Juneau, Alaska's capital.

The townspeople of Haines built the American Bald Eagle Foundation Research Center by raising $108,000 through donations and by holding pancake breakfasts, fairs and flea markets. Affiliated with the University of Alaska's Southeast campus at Juneau, the center occupies seven lots owned by the town.

Dave Olerud, owner of a Haines sporting goods store, chaired the drive to build the research center. He was one of the volunteers working on construction when the last of the 42-foot-long, 21-foot-high walls collapsed. The accident broke his back and paralyzed much of his body.

He directed work on completion of the research center from his wheelchair.

Alaska has an estimated 30,000 to 40,000 bald eagles, three-quarters of America's population of the national bird.

Three eagle experts from the U.S. Department of Fish and Wildlife are credited with doing more to protect and ensure the preservation of Alaska's bald eagles than anyone else. As a result of the work of Sid Morgan, Jim King and the late Fred Robards, Alaskan eagles have never been on the endangered species list as they have in the Lower 48.

Beginning in 1960, the three Juneau residents made surveys by air, by boat and on foot throughout southeast Alaska, recording the giant eagle nests in treetops.

The author spent several days with them surveying eagle nests on Admiralty Island in January, 1974.

At the time, Robards noted there were more eagle nests and more eagles on Admiralty Island than in all the other 49 states combined.

Eagle nests are immense—more than 40 square feet on the top, usually at least five feet deep and exceeding 200 cubic feet in volume. Each weighs several tons.

The bottoms regularly rot out from the ravages of snow, ice and wind in winter. Eagles start refurbishing in April. They haul drift and shed branches up to five feet in length as well as grasses, moss and lichens.

The birds begin laying eggs about the first of May. The average nest contains two eggs. Incubation runs 32 to 34 days. Eagles have a relatively long life span; in captivity they've lived as long as 50 years.

The nests are used year after year. The oldest found by the wildlife biologists dated from 1907.

The Fish and Wildlife trio tagged the eagle-nest trees with yellow fiberglass markers that read: "Bald eagle nest tree. This nest is protected by the Bald Eagle Act. Destruction of eagles or their nests is prohibited by federal law."

Logging is banned within a 330-foot buffer zone around every eagle-nest tree in Alaska.

"If timber companies had harvested the nest trees, it could have wiped out much of Alaska's bald eagle population," Morgan said.

He noted another threat: bounties were paid for killing the birds in Alaska from 1917 to 1952.

"It's hard to believe people were paid to shoot America's national symbol, but it's true," he said. "At first they were paid 50 cents an eagle, later $1 and by 1942, $2."

Bounty hunters killed 128,273 bald eagles during the 45-year period. The eagles were targeted because salmon fishermen and fox-farm owners thought the birds were depleting the fish and fox. But it was later learned the eagles were taking mostly dead and dying fox and salmon.

Today, anyone shooting a bald eagle faces a fine of up to $10,000 and two years' imprisonment.

FIFTY-TWO

PUERTO RICO

Ponce, Mecca for Firemen

IREMEN FROM ACROSS AMERICA beat a steady path to Ponce, Puerto Rico's second largest city. It's named after Juan Ponce de Leon, the Spanish explorer who sought the Fountain of Youth.

It was Ponce de Leon who gave the 110-by-35-mile island its name when he exclaimed, *"¡Que puerto rico!"*—"What a rich port!"—on landing Aug. 12, 1508.

Ponce de Leon didn't discover Puerto Rico. Columbus did, 15 years earlier on his second voyage to the New World. He called the island San Juan Bautista.

But Ponce de Leon's descriptive *"puerto rico"* stuck. Only the commonwealth's largest city, San Juan, retained Columbus' original name.

Fire fighters come to Ponce because of its colorful tributes to the heroism of firemen, or *bomberos*.

They come to see Puerto Rico's oldest fire station, the 1883 Parque de Bombas in Plaza las Delicias. It's one of the most colorful, most unusual fire-houses on earth.

You can't miss it. It's like something out of a fairy tale in the center of the city.

Its whimsical Victorian architecture features small fan-shaped windows and shingles painted bright red and black.

On Sundays, Ponce's municipal band gathers on the large open balcony protruding from the fabled firehouse to serenade the people of Ponce. The audience gathers in Plaza las Delicias, "Delightful Plaza" in English.

Ponce, population 170,000, pays greater tribute to its *bomberos* than perhaps any other city under the U.S. flag.

A street in Ponce commemorates the heroes of the *Fuego del Polvorin*, the "Ammunition Fire," that occurred on Jan. 25, 1899. The street takes its name from the date: 25 de Enero 1899.

Eleven identical homes—all painted red and black, the colors of Ponce's fire department—stand side by side on 25 de Enero 1899. Each of the modest houses has a rooftop weathervane in the shape of a fire-fighting symbol—a fire fighter's hat, a ladder, a nozzle, a fireplug.

Hermina Santos, who resides in one of the houses, explained that the people of Ponce honored the *bomberos* of the city in 1948 by presenting the homes to firemen in appreciation for all the good they had done throughout the history of the city.

Every fireman with at least 25 years' service—"and there were many old-timers in the department," Santos noted—was eligible to enter a lottery for the homes. Her father was one of the winners.

Under the lottery rules, the houses could be inhabited only by the winning firemen and their families. The homes could never be sold, only inherited by descendants of the *bomberos*.

Every day fresh flowers are placed at the monument in Plaza las Delicias honoring the *Heroes del Fuego del Polvorin*.

On one wall of Ponce's fire department headquarters, a few blocks from the plaza and the old fire station, a huge mural shows firemen rescuing people from the 1899 fire. The mural honors the memory of the nine most famous heroes of that blaze.

The largest tomb in Ponce's municipal cemetery has a bigger-than-life-size statue of a *bombero* holding a nozzle and hose. Buried within the huge tomb are the nine heroes of the famous 1899 fire and 60 other firemen. Every Ponce *bombero* with at least five years' service is entitled to burial in the tomb.

The oldest human remains in the tomb—except for the original nine heroes—are reburied elsewhere to make room as new interments occur.

"Let me tell you about the Heroes of the Ammunition Fire," said Capt. Cecilio Pena Ramos, 67, a 41-year member of Ponce's fire department.

"In 1899, a fire began in Ponce and burned several blocks. U.S. forces had occupied the city. The commander of the military base ordered Ponce evacuated for fear the army's ammunition dump would blow up. Nine volunteer firemen ignored the order, kept the fire from spreading to the ammunition dump and, in doing so, saved many lives and most of the city.

"Ironically, the nine firemen were jailed for disobeying orders. But there was such a huge public outcry that the U.S. Congress ordered the firemen freed and decorated them for heroism."

When Pena Ramos started his career as a *bombero* in Ponce, it was an all-volunteer department. "I taught baking in a large bakery for 21 years by day and was a fireman by night," he recalled, "living here in the historic old firehouse. In 1955, we began to get paid—$1 a night."

Henry Perez, 30, for 10 years a Ponce *bombero* and chief of transportation for the department, noted that fire fighters are now paid $660 a month with a maximum of $1,100 a month for a commander with 25 years of service.

"It isn't much money," Perez said. "It's almost a labor of love. But to be a *bombero* of Ponce is a great honor. We have tremendous respect from the people of Ponce.

"It gives us a good feeling that firemen from all over America know about us and come here to see our flamboyant old fire station, to see the red and black houses of the *bomberos* on 25 de Enero 1899, to visit the monument in Plaza las Delicias and the tomb of the *bombero* heroes in the Cemetario Municipal."

FIFTY-THREE

U.S. VIRGIN ISLANDS

Transfer Day and the Chas Chas

T HE SOUND OF CHURCH BELLS echoed through the narrow, twisting streets of Charlotte Amalie, the quaint 325-year-old U.S. Virgin
Islands capital.

The bells celebrated Transfer Day, a territory-wide holiday marking the
anniversary of the transfer of the Caribbean island chain from Danish to
American rule.

For the 100,000 Americans who live in this unincorporated, 133-square-
mile U.S. territory, Transfer Day is one of the biggest holidays of the year.

A reenactment of the transfer began at 4 p.m. on the lawns of the 1874
lime-green, white-shuttered Legislature Building. That's the precise time the

event originally occurred on March 31, 1917.

The United States paid Denmark $25 million for the lush tropical islands embraced by white sand beaches and calm blue-green seas.

The 196-foot-long, three-masted, full-rigged Danish government training ship *Danmark* had sailed from Copenhagen especially for the celebration. The *Danmark's* 18 officers and 80 cadets represented the officers and crew of the *Valkyrien*, the Danish cruiser that carried the last Danish governor and his official party back to Denmark in 1917.

The destroyer *Connolly* represented the *Hancock*, the U.S. ship that brought the first American governor to the Virgin Islands.

Sailors from both ships marched in formation through the streets of Charlotte Amalie as sailors did on the original Transfer Day. They were dressed in military uniforms worn by sailors from both nations in 1917.

Geraldo Guirty, a local historian who witnessed the first Transfer Day, played the part of the islands' first American governor in the pageant. He sat reminiscing on a rock wall beneath the bust of Denmark's King Christian IX in Emancipation Park. "I remember that day so vividly," he said.

"I saw it all, saw the Danish ship *Valkyrien* and the American ship *Hancock* at anchor in the waters off the Legislature Building, then the barracks for Danish soldiers. I had a front-row seat. The island people were calling out to one another: 'Merica goin' to take Sin Tamas.'"

Guirty, a fifth-generation Virgin Islander, described members of the consular corps at the original ceremony perspiring heavily in their Prince Albert coats and top hats. He recalled other dignitaries in linen and white drill suits wearing Panama hats. He was 11 at the time.

"I can still see the Dannebrog, the red Danish flag with the white cross, slowly taken down for the last time. I remember the Stars and Stripes being hoisted and sailors aboard the Danish ship and the American ship firing gun salutes. I can still hear the national anthems of both countries played that day."

Guirty's father was a Danish police officer who wore his dark blue serge uniform and white dress helmet with the royal Danish emblem for the last time on Transfer Day in 1917. That helmet is now on display at a local museum. On Transfer Day, the historian's father became an American policeman.

"It was a big moment in our history," Guirty said. "It ended 245 years of Danish rule. Some of the plain people were sad. Some were glad. Many wept openly. They were saying: 'We know what we have, but we don't know what we be gettin'.'"

The day after Transfer Day in 1917, Hamilton Jackson, the editor of the

Christiansted Herald, wrote in an editorial: "It was a touching sight to see the Old Flag pulled down, but at the same time it was a glorious one to see the Stars and Stripes go up."

In the pageant, several Virgin Island senior citizens took the part of "wailers," crying as one flag was lowered and the other raised.

Muriel Jackson, with the Virgin Islands Department of Conservation and Cultural Affairs, spent months researching, writing and directing the Transfer Day reenactment.

The original proclamations made by President Woodrow Wilson and King Christian X of Denmark were read. Denmark's consul general to New York, Villads Villadsen, flew down to read the king's words in the reenactment.

"All Danes in Denmark and everywhere else in the world know about the Virgin Islands," said Hans Jahn, Danish consul general to the Virgin Islands. "Old-timers remember when St. Thomas, St. Croix, St. John and the 50 or more smaller islands were a Danish colony."

Jahn, who is also president of the West Indian Co., a major Danish Virgin Island firm that owns local shopping centers and serves as agent for many of the cruise ships that call on local ports, said that all Danish schoolchildren learn about the Virgin Islands in history classes.

"After all, we had this part of the world for 245 years," he said. "Our Queen Margrethe has been here. The Virgin Islands are a popular vacation destination for hundreds of Danes every year."

A hundred and twenty members of Dansk Vestindisk Selskab, "Friends of the West Indies," flew in from Denmark for Transfer Day. Inge Mejer Antosen, curator of the Danish National Museum, came for the celebration as well. She brought hundreds of photographs never shown before in the Virgin Islands that depict life at the time of the original Transfer Day.

Danish heritage is evident everywhere throughout the Virgin Islands, in the town buildings' architectural styles of the 1600s, 1700s and 1800s and in the stone ruins of old sugar mills dotting all three major islands.

This is the only place in America where motorists drive on the left side, a holdover from Danish rule.

Charlotte Amalie was named after the Danish queen in 1691. Its principal streets still carry Danish names—Dronnigens Gade ("Main Street"), Norre Gade ("North Street") and Vimmelskafts Gade ("Back Street").

Many elderly residents speak Danish, both black and white (85% of the population is black, 15% white). There are a number of Danish-American families descended from families established in the Virgin Islands since the

1600s and 1700s, especially on St. Croix.

It was not the Danes who called the archipelago the Virgin Islands; it was Columbus. He discovered them on his second voyage in 1493.

After passing a great number islands, he named the group Santa Ursula y las Once Mil Virgenes after the legendary St. Ursula and the 11,000 Virgins.

Gov. Alexander A. Farrelly addressed the Transfer Day celebrants as the Virgin Islands' fourth elected governor (governors have been elected since 1971) and the 70th governor of the islands since Joergen Iversen was appointed by Denmark in 1672.

The governor was interviewed by the author at Government House, a two-story, neoclassic white mansion constructed in 1867 of stuccoed-over Danish ballast brick.

Farrelly, who holds master's and law degrees from Yale, noted that Virgin Islanders have had full American citizenship since 1932. Virgin Island residents, however, may not vote for President or vice president, though island-born citizens may if they live in any of the 50 states.

"We are Americans," Farrelly said. "We do not wish to be anything else. We should be permitted to vote for our President.

"Someday we hope to see the Virgin Islands achieve statehood. I do not believe, however, that I will see it in my lifetime."

The governor said Virgin Islanders are far better off than any of the other Caribbean islanders. "We have the highest per capita income in the Caribbean—$8,000 a year. Transferring from Denmark proved to be exceptionally good for our people."

Locals call Frenchtown, a tiny fishing village on the island of St. Thomas, Cha Cha Town.

That's because, years ago, ancestors of the French-American Virgin Islanders who live in Frenchtown often responded with the unfriendly term *cha cha* when other islanders kidded them about their dress. Their usual attire included black calico shirts and trousers rolled halfway up their legs.

They were also teased about their patois, a mixture of French, Creole and English.

The French islanders response—in their patois, a suggestion as to where the other person might go—earned them the nickname Cha Chas. Their village became known as Cha Cha Town.

The names stuck.

"They call us Cha Chas or Frenchies," explained Francis Bryan, one of Frenchtown's fishermen. "These are friendly nicknames. We call ourselves both names. It's like calling an American a Yank."

The Cha Chas of St. Thomas are a little-known American ethnic group numbering no more than 3,000.

The designation *Cha Cha* has legal recognition in the Virgin Islands. In its coverage of the Virgin Islands, the Encyclopedia Britannica notes:

"The Cha Chas of St. Thomas form a distinct ethnic unit apart from other islanders. They are descended from French Huguenots who came from St. Barthélemy. The Cha Chas maintain themselves as a clannish, aloof, industrious community."

They are fishermen and farmers supplying the island with nearly all its fresh fish and much of its fruit and vegetables.

"Our forefathers came from St. Barthélemy, or St. Barts, as we call it," said Louis Danet, another Frenchtown fisherman. St. Barthélemy is a French Caribbean island 130 miles southeast of St. Thomas.

Danet stood beside a lineup of beached fishing boats on the Frenchtown waterfront. The 16- to 19-foot-long boats had names like *French Boy, Espoir, Jalous, Zozio, Marie Elaine, St. Rose.*

About a thousand Cha Chas live in Frenchtown on the western edge of Charlotte Amalie. A sprinkling of bars and restaurants appear along the fishing village's narrow streets. The establishments have names like Cafe Normandie, Le Bistro and the Coqui Bar.

Another 2,000 Cha Chas live in and around Hull Bay, the other Cha Cha community on the 3-by-13-mile island. Hull Bay is three miles away from Frenchtown, over the steep mountain on the north coast of St. Thomas.

In the 1600s and 1700s, French families from Brittany and Normandy settled on St. Barthélemy. In the mid-1800s, descendants of several of these families began migrating to St. Thomas.

Close ties have been maintained for generations between the French islanders on St. Thomas and St. Barts.

"There are only about 3,000 people living on St. Barts, the same number of Frenchies that live on St. Thomas," noted Sebastian Greaux, bartender for 20 years at the Cafe Normandie in Frenchtown.

"Everybody on St. Barts has relatives here on St. Thomas and vise versa. We are very close. People go back and forth between the two islands all the time."

St. Thomas residents jam the pier at Frenchtown every day. They come to buy fresh fish from the Cha Cha fishermen.

The fishermen set out in their small boats before sunup and return in the afternoon. They unload their catch on the concrete pier—reef fish, snapper, grouper, yellowtail, lobster and much more.

The fishermen of Hull Bay have a similar routine, but they load their catch onto pickups and drive the fish to market for sale mainly to grocery stores, restaurants and hotels.

Over the years, Hull Bay and Frenchtown, although only three miles apart, developed separate dialects of the archaic West Indian French. People here know immediately whether someone lives in Hull Bay or in Frenchtown by his or her manner of speech.

ACKNOWLEDGMENTS

First, my deepest love and eternal thanks to my gorgeous wife Arliene of nearly 50 years who put up with my prolonged absences, always supportive, never once complaining and to Brad and Tori for their understanding, growing up with a dad often out of town.

My appreciation to a special friend throughout my career, Otis Chandler, publisher of *The Los Angeles Times* who made *The Times* one of America's great newspapers and made my travels possible.

I am grateful to Bill Thomas, Editor of *The Times*, who first told me to "stay west of the Mississippi, Charlie" and later relented when I told him the whole world was west of the Mississippi. He gave me the green light to "go anywhere and everywhere you want" to find the human interest features. I traveled the world with Bill's blessing. He also gave me the "America" column.

Thanks to Art Berman, the first editor of the "America" columns, and to numerous other editors I worked with down through the years, to Romeo Carraro, a colleague at the *Chicago Tribune*, who hired me at the *L.A. Times*, to Russ Arasmith, the artist of the astronauts and America's space program who did the Mt. Rushmore rendition on the back cover.

My hat's off to the thousands of men, women and children I met and wrote about, each unique in his and her own way, who gave me their time and friendship, and made it possible for me to have one of the best jobs anyone could ever dream of having.

Thanks to Stan Chambers, Los Angeles' favorite television newsperson, who led me to Noel Young at Capra Press who had the courage to publish this book; to Annette Burden, at Capra, who did the editing; to Frank Goad, Capra's art director, who designed the book and its cover; and to everyone else working with Noel who made this happen.

I am grateful to Marshall Roe who printed all the photographs in the book, and to my son, Brad, and George Jurisich who brought me into the 20th-Century by teaching me how to use a computer to accomplish this writing task.

And, how can I ever thank him enough, and express my heartfelt appreciation to Charles Kuralt, one of America's greatest storytellers, for taking his time and expressing his sentiments in his foreword to this effort.

—C.H.